W9-CCW-479

CULTURAL DIVERSITY AND LEARNING EFFICIENCY

Cultural Diversity and Learning Efficiency

Recent Developments in Assessment

Edited by
Rajinder M. Gupta
and
Peter Coxhead

St. Martin's Press New York

First published in the United States of America in 1988

Printed in Hong Kong

ISBN 0-312-00988-7

Library of Congress Cataloging-in-Publication Data
Cultural diversity and learning efficiency.
Bibliography: p.
Includes index.
1. Learning ability. 2. Children of minorities.
3. Learning. I. Gupta, Rajinder M., 1939-
II. Coxhead, Peter.
LB1134.C79 1987 371.9 87-12925
ISBN 0-312-00988-7

Contents

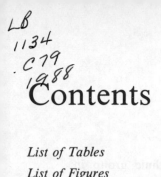

List of Tables

List of Figures

Acknowledgements

Grateful thanks are extended to Professor A. J. Franklin, of the City University, New York, who participated in several discussions during his visits to Britain, while the book was in its infancy. Many thanks also to John Galbraith, a colleague, who, like Professor Franklin, read the first chapter and made very useful comments.

We would also like to acknowledge the secretarial support received first from Tracey Tyler, and later on from Sallie Leamy and Janice Lowe. Their ungrudging assistance saved us hours of painstaking work; we deeply appreciate their help.

RAJINDER M. GUPTA
PETER COXHEAD

Notes on the Contributors

Monique Boekaerts is Professor of Educational Psychology, and is the principal investigator of a national research project on teaching–learning processes. Her specialisations are individual differences in verbal information processing; the measurement of state and trait motivation and state and trait anger and their effect on the selection of learning strategies and grade-point average.

Peter Coxhead is Lecturer in Computing Science at the University of Aston. From 1977 to 1983 he was Lecturer in Research Methods and Statistics at Aston. He received his doctorate in educational research from the University of Cambridge. He has published numerous articles on educational assessment.

Reuven Feuerstein is Professor of Psychology and Education at the Bar-Ilan University, Adjunct Professor at Peabody College of Vanderbilt University and the Founding Director of the Hadassah-WIZO Canada Research Institute. He is a leading exponent of structural cognitive development and mediated learning experience as the foundation of classroom-based and tutorial programmes of enrichment. His textbooks, *Learning Potential Assessment Device* and *Instrumental Enrichment*, have been the basis for ongoing research and experimentation by over 175 independent researchers and doctoral candidates. The programme is applied and studied in the United States, Canada, Venezuela, the United Kingdom, France, Spain, Italy, Belgium, Switzerland, the Federal Republic of Germany, Cyprus, Israel, South Africa and Australia.

Gilbert R. Gredler is Professor of Psychology at the University of South Carolina. Prior to coming to USC Dr Gredler was Professor of Psychology and School Psychology. Other positions have included being Director of Psychological Services for the Atlanta, Georgia school system as well as school psychologist for the Canton, Ohio schools. Dr Gredler is currently on the editorial board of *Psychology in the Schools* as well as book review editor for that journal. He is also associate editor of *Techniques*, a journal dealing with counselling and remediation.

Rajinder M. Gupta is an educational psychologist at the Child Advisory and Psychological Service, Erdington, Birmingham. He was awarded his PhD by the University of Aston for his research on the assessment of the learning efficiency of Asian children. He is the author of several articles on child psychology.

Seamus Hegarty is Deputy Director of the National Foundation for Educational Research. He has conducted research and published widely on the education of pupils with special needs and minority group education. He produced the first commercially available tests of learning ability in this country. Prior to engaging in research, he taught in schools for six years.

Mogens R. Jensen is an Associate Research Scientist at Yale University's Department of Psychology and Director of the Institute for Studies in Cognitive Modifiability in New Haven, Connecticut. Dr Jensen is also a Senior Research and Clinical Psychology Associate at the Hadassah-WIZO Canada Research Institute in Jerusalem, Israel. He received a BA and an MA from the Hebrew University in Jerusalem and a PhD from Yale University. Since 1972 Dr Jensen has collaborated with Dr Reuven Feuerstein on the development, research and presentation of the theory of structural cognitive modifiability.

Shlomo Kaniel is lecturer in Bar-Ilan University, School of Education, engaging in research and teaching, and is a psychologist at Hadassah-WIZO Canada Research Institute, Jerusalem, in individual and group dynamic assessment and interventions on different levels (child, class and school). His areas of specialisation are: cognitive development and modifiability; dynamic assessment and treatment; and application of psychology to school curriculum.

Yaacov Rand is Professor at the School of Education, Bar-Ilan University, and Co-Director of the HWE Research Institute, Jerusalem, Israel. He was previously director of the School of Education and Dean of the Faculty for Social Sciences, Chairman of the Committee for Doctoral Studies, School of Education, Bar-Ilan University, Israel.

Marilyn T. Samuels is the Executive Director of the Calgary Society for Students with Learning Difficulties, where she is responsible for directing research, demonstration and treatment of learning disabled persons. Dr Samuels is an author of a number of research papers and reports and has received several research grants.

Andrew Sutton has a joint background in psychology and Soviet studies and has published a number of articles on Soviet developmental psychology and defectology. He is an Honorary Research Fellow in the Department of Psychology and Associate of the Centre for Russian and East European Studies, University of Birmingham, and is currently working on the Hungarian system of conductive education for the motor disordered.

David Tzuriel is Senior Lecturer in the Early Education Program, School of Education at Bar-Ilan University, Ramat-Gan and Clinical Psychologist and Researcher at the Hadassah-WIZO Canada Research Institute, Jerusalem. His areas of research are cognitive modifiability, mediated learning experience, motivational processes, dynamic assessment procedures especially with pre-school children.

Introduction

Learning is at the centre of all human cultures; indeed, without learning there could be no human culture at all. Learning is also at the heart of the educational process: a teacher has the task of ensuring that his or her pupils learn, which entails ensuring that at some time in the future, they will have knowledge and abilities that they do not have at present. Yet, in Western classrooms at least, access to this *future* learning has been primarily controlled by assessment techniques based on *present* achievement, whether this is achievement in specific academic tasks or in more generalised 'intelligence' tests. In Vigotskii's colourful analogy (see Chapter 5), it is as though a gardener judged the future potential of a garden, the potential it might have after years of careful cultivation, solely by the ripeness of the apples then on the trees.

A concentration on present achievement is shown to be even more misleading when it is considered that, although the ability to learn is clearly a common attribute of people from all classes, cultures and ethnic groups, it is equally clear that *what* is learnt is different. That this is true of detailed *knowledge* is obvious: one would be surprised to find that a villager in India could read a British Ordnance Survey map; one would be equally surprised to find that a British geography professor could not. It is sometimes less obvious that apparently more general *abilities* have also been learnt to different degrees by people from different backgrounds. An anecdote may illustrate this. One of the editors of this book (RMG) asked six postgraduate students, originally from the Indian sub-continent but at that time studying in Cambridge, to fold a spreadout Ordnance Survey map and to find the principle underlying the folding. Each student took a long time to fold the map (an average of nearly 6 minutes), and none could deduce the underlying principle. Since all later successfully completed a PhD, they clearly had no general learning difficulties, nor any lack of general intelligence. Rather, they simply had not learned those manual and spatial-reasoning skills involved in map-folding. Why? Surely because they had never regularly folded maps.

Perhaps to the specialist in this field all this is not new, and may indeed have become utterly obvious. Yet can we honestly say that existing assessment practices reflect this understanding? As Gould (1984, pp. 28–9) reminds us:

> We pass through this world but once. Few tragedies can be more extensive than the stunting of life, few injustices deeper than the denial of an opportunity to strive or even to hope, by a limit imposed from without, but falsely identified as lying within . . . We inhabit a world of human differences and predilections, but the extrapolation of these facts to theories of rigid limits is ideology!

The origins of this book lie in the editors' belief, shared by a growing number of educationalists, that only those forms of assessment which take into account a child's 'learning ability' can provide a basis for educational provision which allows all pupils access to genuine opportunities to learn. However, we must not be too narrow-minded in considering learning ability; individual and cultural differences of all kinds, purely affective as well as cognitive, are likely to be involved. We have to reflect as many of these as possible, both at the practical and at the theoretical level.

This is perhaps the point at which to say a few words about terminology. We have not sought to impose any uniformity on contributors; indeed in this rapidly developing field any such attempt would be unlikely to succeed. However, it is probably true to suggest that the terms 'learning ability' and 'learning efficiency' are used more or less synonymously, denoting the performance of a person in learning specific kinds of knowledge or specific abilities in specific situations. ('Efficiency' perhaps hints more at speed of learning than does 'ability'.) 'Learning potential' on the other hand carries a wider implication, suggesting an extrapolation to all areas of education, and indeed to life in general. The fact that we favour the assessment of learning ability, with the implication that this may say something about learning potential, does not imply that we believe that there is a single general learning ability *per se*, which may be deemed to be at the heart of all types of learning (*cf* Vernon, 1969). Instead, in line with the overwhelming evidence in the literature we subscribe to the view that learning ability is multi-factorial, with no single factor common to all measures of performance on different learning tasks (see, amongst others, Woodrow, 1938a,b, 1939a,b,c; Stake, 1961; Mackay & Vernon, 1963; Duncanson, 1964; Malmi *et al.*, 1979 and a study cited therein by Underwood *et al.*, 1978; also reviews by Guilford, 1967 and Cronbach, 1970). More recently Cronbach (1984, p. 260) has argued that

> to think of a 'general' learning ability – even for organised lessons – oversimplifies. Each method of instruction makes its own demands

for information processing; also there are content-specific learning abilities (for example, in foreign languages).

However, it does not follow that this view, or for that matter any other of the views expressed above, is shared by our contributors. We would not expect it either. As editors, our concern has been to gather material which conveys the richness and variety that has permeated this exciting field.

The book has been organised into three sections, each comprising a number of chapters. The first section of the book presents the **concept of learning ability**, together with the history of, and rationale for, its use in assessment. Three chapters provide accounts of the varied approaches which have been, and are currently being, used to assess the child's learning ability; these approaches are reviewed and critically analysed. This also involves contrasting the assessment of learning ability with more traditional assessment procedures (such as IQ measures), and displaying the unacceptable (because unjust) consequences which follow from the use of these traditional procedures, particularly when applied to children from diverse cultural backgrounds. The three chapters, Chapter 1 by the editors, Chapter 2 by Seamus Hegarty, and Chapter 3 by Gilbert Gredler, inevitably overlap slightly, but use varied research evidence to argue that, for the purposes of decision making, determining educational provision, and curriculum planning, practitioners should favour assessment related to children's learning potential as opposed to their achievements or 'intelligence'. However, such assessment is not a universal panacea, and some difficulties in using currently available measures are pointed out by Professor Gredler in particular.

The second section considers some of the **theoretical frameworks** which can provide a setting for the assessment of learning ability. It may seem to put the cart before the horse to consider concept before theory, but at present it is not unfair to say that, whatever the arguments against this practice, the assessment of learning ability is based more on an *ad hoc* use of diverse psychological theories and on empirical success than it is on a more general, broadly-based framework. (The best that can be said is that conventional IQ tests seem to have even less in the way of theoretical foundations.)

Professor Reuven Feuerstein's framework, which is discussed by Mogens Jensen, Reuven Feuerstein, Yaacov Rand, Shlomo Kaniel and David Tzuriel in Chapter 4, has generated considerable research interest, particularly in Europe, Israel and the United States. 'Structural Cognitive Modifiability' makes a clear distinction between those individuals and groups who are 'culturally different' and those who are 'culturally deprived'. Although under some circumstances the manifest level of functioning of both groups may be quite similar, and in both cases may require mediation and educational intervention, the underlying etiology (cultural difference vs. cultural deprivation) will indicate considerable differences in the nature, intensity and mode of this intervention. The key factor is 'Mediated Learning':

> the interactional process between the developing human organism and an experienced adult who, by interposing himself between the child and external sources of stimulation, mediates the world to him by framing, selecting, focussing and feeding back environmental experience in such a way as to create appropriate learning sets!
>
> (Feuerstein, 1970, pp. 358–9)

The culturally deprived, through lack of sufficient exposure to mediated learning, will often lack important cognitive skills, and in particular flexibility and modifiability, whereas the culturally different, with adequate exposure to mediated learning, may initially have similar difficulties when immersed in a strange culture, but these are essentially due to a lack of knowledge rather than a lack of cognitive skills. The Learning Potential Assessment Device (LPAD) which is firmly based in this theoretical framework, is crucial both in diagnosis and in defining appropriate remediation.

Vygotskii's work and his Cultural Historical Theory of mental development, described by Andrew Sutton in Chapter 5, is less familiar to Western academics, although beginning to receive more attention. The different historical and political origins of Vygotskii's work (accompanied by difficulties in translation), should not hide from us the underlying similarities with many of the views expressed in earlier chapters. The focus on the 'Zone of Next Development' in particular expresses exactly the central thrust of the argument in favour of assessing, however imprecisely, a child's future learning potential rather than his or her current status. (It should not however be assumed that the Vygotskian tradition is necessarily in sympathy with attempts to reduce this assessment to procedures possessing, at least in some measure, psychometrically desirable properties.) If societies do undergo predictable historical changes, along with related cultural developments, history, sociology and politics interact with psychology much more than non-Marxist scholars in the West have been prepared to consider.

The final section considers some **current research and practice**. The editors, in Chapter 6, show how a particular instrument, the Learning Efficiency Test Battery, was designed, developed and psychometrically validated. Although this particular assessment device was specifically constructed with Asian children living in Britain in mind, some evidence is presented that it is of wider application. Part of the purpose of this chapter is to provide an example (not necessarily perfect!) so that others may be encouraged to develop a variety of high-quality measures of learning ability. The existence of a range of good measures of learning potential might encourage more practitioners and researchers to use them in their work as sheer availability accounts for some of the continued use of intelligence tests.

Presenting learning tasks without considering affective factors, is, in our judgement, extremely unwise. Many children referred for assessment may have a long history of failure, particularly in basic school subjects. Presenting such children with learning tasks with the intention of assessing their learning ability, but where those tasks are culled from a subject domain in which they have a history of learning failure, can generate feelings of anxiety, fear of betraying inadequacy, and poor self-esteem, leading to avoidance behaviour. Any child experiencing such feelings is unlikely to be able to concentrate well on the task in hand, and hence his or her performance will be adversely affected (see also Bloom, 1976; Spielberger, 1975). In Chapter 7, David Tzuriel, Marilyn Samuels and Reuven Feuerstein discuss the influence of non-intellective factors during the administration of the LPAD. They consider how these influences can be understood and evaluated, and suggest some useful strategies for modifying their influence during a dynamic assessment procedure. Such an understanding is important, not only in respect of children's test performances, but also in understanding the learning difficulties which they may be experiencing in school and everyday life.

It seems likely there are distinct cultural differences in those affective factors which relate to varied learning tasks. Only by understanding and responding to these can we hope to achieve some measure of fairness across different cultural backgrounds. Monique Boekaerts, in Chapter 8, shows that in some important respects, even Flemish and Dutch pupils, who might be thought to be reasonably culturally similar, differ in the way they think about learning. Some implications for the classroom are discussed.

References

Bloom, B. S. (1976), *Human Characteristics and School Learning* (New York: McGraw-Hill Book Company).

Cronbach, L. J. (1970), *Essentials of Psychological Testing*, 3rd edn (New York: Harper International Edition).

Cronbach, L. J. (1984), *Essentials of Psychological Testing*, 4th edn (New York: Harper & Row).

Duncanson, J. P. (1964), *Intelligence and the Ability to Learn* (Princeton: Educational Testing Service.)

Feuerstein, R. (1970), 'A dynamic approach to the causation, prevention and alleviation of retarded performance' in H. C. Haywood (ed.) *Social-Cultural Aspects of Mental Retardation* (New York: Appleton-Century Croft).

Gould, S. J. (1984), *The Mismeasure of Man* (Harmondsworth: Penguin Books).

Guilford, J. P. (1967), *The Nature of Human Intelligence* (New York: McGraw, Hill Book Company).

Mackay, G. W. S., Vernon, P. G. (1963), 'The measurement of learning ability', *British Journal of Educational Psychology,* **33,** 177–186.

Malmi, R. A., Underwood, B. J., Carroll, J. B. (1979), 'The interrelationships among some associative learning tasks', *Bulletin of the Psychonomic Society,* **13,** 3, 121–3.

Spielberger, C. D. (1975), 'Anxiety: state: trait-process' in C. D. Spielberger and I. G. Sarason (eds) *Stress and Anxiety*, vol. 1 (New York: John Wiley & Sons).

Stake, R. E. (1961), 'Learning parameters, aptitudes and achievements'. *Psychometric Mon.* No. 9.

Vernon, P. E. (1969), *Intelligence and Cultural Environment* (London: Methuen).

Woodrow, H. (1938a), 'The effect of practice on test intercorrelations', *Journal of Educational Psychology*, **29**, 268–278.

Woodrow, H. (1938b), 'The relation between abilities and improvement with practice', *Journal of Educational Psychology,* **29,** 215–30.

Woodrow, H. (1939a), 'Factors in improvement with practice', *Journal of Educational Psychology,* **I,** 55–70.

Woodrow, H. (1939b), 'The application of factor analysis to problems of practice', *Journal of General Psychology,* **21,** 457–60.

Woodrow, H. (1939c), 'The relation of verbal ability to improvement with practice in verbal tests', *Journal of Educational Psychology,* **30,** 179–86.

1 Why Assess Learning Potential?

Rajinder M. Gupta and Peter Coxhead

INTRODUCTION

In this chapter, we attempt to set out the reasons why the assessment of learning efficiency is frequently to be preferred to the more traditional forms of assessment widely used hitherto. There are two main directions to the argument. Firstly, traditional assessment procedures are demonstrably unfair to many ethnic minority groups. Secondly, there are sound theoretical reasons, increasingly backed by research evidence, for believing that the assessment of learning efficiency is more relevant to the determination of the appropriate educational provision for a child than are traditional procedures.

It is important to set out clearly from the start our reasons for attaching considerable importance to the issue of educational decisions relating to ethnic minority children. It is emphatically *not* that we believe that traditional procedures are acceptable for the cultural majority but somehow uniquely unfair to ethnic minority children. Nothing would be gained, and much lost, by having a separate set of assessment procedures used for ethnic minorities only; inevitably these procedures would come to be seen as second-rate. Rather, it is that traditional assessment methods implicitly pre-suppose a certain set of family and community inputs to a child's prior learning experiences. It has always been the case that many children within the majority community have not had these experiences; perhaps for socio-economic reasons, perhaps because of different traditions of child-rearing. However, in the absence of clearly identifiable ethnic minorities, it has always been possible for educators to minimise and even ignore such differences in children's prior experiences, and to believe, however incorrectly, that at least the principle of the unitary model held; individual differences being due solely to so-called 'cultural deficits'. Faced with distinct ethnic groups with their own developed and autonomous cultural practices, it becomes impossible to sweep away these prior differences; instead it is essential to ensure that assessment procedures are used which are demonstrably fair, regardless of prior cultural experience. In our view, assessing learning efficiency takes a major step towards this goal.

ETHNIC DISPROPORTION IN SPECIAL SCHOOLS

In Britain, Coard (1971) was probably amongst the first to voice disquiet concerning the over-representation of West Indian children in special schools and/or units. Referring to the figures from the Inner London Education Authority survey (1968), *The Education of Immigrant Pupils in Special Schools for Educationally Subnormal Children*, Coard drew attention to the survey's findings that in 1967 in five of their ESN secondary schools there were 30 per cent 'immigrant' children, and that by January 1968 in one of these special schools the numbers rose to 60 per cent. In 1970, while there were only 17 per cent 'immigrant' children in ordinary schools, there were nearly 34 per cent 'immigrant' children in ESN schools; of all 'immigrant' children in ESM(M) schools, 80 per cent were of West Indian origin (see also Townsend, 1971). The Department of Education and Science's statistics (1972) further confirm that in almost all categories of special schools the number of West Indian children far exceeds the rest of the groups: compared to children from the 'rest of the commonwealth', there were nearly 66 times more West Indian children in special schools – surely an unacceptable and alarming figure by any standards.

The findings of a recent investigation (reported by Roberts, 1984) carried out in a Midlands town in England furnish further evidence that children from West Indian and Indian backgrounds are over-represented in remedial classes compared to their 'white' peers. These figures are summarised in Table 1.1.

Table 1.1 Percentage of children of each ethnic group in remedial classes

	West Indian	*Indian*	*Majority*
Remedial English	17%	12%	5%
Remedial Maths	19%	12%	8%

Source: Adapted from Roberts, 1984.

Compare the figures in Table 1.1 with those in Table 1.2. Table 1.2

shows the number of children in the same town with West Indian background, compared to their indigenous peers, who went to grammar schools or were placed in grammar school streams (including sixth formers). The comparison is quite striking.

Table 1.2 Percentage of children of each ethnic group attending grammar schools/streams including sixth formers

West Indian	*Indian*	*Majority*
2.5%	17.5%	30.1%

Source: Adapted from Roberts, 1984.

'Majority' children were nearly fifteen times as likely to be selected for grammar school education as West Indian children and almost twice as likely as Indian children. (See also Wilce, 1985, who reports Taylor's research suggesting that the verbal reasoning tests used at the 11+ selection may be biased against ethnic minority groups).

It is, however, not only in Britain where over-representation of children from ethnic minority groups in special schools has been observed. This has been noted in the United States too (Brady, *et al.*, 1983, and several studies cited therein; Tucker, 1980). In fact, in America the issue of the misclassification and over-representation of ethnic minority children has been studied at a greater depth than in Britain. Brady *et al.* (1983) quote an earlier survey conducted in the United States, concerned with the issue of the over-representation of ethnic minority children in special schools. They state:

> Eugene Doll, in a 1962 historical review of this country's management of mental retardation, wrote that 'many subcultures and economically marginal groups contribute to the problem of retardation all out of proportion to their number' (Doll, 1962, p. 81). It is twenty years later and this statement is still true.
>
> (Brady *et al.*, 1983, p. 295)

To illustrate their point Brady *et al.* refer to a study conducted by the New Jersey State Department which found that 43 per cent of black children were categorised as EMR (Educable Mentally Retarded) whilst they constituted only 17.8 per cent of the public school population; comparable figures for Hispanic children were 13.3 per cent labelled as EMR whilst they constituted only 7.4 per cent of the total school population. Brady *et al.* also add that such data is not peculiar to states such as New Jersey, but is typical 'of the Nation as a whole' (p. 296). (See also Argulewich and Sanchez, 1983. Tobias *et al.* (1983) cite findings of their earlier investigations (Tobias *et al.*, 1982) which add a further dimension to the issue of over-representation of ethnic minority children in special schools and units in that they show that teacher differ by race in the extent of referrals.)

Referral of a child of any ethnic group for special educational provision, either by a teacher or other agency, is an important part of the procedure but it is not the sole basis for placing children in special schools and units. What really determines the placement of a child in a special school is the outcome of the assessment procedure employed. If the assessment procedure employed is biased against the child, then the probability of the child's being incorrectly placed is very high. Commenting on the assessment practices which were employed by many practitioners – and probably still are – Hegarty (1977) observed that children from non-English speaking homes were at a disadvantage in British schools. Pointing particularly to their linguistic handicap, Hegarty argued that they performed poorly in schools compared with indigenous children; this in turn meant that they were liable to be sent for remedial assessment. The assessment procedures which were employed were unfair and inappropriate for these children, resulting in the disadvantage being compounded. Little wonder the outcome of such an assessment was that there were many more 'immigrant' children in ESN(M) schools in relation to their English counterparts (see also Tomlinson, 1981).

ETHNIC MINORITIES VERSUS TRADITIONAL ASSESSMENT PROCEDURES

There are many reasons why traditional assessment procedures, IQ tests in particular, have become a focus of criticism. Among some of the well rehearsed and acknowledged reasons for this criticism are two that we consider relevant here. First, IQ tests assess the products of previous learning and thus penalise children from diverse cultural and home backgrounds who may have had different learning experiences compared to those on whom the tests have been standardised. Since a majority of the existing IQ tests have been mainly designed for and standardised on western type populations, they should not really be used to make crucial decisions about children where previous experiences and culture differ substantially from the former group.

There is ample cross-cultural evidence which suggests that different cultures tend to stimulate and favour the development and application of different cognitive skills and strategies for coping with their environments (Anastasi and Foley, 1949; Berry, 1981; Bruner, 1966; Cole *et al.*, 1971; De Vos and Hippler, 1969; Ferguson, 1954; Ghuman, 1975; Vernon, 1969).

For instance, the recent study of Farquhar *et al.* (1983) has shown that there are differences between 'white' and 'black' parents in the skills which they encourage during the early development of their children. Farquhar *et al.* found that 'white' parents tended to encourage activities like drawing, whilst 'black' parents placed emphasis on teaching self help skills. Sharron (1985) referring to the work of Professor R. Feuerstein in Israel with the Falashas (Ethiopian children airlifted to Israel) reports that these children's ability to learn new concepts (it is not made clear what type of concepts) far exceeded expectations. At the same time, there were domains where the Falashas showed certain weaknesses, for example, these children's ability to grasp complex drawings was not commensurate with their general potential to learn some other types of concepts.

In addition there is also evidence which suggests, though contrary to popular belief, that even if children from minority cultures are brought up and educated in a dominant culture all their tested skills and abilities are not equally affected. Ghuman (1975) found that as a result of exposure to the British educational system West Indian and Indian children showed significant improvement on a range of verbal and educational abilities but *not* on spatial and perceptual abilities. Gupta (1983) too, found that unlike some of the other domains of mental skills (for example maths, English, and mental maturity as measured by the Draw-a-Man test (Harris, 1963) which are sensitive to English education) short-term memory was least influenced either by English schooling or Western culture. In fact, what Gupta found was that short-term memory was *better* developed both in Asian children and in children living in India compared to English children. Short-term memory would appear to be an area where the influence of the home on Asian children is stronger than outside influences. It is an important point because it challenges the common but erroneous thinking regarding children from different ethnic and cultural backgrounds who are born and brought up in Britain, as being likely to have developed similar types of cognitive processes as the children of the dominant culture: the rationale behind this type of thinking being that all these children have had equal opportunities to learn and have been exposed to the dominant culture. Unfortunately, this type of fallacious thinking grossly underestimates the powerful influence of home and one's culture on abilities.

A second major criticism is that information about the child's IQ is hardly an aid in designing a curriculum appropriate to the child's developmental level. This limitation of IQ tests has received considerable attention these days as the demands of test results have changed. Tests must now be useful in planning educational programmes rather than just being tools of prediction or identifying which children need special education and which would benefit from receiving education in the mainstream of education. (See also Jones and Jones, 1985, who also state several other limitations of IQ tests.) Carroll and Horn (1981) (see also McReynolds, 1982) also point out that:

> The IQ for one individual can be based on a combination of high and low scores for component abilities that is different from the combination for the same IQ for another individual, and there is insufficient evidence that such combinations have the same implications. (p. 1017)

Vernon (1969) hits at the fundamental misconception about IQ tests and at those who consider IQ tests as measures of learning potential. He states that it is amazing that IQ tests are used for predicting potential for learning notwithstanding that none of the subtests in IQ test batteries assess the child's learning ability.

It is possible to add to this several other reasons for not using IQ tests on ethnic minority children. The intention here is not to be exhaustive but just to highlight some of the well known pitfalls of employing IQ tests on ethnic minority children for assessing their potential to profit from instruction or for the purposes of decision making. Although a large majority of psychologists are aware that the traditional IQ tests are inappropriate for ethnic minority children (*cf.* Mackenzie, 1980), such tests continue to be used as one of the important criteria for the purposes of classifying and placing these children in special schools and units. Commenting on the use and relative importance of IQ tests for the purposes of decision making, Tomlinson (1981), says:

> Although the psychologists regard IQ as only one factor in the assessment process; it is still seen as an important factor and the dubious history of the application of IQ testing ... does not seen to worry psychologists unduly. (p. 294)

The Warnock report (DES, 1978) and the DES (1983) document, *Assessments and Statements of Special Educational Needs* (both UK studies) do not appear to provide any firm guidelines with regard to the use of IQ tests on ethnic minority children either. What impact these two documents have had on practising psychologists with regard to their use of IQ tests on ethnic minority children is difficult to gauge in the absence of published evidence. Notwithstanding any empirical evidence, one view is that 'the concept of "special Needs"', which is enshrined in the Warnock Report and the DES (1983) document, fails to provide any direction for the evaluation of not only ethnic minority but the rest of the children as well (Tomlinson, 1984).

In the United States, the indictment of racial, ethnic and cultural bias against the testing procedure and assessors has led to the involvement of the judicial system (e.g. Diana vs. California State Board of Education, 1969; Hobson vs. Hanson, 1967; Larry P. vs. Wilson Riles, 1979, cited in Brady *et al.*, 1983). The findings of the judiciary appear to confirm the evidence of discriminatory practices in the procedures followed in the assessment of black children and Franklin (1984) observes that there have been cases of the 'horrendous unethical use of tests' involving testing children in a language or dialect which is unfamiliar to the test takers, and then basing decisions on such test results (p. 10).

Little wonder, then, that the use of standardised IQ tests for the purposes of identifying and placing ethnic minority children in educable mentally retarded classes has been prohibited by judicial order (Duffy, *et al.*, 1981). Remarking on current American attitudes towards the use of intelligence tests on ethnic minority children, Vernon (1979) stated that they were no longer perceived as 'veridical'; rather they were now criticised and distrusted, and several states were considering banning them from use in schools on the grounds of being culturally biased and inappropriate measures of intelligence. Vernon continues that in the present milieu the use of low IQ scores for placing children in special schools or rejecting them for employment had also been successfully challenged. Thus, the growing concern with the use of IQ tests in general, and in particular on children from diverse cultural backgrounds, has inspired several workers to develop alternative forms of assessment: some of them will be considered in the next section.

ALTERNATIVE FORMS OF ASSESSMENT

Some psychologists, who are acutely aware of the pitfalls of using traditional assessment procedures to evaluate the mental processes of ethnic minority children and the attendant problem of their over-representation in special schools, have started examining alternative forms of assessment to ensure non-biased outcomes of evaluation procedures. In America in order to eliminate bias in assessment two methods of evaluation have been recommended in the 'Protection in Evaluation Procedures' (see Brady *et al.*, 1983). The first procedure is concerned with a multi-disciplinary team approach for the purposes of decision making; the other includes the assessment of adaptive behaviour. Brady *et al.* (1983) refer to several studies which provide some support for a multi-disciplinary team approach for the purposes of decision making; they also refer to a considerable body of literature which shows practical difficulties with the implementation of this approach. To date, there is a paucity of data with regard to the actual influence this particular assessment model has had on ethnic representation in special educational schools and units. However the limited data that is available would suggest that, where this approach has been in use for a number of years, ethnic disproportion has not decreased relative to places where multi-disciplinary teams are not employed for the purposes of assessment.

So far as the second recommended assessment procedure is concerned, the assessment of adaptive behaviour, Brady *et al.* (1983) state that there is some evidence which suggests that this procedure does in fact reduce the ethnic disproportion in special schools. Unfortunately, though, there is little evidence which verifies its use by practitioners. Consider Table 1.3 which clearly shows that many districts do not collect data about adaptive behaviour despite the legal requirement.

Brady *et al.* conclude that although the two assessment approaches have had the backing of the Federal government, neither of them is

Table 1.3 School districts cited by level II monitors for failure to collect adaptive behaviour data over 3-year period

School Year	*Level II Evaluations*	*No. of school districts cited for failure to collect adaptive-behaviour data*
1978–79	6	3 (50%)
1979–80	10	7 (70%)
1980–81	7	6 (85%)

Source: After Brady, *et al.*, 1983.

proving effective (see also Reschly, 1984, and the studies cited therein for their critical evaluation of the assessment of adaptive behaviour).

In Britain, attempts to devise alternative forms of assessment have been much more modest and the government has not been involved to the same extent as in the United States. Haynes (1971) was among the pioneer workers who provided a lead by developing a battery of tests which attempted to circumvent many of the now well recognised objections to the current practices of assessing minority children (see also Feuerstein, 1980; Haywood *et al.*, 1975; Hegarty and Lucas, 1978; Lambert *et al.*, 1974). The result was an unpublished test battery based on the concept of learning ability.

Haynes' research involved 7- to 8-year-old children (125 Indian and 40 English) from the Southall district of the London Borough of Ealing. As well as attainment and IQ tests, Haynes also administered five self-devised learning tasks to her total sample. The results revealed significant differences on four out of five learning tasks in favour of English children. Significant differences were also found on all the attainment and most of the IQ tests used in the study except for the WISC Coding and Draw-a-Man Tests.

The key finding of this investigation was that Haynes' battery of learning tasks was a better predictor of 125 Indian children's academic progress than the Performance Scale of the WISC (Wechsler, 1949). Although Haynes made a significant contribution by highlighting the importance of assessing the learning ability of children with diverse cultural backgrounds, rather than relying on the use of IQ and attainment tests, her results suggest that her learning tasks seem to suffer from a similar kind of cultural bias to that reported in many of the commonly used IQ tests. If Haynes' learning tasks had tapped mental processes which are fairly equally favoured in the two cultures, it is reasonable to speculate that there would not have been significant differences in favour of English children on four out of five learning tasks. Despite this weakness in Haynes' learning tasks, its 'novel approach to testing offered a way round some of the obstacles associated with assessment in multicultural situations' (Hegarty, 1977, p. 4).

This study led to the Department of Education and Science commissioning the National Foundation for Education Research (NFER) to develop and validate test materials for predicting the learning potential of children for whom conventional forms of assessment were unsuitable on the grounds of their linguistic and cultural backgrounds (Hegarty and Lucas, 1978; see also chapter 2).

Haynes (1971) and Hegarty and Lucas' (1978) work have provided significant advances in the field of testing, but unfortunately their work, or for that matter the notion of learning ability as an assessment tool, has, on the whole, generated very little interest in the United Kingdom. Between 1960 and 1980, apart from Haynes and Hegarty and Lucas' investigations, just two more studies have been conducted where the notion of learning ability plays a key role.

The first is by Mackay and Vernon (1963). The main aim of the study was to devise tests of 'actual learning' and compare their validity in predicting children's future academic progress in the basic subjects with conventional IQ tests – which hardly ever have items which really test the child's ability to learn. The sample consisted of two groups of 8–9 year old and 10–11 year old children with a good middle class background. All these children were administered nine self devised learning tests and ten reference tests which included tests of intelligence, attainment, memory for digits and spatial ability and the Bender Gestalt Test. For the purposes of the analysis of the data the authors used terminal scores. The results were in the expected direction with the 10–11 year old children, but somewhat 'disappointing' with the younger group. With the 8–9 year olds, the results tended to be 'specific' and less predictive. Despite the disappointing results, the authors seem quite optimistic in that they go on to recommend that it should be possible to devise a battery of learning tasks which should be based on a large sample, and such a battery of learning tasks would not only provide information about children's future academic progress but would also be useful in providing information about their style of working, level of concentration, etc. Mackay and Vernon (*op. cit.*) do not speculate in favour of individual learning tests on two grounds. Firstly, they would need to be prohibitively lengthy to permit sufficient practice; secondly, there may be significant differences in the child's reaction in the learning situation on the one hand and the classroom situation on the other.

In this study, although Mackay and Vernon are fully aware of the fact that their results are based on a small sample, and that any interpretations therefore need to be made with considerable caution, the authors seem to be making claims which a study based on such a small sample does not warrant. For instance, they offer quite unguarded or unqualified opinions about the use of gain scores and whether tests of learning should be individual tests, or a group test. However, Mackay and Vernon deserve credit for being ahead of their time, at least in Britain, in questioning the common, but in our view fallacious, notion of equating intelligence with learning ability.

The interested reader is also referred to another study by Kroeger

(1980). Briefly, the major goal of this study was to examine the role of teaching in the evaluation of learning ability in 'migrant' children. The study was concerned with a number of issues but pertinent to the present discussion is the author's argument in favour of using learning test scores for the purposes of predicting future academic performance, as opposed to conventional IQ tests.

This would seem to be the sum total of research effort in the domain of learning ability in Great Britain. Although there is clearly a dearth of literature in this field, studies which have been carried out, irrespective of their constraints, shortcomings, and disappointments, seem to reiterate the point that *in order to measure children's ability to learn, especially that of ethnic minority groups, tests of learning ability should be used rather than conventional IQ tests, which provide little information about the child's ability to learn*.

In the United States, unlike Britain, the area of learning ability has been a subject of much more theoretical as well as research interest. This may well be due to the fact that American psychologists have a wider experience of assessing the needs of individuals with diverse backgrounds (Anastasi, 1976), and they have also long recognised the limitations of IQ tests (Jensen, 1961, 1963), as measures the abilities of children with different backgrounds and experiences. Criticising the use of IQ tests on ethnic minority children and high-lighting the positive aspects of assessing their learning potential, Jensen wrote:

> The standard intelligence tests currently in use are actually static measures of achievement which sample the knowledge and skills the child has acquired in the past. Often this sampling can be quite inappropriate for children who have not had much exposure to the Anglo-American culture of the normative group. It would seem that a better way to measure learning potential, or to decide whether a child is inherently a slow learner, would be to give the child a standard task and observe how fast he learns it, whereby we may note how readily the child's behaviour changes through the trial-and-error of experience. (Jensen, 1961, p. 148)

This was over two decades ago and perhaps over the years Jensen has revised his views about the inappropriateness of using IQ tests on ethnic minority children. Notwithstanding Jensen's present views about IQ tests and learning tasks, the current climate in the United States would appear to be that the justification for using IQ tests on ethnic minority children is being examined and questioned not just from the psychometric standpoint but also from the social, economic, ethical, political and legal standpoints as well (see *American Psychologist*, 36, 1981; the whole issue was devoted to various aspects of assessment including the assessment of ethnic minority groups).

Hegarty and Lucas (1978) advance several reasons in favour of assessing learning efficiency. Unlike in conventional assessment where the main emphasis is on performance, in the assessment of learning efficiency the main focus is on the processes that underly it. Hegarty and Lucas also believe that with learning tasks it is possible to equate previous experiences by using tasks which, as far as possible, are equally unfamiliar to all children. Vernon (1969) also supports this view when he states that the assessment of learning ability:

> should overcome the difficulty that different groups of individuals within a group will always be at different stages of familiarisation. (Vernon, 1969, p. 106)

Yet another advantage posited by Hegarty and Lucas is that since IQ is not an index of a child's rate of learning, then with a measure of learning efficiency we can identify children of different learning abilities but in the same IQ range (see Chapter 2). Gupta (1983) too obtained similar findings when developing the Learning Efficiency Test Battery (see also Gupta and Coxhead, Chapter 6 in this volume).

Hegarty and Lucas also claim that for certain groups of children tests of learning ability are more effective than IQ tests in predicting school achievement. The development of their learning ability tests provide empirical support to their claim (see also Haynes, 1971). Gupta too found that, particularly in the case of his specially selected sample (children who according to the conventional assessment procedures, that is IQ measures and/or teachers' ratings, were in the bottom 5 per cent of the population) the Learning Efficiency Test Battery, in the main, was better relative to conventional measures of assessment in predicting gains in reading whether measured directly or indirectly through the covariance approach (for details see Gupta, 1983, 1984).

A further advantage of results obtained from a child's performance on learning tasks lies in determining his future educational needs and in inferring the teaching effort he is likely to require in order to master or grasp new concepts or skills. Efficient performance on learning tasks is likely to be inversely related to teaching effort; in other words, high scorers would require less teaching input to reach mastery level as opposed to low scorers. In the testing situation, were the child to require an inordinate amount of teaching effort to reach criterion, this would suggest that in the classroom situation he would be likely to need a substantial amount of teaching help in order to grasp new concepts. For any decision making then the central question would be: can the teacher concerned provide the teaching input the child is likely to require or does the psychologist need to explore some kind of special educational provision where the teaching could be carried out at the child's pace of learning?

Learning tasks, as opposed to IQ tests, offer a better opportunity to the psychologist to observe such attributes as the child's attention span, perseverance, learning style – all of which are of considerable importance to future success or failure (Cattell, 1965; Mackay and Vernon, 1963).

SOME STUDIES CONCERNING THE VALUE OF LEARNING EFFICIENCY IN THE UNITED STATES AND ISRAEL

Milton Budoff and his associates at the Cambridge Laboratory, Haywood and his associates at the Nashville Laboratory (both of these groups in the United States) and Feuerstein in Israel are among the leading psychologists who have made significant contributions in the field of learning ability. Budoff has studied 'educable mentally retarded' children, Haywood has studied 'cultural-familially retarded' and Feuerstein 'immigrants' in Israel. Although each of these workers has offered different explanations as to why their subjects' performance was considerably lower on traditional standardised tests, they all came to the same conclusion that conventional IQ tests were unsuitable for assessing these children's intellectual ability or for drawing inferences about their learning potential regarding IQ as an invalid and biased index (see also Rohwer *et al.*, 1971). In the succeeding pages, some of the work of Budoff, Haywood and Feuerstein which highlights their views on the issue of learning potential will be reviewed (for further details of their work see Haywood *et al.*, 1975; Hegarty and Lucas, 1978; see also Feuerstein, 1980).

Haywood and his associates

At the Nashville Laboratory, Haywood and his associates discovered that standard intelligence tests under-estimated the ability of 'cultural-familially retarded' individuals to form verbal abstractions. These writers claim that such individuals are not necessarily deficient in forming verbal abstractions, but suffer from information deficit. Haywood *et al.* (1975) regard verbal abstractions as being at the heart of social interaction in our day-to-day living. By verbal abstraction they mean those activities which involve grouping and classifying isolated events and giving them abstract labels on the resultant categories. For instance, various fruits such as banana, grape, plum, apple, etc., can be grouped into a single category and given the abstract label fruit. Haywood *et al.*, further explains:

> In a sense, the individual performs a factor analysis on the data that impinge upon his senses; that is, he uses a central process to reduce a large number of isolated events to a small number of abstract categories to determine whether a new event can be assimilated into an existing category. If so, the new event can be understood more easily. (Haywood *et al.*, 1975, p. 104)

In order to provide empirical evidence for the hypothesis of information deficit in cultural-familially retarded persons Gordon and Haywood (1969) administered a 22 item similarities test (a subtest from the WISC) under two conditions to known organically retarded and cultural-familially retarded institutionalised subjects. The two conditions of administration of the test were: standard and 'enriched'. In the latter condition, there were five exemplars instead of two as in the standard condition. In addition to organically retarded and culturally retarded groups, the authors also included a group of non-retarded children who were equated with the retarded children on mental age. The results of this experiment supported the prediction. Under the standard condition the performance of the mental-age matched, non-retarded group was significantly better than both retarded groups.

However, under the enriched condition the scores of the culturally deprived group were significantly better than their own scores under the standard condition; significantly better than the enriched condition scores of the organically retarded group; and there were no significant differences between the non-retarded and culturally deprived children on the the conditions which employed five exemplars. From these results, Gordon and Haywood conclude that children from culturally deprived backgrounds are not retarded in their ability to form verbal abstractions but suffer from an information input deficit. This deficit is modifiable by enriching the information presented to such children. With regard to non-retarded subjects, the authors maintain since information deficit is not assumed one should not expect that such a group is likely to benefit from enrichment procedure. In the case of the organically retarded group, Gordon and Haywood explain their performance as follows:

1. either brain damage might have actually caused damage to the central abstracting processes; or
2. the enrichment procedure was not sufficient to surmount the deficit that might have been present in these children.

Other workers at the Nashville Laboratory (e.g. Call, 1973; Foster, 1970; Tyrnchuk, 1973) have several times tested the input-deficit hypothesis of Gordon and Haywood involving different samples and found results in line with the earlier study of Gordon and Haywood (1969).

The aforementioned studies provide empirical evidence to the Haywood *et al.* (1975) hypothesis of input deficit amongst culturally deprived children and to their claim that by enriching the supply of information these children can be helped to perform verbal abstracting tasks at a normal level. However, the authors are careful in their claim in that they do not infer that given enriched input, mildly culturally deprived children would be able to perform as well as their normal peers in any domain. These findings nevertheless, have an important bearing on actual classroom teaching practice. For instance, in the light of the input-deficit model, teachers could try enriching their traditional way of presenting teaching materials to culturally deprived or culturally different children, to see, if by so doing, their level of performance in basic subjects can be brought up to par with indigenous children. Although the authors of the input deficiency model present an intriguing hypothesis and support it with well designed empirical evidence, it is difficult to imagine that this alone could be at the heart of the difference that one finds in the the performance of ethnic minority children and children from the dominant culture.

Budoff and his associates

At the Cambridge Laboratory (Massachusetts, America) Budoff and his colleagues have been concerned with determining the learning potential of children who have been diagnosed as educable mentally retarded (EMR) by standardised tests. They found that by assessing these children's learning potential they could identify children who were essentially and intrinsically EMR; whilst others, although identified as EMR by standardised tests, were functioning at that level due to verbal deficiencies (Budoff, 1967; 1969). In order to obtain an index of these children's learning potential Budoff and his associates have adapted some of the existing non-verbal tests, e.g. Kohs Blocks, Feuerstein's Learning Potential Assessment Device, and the Raven's Matrices (see Johnson, 1976).

Budoff has carried out several studies (e.g. 1967, 1969) in order to test his hypothesis concerning verbal deficiencies in educable mentally retarded children. In one of his earlier studies Budoff (1967) presented Koh's Blocks three times to a group of educable mentally retarded (EMR) adolescents. During the first administration the child's base level of functioning was obtained, followed by a period of training with a view to coaching the children in such activities as the analysis of each design into simple elements, the concept of two colour blocks as the components of more complex designs and a systematic comparison with the standard design. After completion of the training period, the children were re-tested: first a day after the training period, and then a month after the training period. The pattern of results that emerged as a result of presenting Koh's Blocks this way, was that there was a small group of children amongst this sample who achieved fairly high scores during the first testing and were able to solve difficult problems; this group showed little evidence of benefiting from the coaching. Budoff called them high scorers. There were some children amongst the EMR group who obtained quite low scores during the first testing but made substantial gains as a result of the coaching. They were described as gainers. There emerged yet another group: this group's performance was quite poor on all three occasions (non-gainers). From these findings and on the basis of another study (Budoff, 1969) where he followed the same procedure as in the earlier study (except that in this second study Budoff used the Raven's Matrices, Wechsler's Performance Test and concept shift tasks) Budoff found that, in the main, the performance of gainers was superior to non-gainers both in speed and efficiency of learning. From these two studies Budoff advanced the idea that there are two categories amongst EMR children: some who may be considered as 'truly intrinsically mentally retarded' (Budoff, 1969, p. 286), whilst others are not essentially mentally retarded in this sense but their retardation could be associated with verbal deficiencies. Furthermore, individuals who demonstrate greater gains on Budoff's assessment devices are significantly more competent compared to non-gainers in all aspects of social functioning.

Budoff (1969) maintains that the results obtained from assessing the child's potential have a useful implication for the practitioner. Once the 'gainers' have been identified on the basis of their learning potential score then this information can be used in designing a curriculum appropriate for the need of these children. The provision of the appropriate curriculum for these 'gainers' would enable them to benefit from schooling at least as much as their low achieving peers in the mainstream of education. The assessment of learning potential would also help to identify able children who may be likely to be at risk.

Feuerstein

Feuerstein's work in Israel developed for more or less the same reasons as Gupta's (1983) research in the UK: to resolve the problem of assessing 'immigrants' with a diverse cultural and educational background. The use of conventional IQ and attainment tests on these adolescent immigrants showed, in the main, the same kind of results as have been observed in Britain and the United States, i.e. their performance on scholastic-achievement tests was very low and they also demonstrated a developmental lag ranging from nearly four to six years in several cognitive areas (Feuerstein, 1980). Disenchanted with conventional assessment procedures, Feuerstein developed his own theory and an assessment device (Learning Potential Assessment Device, Feuerstein, 1968), rooted in 'a theory of the nature and development of intelligent functioning' (Haywood *et al.*, 1975). One of the key features of this assessment device is that assessment is not carried out in a void. It is linked with intervention and the remediation of areas found deficient as a result of assessment. It is claimed that Feuerstein's approach, which embraces both assessment and remediation has benefited thousands of academically retarded immigrants who emigrated to Israel (Haywood *et al.*, 1975; see also Feuerstein, 1980; Hegarty and Lucas, 1978, and Chapters 4 and 7 in this book).

In conclusion, what we have attempted to show in this chapter is that assessment practices which are currently in vogue for testing children from ethnic minority groups, are less than satisfactory and should not be employed. There is a danger that continued reliance on these practices can result in these children's over-representation in special schools which is socially and ethically indefensible. It has also been highlighted that it is erroneous to use IQ tests as measures of learning efficiency. In order to assess learning efficiency instruments designed to measure this process should be used. Several benefits which can accrue as a result of the assessment of learning efficiency have also been noted. There has been some modest effort in this direction in Britain, but more research is required.

References

Anastasi, A. (1976), *Psychological Testing*, 4th edn (New York: Macmillan).

Anastasi, A., Foley, J. P. (1949), *Differential Psychology* (New York: Macmillan).

Argulewich, E. N., Sanchez, D. T. (1983), 'The special education evaluation process as a moderator of false positives', *Exceptional Children*, **49**, 5, 452–4.

Berry, J. W. (1981), 'Cultural systems and cognitive styles' in Friedman, M. P., Das, J. P., O'Connor, N. (eds), *Intelligence and Learning* (New York: Plenum Press).

Brady, P. M., Manni, J. L., Winnikur, D. W. (1983), 'Implications of ethnic disproportion in programs for the educable mentally retarded', *Journal of Special Education*, **17**, 3, 295–302.

Bruner, J. S. (1966), 'On cognitive growth' in Bruner, J. S., Oliver, R., Greenfield, P. M., *Studies in Cognitive Growth* (London: John Wiley).

Budoff, M. (1967), 'Learning potential among institutionalised young adult retardates', *American Journal of Mental Deficiency*, **72**, 404–11.

Budoff, M. (1969), 'Learning potential: a supplementary procedure for assessing the ability to reason', *Seminars in Psychiatry*, 1, 278–90.

Call, R. (1973), 'Verbal abstracting performance of low SES children: an exploration of Jensen's theory of Mental Retardation', unpublished doctoral dissertation, George Peabody College.

Carroll, J. B., Horn, J. L. (1981), 'On the scientific basis of ability testing', *American Psychologist*, **36**, 10, 1012–20.

Cattell, R. B. (1965), *The Scientific Analysis of Personality* (Harmondsworth: Penguin Books).

Coard, B. (1971), *How the West Indian Child is made Educationally Subnormal in the British School System* (London: New Beacon).

Cole, M., Gay, J., Glick, J. A., Sharp, D. W. (1971), *The Cultural Content of Learning and Thinking: An Exploration Experimental Anthropology* (New York: Bane Books).

Department of Education and Science (1972), *Statistics in Education*, vol 1 (London: HMSO).

Department of Education and Science (1983), *Assessments & Statements of Special Educational Needs*, Circular 1/83 (London: DES).

Duffy, J. B., Salvia, J., Tucker, J., Ysseldyke, J. (1981), 'Non biased assessment: A need for operationalism', *Exceptional Children*, **47**, 6, 427–34.

Farquhar, C., Blachford, P., Burke, J., Plewis, I., Tizard, B. (1983), 'A comparison of the views of parents and reception teachers'. An adaptation of a paper presented to the British Psychological Society's London Conference.

Ferguson, G. A. (1954), 'Learning and human ability' in Wiseman, S. (ed.), *Intelligence and Ability* (Harmondsworth: Penguin Books).

Feuerstein, R. (1968), 'Learning potential assessment device' in Richards, B. W. (ed.), *Proceedings of the First Congress of the International Association for the Scientific Study of Mental Deficiency* (Reigate, Surrey: Michael Jackson).

Feuerstein, R., Hoffman, M., Shalom, H., Kiram, L., Narrol, H., Schachter, E., Katz, D., Rand, Y. (1972), 'The dynamic assessment of retarded performers: the Learning Potential Assessment Device, theory, instruments, and techniques', *Studies in Cognitive Modifiability*, report No. 1, vol. 1 (Jerusalem: Hadassah-Wizo- Canada Research Institute).

Feuerstein, R. (1980), *Instrumental Enrichment. An Intervention Program for Cognitive Modifiability* (Baltimore: University Park Press).

Foster, M. (1970), 'The effects of different levels of enriched stimulus input on the abstracting ability of slow learning children', unpublished master's thesis, George Peabody College.

Franklin, A. J. (1984), 'Contemporary psychology in a multicultural society', *Educational and Child Psychology*, **1**, 1, 5–13.

Ghuman, P. A. S. (1974), 'A cross-cultural study of the basic thinking processes of English "British" Punjabi and indigenous Punjabi boys', unpublished Ph.D. thesis, University of Birmingham.

Ghuman, P. A. S. (1975), *The Cultural Context of Thinking* (Windsor: NFER).

Gordon, J. E., Haywood, H. C. (1969), 'Input deficit in cultural-familial retardation: effect of stimulus enrichment', *American Journal of Mental Deficiency*, **73**, 604–10.

Gupta, R. M. (1983), 'The assessment of the learning efficiency of Asian children', unpublished Ph.D. thesis, Aston University.

Gupta, R. M. (1984), 'The longitudinal predictive validity of the Learning Efficiency Test Battery', paper presented at the DECP Symposium, on Psychologists and ethnic minority groups at the 1984 Annual Conference of the British Psychological Society, held at Warwick University, Coventry.

Harris, D. B. (1963), *Goodenough-Harris Drawing Test Manual* (New York: Harcourt, Brace & World Inc.).

Haynes, J. M. (1971), *Educational Assessment of Immigrant Pupils* (Slough: NFER).

Haywood, H. C., Filler, J. W., Shifman, M. A., Chatelanat, G. (1975), 'Behavioural assessment in mental retardation', in McReynolds, P. (ed.). *Advances in Psychological Assessment*, vol. 3 (San Francisco: Jossey-Bass Publishers).

Hegarty, S. (1977), *Test of Children's Learning Ability: Individual Version* (Slough: NFER).

Hegarty, S., Lucas, D. (1978), *Able to Learn? The Pursuit of Culture-Fair Assessment* (Slough: NFER).

Inner London Education Authority (1967), *The Education of Immigrant Pupils in Special Schools for ESN Children* (London ILEA Report 657, 10 September.

Jensen, A. R. (1961), 'Learning abilities in Mexican-American and Anglo-American children', *California Journal of Educational Psychology*, **XII**, 4, 147–59.

Jensen, A. R. (1963), 'Learning ability in retarded, average and gifted children', *Merrill-Palmer Quarterly of Behaviour and Development*, **9**, 2, 123–40.

Johnson, O. G. (1976), *Tests and Measurements in Child Development: Handbook II*, vol. 2 (San Francisco: Jossey-Bass Publishers).

Jones, R. L. Jones, J. M. (1985), 'Assessment and special education of minority and immigrant children in the United States: Issues and developments'. Paper presented at the First Circum-Mediterranean Regional IACCP Conference: Ethnic Minority and Immigrant Research (Malmö: Sweden).

Kroeger, E. (1980), 'Cognitive development in the acculturation of migrant children: the role of training in the assessment of learning ability', *International Review of Applied Psychology*, **29**, 1/2, 105–18.

Lambert, N. M., Wilcox, M. R., Gleason, W. P., (1974), *The Educationally Retarded Child* (New York: Grune & Stratton).

Mackay, G. W. S., Vernon, P. E. (1963), 'The measurement of learning ability', *British Journal of Educational Psychology*, **33**, 177–86.

Mackenzie, A. (1980), 'Are ability tests up to standard?' *Australian Psychologist*, **15**, 3, 335–48.

McReynolds, P. (1982), 'The future of psychological assessment', *International Review of Applied Psychology*, **31**, 117–39.

Reschly, D. J. (1984), 'Beyond IQ test bias: the National Academy Panel's analysis of Minority EMR Overrepresentation', *Educational Researcher*, **13**, 15–19.

Roberts, J. R. (1984), 'The relative development and educational achievement of ethnic minority children in a Midlands town', *Educational and Child Psychology*, **1**, 14–22.

Rohwer, W. D., Ammon, M. S., Suzuki, N., Levin, J. R. (1971). 'Population differences & learning proficiency', *Journal of Educational Psychology*, **62**, 1, 1–14.

Sharron, H. (1985), 'Bridging the culture gap', *Times Educational Supplement*, 18 Jan., p. 17.

Taylor, J. H. (1973), 'Newcastle upon Tyne: Asian pupils do better than whites', *British Journal of Sociology*, **24**, 4, 431–47.

Tobias, S., Zibrin, M., Menell, C. (1983), 'Special education referrals: failure to replicate student-teacher ethnicity interaction', *Journal of Educational Psychology*, **75**, 5, 705–7.

Tomlinson, S. (1981), *Special Education* (London: Harper & Row).

Tomlinson, S. (1984), *Home & School in Multicultural Britain* (London: Batsford).

Townsend, H. E. R. (1971), *Immigrant Pupils in England* (Slough: NFER).

Townsend, H. E. R., Brittan, E. M. (1972), *Organisation in Multiracial Schools* (Slough: NFER).

Tucker, J. A. (1980), 'Ethnic disproportions in classes for the learning disabled issues in non-biased assessment', *Journal of Special Education*, **14**, 93–105.

Tyrnchuk, A. J. (1973), 'Effects of concept familiarization vs. stimulus enhancement on verbal abstracting in institutionalized retarded delinquent boys', *American Journal of Mental Deficiency*, **77**, 551–5.

Vernon, P. E. (1969), *Intelligence and Cultural Environment* (London: Methuen).

Vernon, P. E. (1979), *Intelligence: Heridity and Environment* (San Francisco: W. H. Freeman & Company).

Vos, G. A. de, Hippler A. (1969), 'Cultural Psychology: comparative studies of human behaviour' in Lindzey, G., Aronson, E. (eds) *Handbook of Social Psychology*, vol. IV (Cambridge, Mass.: Addison-Wesley).

Warnock, H. M. (1978), *Special Educational Needs: Report of the Committee of Enquiry into the Education of Handicapped Children and Young People* (London: HMSO).

Wechsler, D. (1949), *The Wechsler Intelligence Scale for Children* (New York: The Psychological Corporation).

Wilce, H. (1985), 'Grammar place tests may be biased against minorities', *Times Educational Supplement*, 19 July, p. 8.

2 Learning Ability and Psychometric Practice

Seamus Hegarty

INTRODUCTION

Assessing children from minority backgrounds – be they ethnic, socio-economic or disability-related – poses particular problems. Ironically, these children are the ones who have most to gain – or lose – from the assessment process. On the one hand, they stand to benefit from modified curricula and teaching approaches; these modifications have to be devised and implemented on the basis of assessment, and if their needs are to be met it is essential that accurate and relevant information be forthcoming. On the other hand, they can be the victims of inaccurate assessments which damage their self-concepts, lower teachers' expectations of them and confine them to inappropriate educational programmes.

These assessment difficulties are especially acute where norm-referenced assessment is concerned. Bailey and Harbin (1980) summarise the numerous criticisms that have been levelled at the use of standardised tests in the United States. Standardised tests (a) are loaded with items based on white middle-class values and experiences, (b) penalise children with linguistic styles different from that of the dominant culture, (c) sample cognitive styles directly opposed to those found in many children from low income families or culturally diverse groups, (d) are often administered in an atmosphere that may penalise culturally diverse children; and (e) are scored on norms derived from predominantly white middle class standardisation groups.

Criterion-referenced assessment might appear to be the resolution of these difficulties. Comparisons are with the individual's own previous performance, not with other individuals, so that their different circumstances become irrelevant. There is also a strong curriculum orientation in that criterion-referenced assessment provides information that is directly relevant to teaching and can help to ensure that children from minority backgrounds receive appropriate educational experiences.

While criterion-referenced assessment may mitigate the difficulties associated with assessing children from minority backgrounds it should not be seen as offering a total solution. First, many of the problematic features, e.g. selection of items, test administration, diversity of linguistic and cognitive styles, persist across norm- and criterion-referenced assessment. Secondly, there is still a great deal of work to be done in developing criterion-referenced tests, particularly if they have to relate to minority contexts. Thirdly, criterion-referenced assessment cannot totally replace norm-referenced assessment since it has different purposes and is doing different tasks. Apart from the fact that norm-referenced tests continue in widespread use, they also provide diagnostic and other information that cannot readily be obtained from criterion-referenced tests.

INTELLIGENCE AND LEARNING ABILITY

The problems associated with standardised testing are notoriously evident in respect of intelligence tests. Hegarty and Lucas (1978) point out a range of both theoretical and practical difficulties where the use of intelligence tests with ethnic minority children is concerned.

This is not the place to elaborate a theory of intelligence, and indeed the theoretical background is discussed elsewhere in this book. Suffice it here to note that measured intelligence is a socio-cultural entity. Intelligence cannot be operationalised or incorporated into tests independently of social and cultural constructs. This means that intelligence tests are oriented toward particular constructs and values – which in the nature of things tend to be those of the dominant majority culture. This in turn means that IQ scores have to be interpreted in terms of socio-cultural differences and modified appropriately. In the absence of a detailed understanding of how measured intelligence is related to socio-cultural differences any such enterprise must be viewed in a very tentative light.

An alternative way of dealing with this is to relate measured intelligence and socio-cultural differences on *empirical* grounds. Given the difficulty of producing an adequate theoretical account, this may well be the best way forward. Such an approach is in fact adopted by Mercer and Lewis (1978) in the SOMPA battery described below.

The practical difficulties can be illustrated by looking at the content and the mode of construction of actual tests in use. Intelligence tests are samples of tasks requiring 'intelligent' responses. They are constructed so as to allow the possibility of inferring a subject's likely responses in situations outside the test itself. For this to be possible the test tasks must be representative of what constitutes intelligent behaviour in these situations. Such behaviour requires a context however; a socio-cultural context which is particular and is not common to everybody. The test constructor has of necessity to choose tasks that are socio-culturally specific. What has happened traditionally is that these choices have been made from the mainstream majority culture. Other things being equal, a test constructed in this way will be valid for members of the mainstream grouping, and their performance on it can be taken as a valid measure. This is not necessarily true however for members of ethnic minority groups. What constitutes intelligent behaviour in their case may be significantly different, and a sample drawn from majority culture behaviour will therefore not represent it adequately.

The force of this can be seen more clearly by looking at the actual content of some tests. Individual test items can be highly culture-specific. A major intelligence test in common use has questions like: 'How far is it from London to Glasgow?' 'Who wrote *A Midsummer Night's Dream*?' 'Why is it good to pay bills by credit card?' Correct answers to these and similar questions may signify intelligence on the part of children from the majority culture, but it would be wrong to assume of many children that they are failing to display intelligence if they cannot answer them.

These are gross examples of cultural bias, and hence relatively easy to rectify or discount. Less evident but more pervasive bias arises from the *nature* of the activities that comprise a test. One subtest of the WISC for instance requires children to assemble a complete object from wooden cut-outs. Clearly children used to playing with jigsaws will find this far easier than children who have never seen a jigsaw. Many similar examples can be found where the level and type of stimulation and learning experiences available to some children put them at a disadvantage in attempting certain test items.

This relates to a further more general difficulty, viz. that intelligence tests are to some extent a measure of previous learning. Successful performance on an intelligence test requires considerable prior learning. If this learning is absent then performance will be low, regardless of the individual's intellectual ability. The requisite prior learning can however be absent for a number of reasons unconnected with intellectual ability. In the present context, these refer specifically to the differential learning opportunities associated with ethnic minority and mainstream group memberships. The requisite learning tends to be oriented toward middle-class majority culture values. Many ethnic minority children will not have had the requisite learning experiences. They may have engaged in other, no less worthwhile, learning but to the extent that their previous learning does not match what is presumed by a particular test their performance on it cannot be taken as a valid indicator of their intellectual ability.

Some of these difficulties can in fact be met by using tests based on the notion of learning ability. First, tests based on the notion of learning ability are tests of potential rather than achievement. By contrast with intelligence tests which focus on performance, learning ability tests are concerned with the processes that underlie performance. This difference is one of emphasis, not an absolute difference in kind. Intelligence tests can give information on the child's mental processes, especially in the hands of a skilled user, and tests of learning ability do provide information on level of performance. If the principal interest however is in a child's potential for learning rather than present level of performance, it makes sense to use tests that measure it directly rather than ones that only provide indirect information.

Secondly, tests of learning ability help to equate to some extent the amount of relevant learning experience. This is achieved in part by selecting for the test learning tasks which are unfamiliar. In addition, test procedures routinely begin with a practice element; this can be quite extended and serves to correct any misunderstandings the children may have. It also however helps to compensate for inadvertent differential familiarity with the tasks or materials. Some such procedure is clearly advantageous where ethnic minority children are concerned since their learning backgrounds can be quite different from those of children from the majority population.

Thirdly, tests of learning ability need not rely to the same extent as intelligence tests on materials that are specific to a given culture. This is because of the teaching element they incorporate. Test items can be based on quite unfamiliar material if preliminary teaching is based on it. Intelligence tests have less scope in this respect since they rarely involve explicit teaching and are obliged to assume a far larger core of common experience. Test items must be based on relatively familiar material which will inevitably be drawn from the majority culture.

Fourthly, there is evidence to suggest that tests of learning ability can discriminate between children with uniformly low IQ scores. In other words, low IQ does not define a homogeneous group with respect to learning ability. Jensen (1963) reports a study where tests of learning ability were administered to three groups of children with low, average and high IQ. Children with average and high IQs returned average and high learning ability scores. Quite a different picture emerged from the children with low IQ: their learning ability scores were not uniformly low and indeed spanned the whole range of scores obtained. Some had very low scores but others obtained scores that exceeded the mean score of the high IQ group. (In fact, the highest learning ability scores were recorded by children who were ascribed IQs respectively of 147 and 65!).

Hegarty and Lucas (1978) report similar though less dramatic findings using the NFER Test of Learning Ability. There were many misclassifications in terms of IQ as measured by simultaneous learning ability scores and by attainment scores after a year's interval. For example, the child with lowest IQ (64) scored better than average on two of the learning ability subtests. A child with an IQ of 72 scored better than average on all but one of the learning ability subtests and the attainment tests; on two of them his scores were much better than average, i.e. more than two standard deviations above the mean. Of the 28 children with IQs below 75 twenty scored better than average on at least one of the ability or attainment tests, and 14 did so on two or more of the eight tests.

The System of Multi-Pluralistic Assessment (SOMPA) described below is actually based on modifying IQ scores in accordance with socio-cultural variation in order to produce learning potential or learning ability scores. So, individuals with similar IQs will by definition have different learning potential scores if their sociocultural situations are different. Beck (1984) applied SOMPA to 120 students receiving special education services in the United States, looking at how the students would be categorised by SOMPA and by WISC-R and at how they were classified by a placement team. Considerable differences emerged; in particular, 15 per cent of students would be declassified as not needing special education services if SOMPA were used.

Fifthly, there is evidence to suggest that for certain groups of children tests of learning ability predict better than intelligence tests to school achievement. The case is not simply that learning ability tests can be used to obtain *some* information in situations where intelligence tests can readily be used and no information is available. That situation does arise of course but is not the burden of the argument here. Evidence is now available from a number of studies that shows how tests of learning ability can out-perform intelligence tests in predictive power. The NFER Test of Learning Ability was compared with the WISC in terms of predicting to subsequent school performance and, as described below, was found to perform considerably better.

MEASURING LEARNING POTENTIAL

The history of learning ability measurement goes back to Russia in the 1930s. Vygotsky (1934) was one of the first to criticise traditional tests for their exclusive emphasis on a person's present intellectual state. They gave information on the individual's 'zone of present development', when what was generally needed was a measure of the 'zone of next development'. Vygotsky's approach to this was through a rather narrow focus on imitation of how adults solved tasks. Because of language difficulties and the rejection of psychometric procedures in Russia, Vygotsky's ideas were rejected and for nearly 30 years little thought was given to how they might contribute to assessment practice.

A different approach to measuring learning ability, based on level and rate of performance in learning tasks, was explored by US psychologists in the 1940s. This is summarised by Guilford (1967) and, briefly, by Klein (1983). The work was conducted in a context of investigating the nature of intelligence. It was particularly concerned with the relationship between learning ability and intelligence and with the extent to which learning ability was a unitary trait or was composed of distinct components.

Learning ability was conceptualised in two different ways for purposes of these studies: as performance on learning tasks (Husband, 1939); and as rate of learning when other variables were held constant. The learning tasks used were generally based either on simple cognitive functioning (computation, memory for names and faces) or on psychomotor functioning (mirror drawing, reaction time, two hand co-ordination). The rate of learning was measured in terms of gain scores, i.e. the difference between initial score and final score when subjects were measured before and after engaging in a standard learning task.

Numerous studies were conducted into gain scores and the intercorrelations of the various factors associated with learning (Heese, 1942; Woodrow, 1938). It has to be said however that the outcome was a contribution to the psychological understanding of intelligence and learning ability rather than any advancement of psychometric practice. The essential conclusions were that intelligence and learning ability were separate albeit linked entities and that learning ability involved many different component abilities. The studies did not lead to the development of practical tests which could be used outside the psychological laboratory nor did the underlying thinking feed into assessment practice in any significant way.

There was a revival of psychometric interest in learning potential in the 1960s and 1970s. Pockets of work, much of it going on in isolation, emerged in Israel, Hungary, the German Democratic Republic, England and the United States. Most of the tests developed were used primarily as research instruments, and there was little commercial publication of tests for practitioner use.

The common feature of these tests was that they incorporated teaching into test procedures. Structured teaching activities and standard response cues were devised. This was in order to measure how children responded to teaching, i.e. how well they could learn. The teaching was done in a variety of ways. A basic distinction can be made between *reactive* and *proactive* teaching. (This corresponds in part to Guthke's 1982 distinction between long-term and short-term learning tests.) Reactive teaching in this context can mean:

1. Giving the correct answer immediately after each question has been tackled. This corresponds to an elementary form of programmed learning. It is based on the assumption that each answer is a learning probe as it were by the student, designed to test out a specific hypothesis. By being told the correct answer the student can confirm or reject the hypothesis and thus engages in relevant learning before proceeding to the next question. There is of course the further assumption that successive questions are related to each other and that initial learning has some bearing on subsequent questions.
2. Guiding the testee to a correct response by means of answer-until-correct techniques. This is the procedure adopted by Henning (1975). This is based on the same assumption as 1. The feedback is more gradual however: instead of being told that an answer is wrong and what the correct answer is, the testee is given an indication as to how near being correct the answer is and invited to try again, until the correct answer is obtained.
3. Giving prompts when an incorrect answer has been given or no answer is forthcoming. This procedure corresponds to an elaboration of programmed learning. It is utilised in the NFER Learning Ability Test described below. This is a further refinement of reactive teaching: testees have their mistakes corrected in a standardised way and are given additional cues or prompts that will lead them toward the targeted learning.

Proactive learning, as the name implies, takes the initiative in instructing testees in ways that are relevant to test performance. Rather than waiting for mistakes to be made, it seeks to prepare beforehand in a standardised way. The main form it takes is giving prior instruction that is geared toward the test activities. This might be explaining problem-solving strategies, elucidating cognitive principles or drawing attention to patterns of relationships and classification criteria. It is illustrated by Budoff's work outlined below.

A radically different approach to the assessment of learning potential has emerged in recent years. This is based on the statistical manipulation of children's actual scores on an achievement test. Since achievement scores are culture-specific they must be modified in the light of socio-cultural differences. Such a procedure depends on the assumption that all groups have the same learning potential regardless of their ethnic or cultural diversity: if the average performance of a given group is lower this is because members of that group have diminished learning opportunities (as far as the test is concerned). It also depends on there being an adequate means of linking the achievement scores of a given socio-cultural grouping with those of the majority population. (The best-known contender here is Mercer's System of Multi-Pluralistic Assessment outlined below.) If the assumption on parity of learning potential holds true and a means of linking achievement scores across socio-cultural groupings is available, then the adjusted scores can be taken as a measure of estimated learning potential.

Examples

Various efforts have been made to incorporate learning potential ideas into psychometric practice. Examples in this book include work by Feuerstein (Chapter 4) and Gupta (Chapter 6) as well as the assessment procedures embodied in Soviet defectology described in Chapter 5. Some other examples will be presented here based respectively on the work of Budoff, Henning, Hegarty and colleagues at NFER, and Mercer and Lewis.

Budoff drew stimulus for his work from the learning difficulties and frequent academic failure of disadvantaged children in America. He attributed this failure in particular to the difficulty these children had with the required problem-solving strategies. They might be able to reason adequately but their experiences tended not to prepare them for the demands of middle-class schools and middle-class tests. When they were being assessed in conventional ways they did not develop the most effective strategies (by middle-class criteria) to solve the problems.

He developed a learning potential procedure, based on a process-oriented conceptualisation of intelligence. Changing the contents of problems so that they conform to children's experience is not enough; one has to attend to *how* the problems are to be solved. The emphasis is on the child's trainability, on the capability to improve performance on tasks following a systematic learning experience.

The tasks used are reasoning problems, administered in a 'test-train-test' sequence. The child is taught how to solve these problems: s/he is given a suitable strategy and has an opportunity to put it into practice. This training allows the child to understand how to solve problems when their contents are strange and an appropriate strategy is not readily apparent. Such training is particularly important for children from minority backgrounds. It helps to narrow the cognitive gap between their previously learned problem-solving strategies and those implicit in the problems encountered in formal testing.

Budoff has used three kinds of learning task to carry out his assessment programme: an altered version of Kohs Block Designs (Budoff, 1969); Raven's Progressive Matrices (Budoff *et al.*, 1973); and the Series Learning Potential Test (Babad and Budoff, 1974a). The first two of these are discussed in Chapter 1; what is novel is the way in which thcy are used. This can be described equally well in respect of the third set of materials.

The Series Learning Potential Test is a group test for use with younger children. It involves completing a series of pictures or geometric forms arranged in a pattern in which figures change systematically. Its efficacy as a test of learning ability was measured by comparing children's scores before and after training. Disadvantaged children whose learning opportunities would have been diminished or different should register the greatest gains since the gap between present performance and potential is likely to be greatest in their case.

In one study described by Babad and Budoff (1974b) the Series Potential Learning Test was administered three times to groups of bright (average IQ 133), dull-to-average (85) and retarded (68) children. Training on relevant strategies was given after the *second* administration. This meant that a practice effect (difference between second and first scores) as well as a training effect (difference between third and second scores) could be measured. All groups gained from practice; the gains were slight in the case of the retarded and bright groups but significantly greater in the case of the dull-to-average group. All groups likewise benefited from training but the pattern was different. The highest gain was obtained by the retarded group, followed by the dull-to-average group with the bright group again showing only a small increase.

A further study was carried out to compare the predictive power of the Series Potential Learning Test with that of an intelligence test. The criterion for the comparison was school success as measured by (concurrent) teacher ratings on an 11-point scale. The IQ and learning potential predictions were almost identical for the bright group, but for the other two groups the learning potential predictions were higher.

Henning's work is distinguished by its focus on adults and the fact that it is oriented to vocational as well as educational decision making. The Learning Ability Profile (Henning, 1975) comprises 80 pencil-and-paper items based on abstract symbols, numbers and letters but also language. The partial dependence on language clearly limits its culture fairness.

A significant feature of the Profile is its early use of answer-until-correct techniques. The testee is given feedback on every response made. Only multiple-choice answers are available and the testee is given information on the quality of each answer selected – whether correct or not, and if not how near to being correct. Each question must be answered correctly, by successive choice of responses if necessary, before the next question is attempted.

The Learning Ability Profile has been tried out on groups of varying educational, socio-economic and cultural backgrounds. Henning claims that there were 'no significant differences among racial groups, males and females, and between persons in their prime occupational years and persons 50 years of age and older'. The Profile was published commercially and has been used in education, industry and government in North America. It is unfortunate that there has been so little published study of the Profile in use since, despite some evident limitations, it offers a distinctive way of assessing learning potential in the adult population.

The work of Hegarty and colleagues at the National Foundation for Educational Research (NFER) has resulted in one of the few commercially available test batteries based on learning ability (Hegarty, 1978). The context for this work was the growing number of immigrant children and children from immigrant backgrounds in British schools in the 1960s and early 1970s. There was particular concern over the provision for remedial and special education. This was arranged, frequently in self-perpetuating segregation, so that ethnic minority children were represented in what seemed to be disportionate numbers. At one point for instance there were four times as many West Indian pupils, relative to their number in the population, in schools for the educationally subnormal as there were indigenous pupils. A main reason given for this was that the means by which pupils were ascertained for placement in such schools were biased against ethnic minority children; they did not discriminate sufficiently between children who were backward because of cultural difference or disadvantage and children who were backward for other reasons.

The work at NFER was based on an earlier study by Haynes (1971). This was designed to 'assess the abilities of children from a different cultural background and with a poor knowledge of English'. Haynes developed a battery of tests based on the notion of learning ability and tried it out on a sample of Sikh children in West London. In the event, the battery predicted moderately well to subsequent school attainment.

The NFER study grew out of this initial material, with changes being made to reflect the experience obtained with the Haynes material and theoretical inputs. The final battery comprises five subtests: Analogies; Concept Formation; Number Series; Verbal Learning of Objects; and Verbal Learning of Syllables. These cover different aspects of the ability to learn. Analogies is a test of the grasp of relationships. Concept Formation requires the child to sort sets of objects according to various perceptual characteristics. Number Series is a test of number seriation. Verbal Learning Objects and Verbal Learning of Syllables are tasks in paired-associate and auditory rote learning respectively.

Each subtest is structured so as to contribute to the overall objective of the test, viz. to assess the child's ability to respond to structured teaching and so benefit from instruction. There is a common pattern recurring through each one:

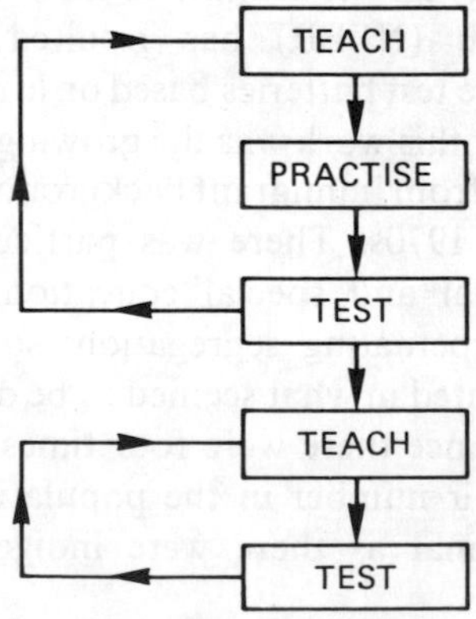

The child is first taught a simple task by demonstration and given practice on related material until the instructions have been clearly understood. Testing proper then commences, with each test trial preceded by further practical teaching. This procedure makes it possible to dispense with verbal instructions and also helps equate to a certain extent the amount of relevant prior learning experience.

The technical studies carried out to examine the psychometric characteristics of the battery are reported in detail in Hegarty and Lucas (1978). They are summarised briefly here. The particular interest was in knowing how the battery predicted subsequent school achievement. It was administered to a sample of some 400 seven-year-old children of immigrant background. At the same time a short form of the WISC was administered. A year later, when all the children had been in the British education system for at least a year, school attainment tests in vocabulary, maths and reading were administered.

This design made it possible to compare the respective performances of the learning ability test battery and the WISC in terms of prediction of subsequent achievement. Three forms of comparison were used: simple correlation matrices; canonical correlation coefficients; and stepwise regression analyses. The consistent picture that emerged was that the learning ability test predicted subsequent school achievement well and did so considerably better than the WISC (short form).

A radically different approach to assessing learning potential is offered by the System of Multi-Pluralistic Assessment (Mercer and Lewis 1978). Known as SOMPA, this is a comprehensive battery of existing and original instruments designed to assess children from culturally different backgrounds. There are nine instruments in total which are used to collect information from both child and parents in order to build up a comprehensive picture from medical, socio-cultural and educational perspectives.

SOMPA is based on three basic models of assessment practice, each with its own subsystem of measuring instruments: the medical model (physical dexterity tests, Bender Gestalt test, health history inventories, measures of visual and auditory acuity and of weight by height); the social system model (Adaptive Behaviour Inventory for Children and WISC-R); and the pluralistic model (socio-cultural scales and WISC-R). The assessment based on the medical model follows a relatively traditional pattern, though some norms relate to culturally different populations. The social system model relates to behaviour in the various roles the child is called upon to fulfil at home, in the community, with peers and so on. (WISC-R in this context is seen as a measure of social behaviour and not of ability or intelligence.)

The pluralistic model, which is the most innovative part of the system, tackles learning potential directly. It assumes that all socio-cultural groups have the same average potential for learning and that any differences observed are the result of different learning experiences. Direct comparisons can only be made between individuals who occupy the same 'socio-cultural space'. Otherwise, scores have to be adjusted to take account of socio-cultural differences.

There are four socio-cultural scales – family size, family structure, socio-economic status and urban acculturation – which attempt to measure how the child's socio-cultural situation relates to, and in particular differs from, the majority culture. This measurement makes it possible to predict the distribution of WISC-R scores for children in that socio-cultural setting. By comparing the individual's actual WISC-R score with the pattern of predicted scores for that group, it is then possible to compute that individual's 'estimated learning potential'. Thus, if two individuals had WISC-R scores of 95 but belonged to different socio-cultural groups whose predicted WISC-R scores were distributed around means of 85 and 90 respectively, the first would have a higher estimated learning potential than the second – and both would have higher estimated learning potentials than a majority group member with a WISC-R of 95 since the predicted scores would in that case be presumed to be normally distributed around a mean of 100.

SOMPA has generated a good deal of literature and not a little controversy since its publication in 1978/9. Its advocates point to its comprehensive nature and its direct assault on ethnic and socio-cultural differences. Figueroa (1979) is one of many pointing to its relevance for assessing children with learning difficulties and in particular meeting the growing legal requirements for non-discriminatory assessment (e.g. the US legislation on the education of handicapped children, PL 94–142). It has been roundly criticised as well on conceptual, technical and practical grounds. Jirsa (1983) takes issue with the sociology of knowledge ideas underlying SOMPA, though without developing a detailed critique. Yonge (1982) argues that the score adjustments produced are based on statistical artefacts that are not relevant to individual children or their educational requirements. Oakland (1979) and Beck (1984) report on empirical studies where the use of SOMPA made little useful contribution to decision making in respect of children receiving or being considered for receiving special education services.

Whatever the resolution of the controversies, it is clear that SOMPA offers a novel and distinctive way of estimating learning potential. The empirical data must be expected to be contentious, because SOMPA is operating at the thorny interface between special education provision and ethnic minority group membership, and it is unlikely that any practical application would be free of extraneous factors which complicate the interpretation of findings. It is to be hoped however that the evidence from practical applications will lead to a coherent pattern and that, if it is found wanting in technical details, more adequate batteries will be built on the underlying rationale.

THE FUTURE

The assessment of learning ability has major implications for children from minority groupings. It offers the possibility of a dynamic statement of potential as distinct from a static record of current achievement. It makes it possible to take account of the disadvantage associated with constrained learning opportunities. Above all, it furnishes a basis for matching educational provision to children's actual teaching needs so as to maximise their learning.

These benefits are slow in being realised. Psychometric interest in learning ability has been limited to a few enthusiasts, and there has been far more awareness of the difficulties of adequate measurement than determination to resolve them. Some headway has been made in recent years but a great deal of new work, and consolidation of existing work, is necessary.

There are not enough tests of learning ability commercially available, and the first priority must be to rectify this – either by developing new tests or by preparing existing research instruments for publication. Learning ability will remain peripheral to the psychometric enterprise until practitioners have the means regularly to include it in their perspective on children.

Given a reasonable selection of tests in widespread use, the next concern must be to study the tests in use. Three aspects may be noted. First, when tests are used on actual populations, for purposes of planning and decision making that lead to real changes in children's lives, major opportunities for further test development are presented. These range from clarifying and tightening up on test administration procedures to articulating construct validity and relating the assessment to relevant practice. This study of tests in use is an essential part of developing them so that they make an effective contribution to assessment practice.

Learning ability tests are based on certain teaching and learning activities which though quite familiar have not been subjected to close psychometric scrutiny. This suggests that there is need for a further type of study, viz. one that isolates the significant cognitive activities going on in learning ability assessment and studies their psychometric characteristics. These activities include giving feedback – in different modes – to testees, explaining problem-solving techniques and rehearsing item types without teaching. The psychometric investigation of these activities can be incorporated into the study of tests in use or it can be conducted in its own right separately from actual tests.

A good example is Whetton and Child's (1981) study of answer-until-correct (AUC) procedure. This is a particular form of item-by-item feedback on multiple-choice tests. Following a review of earlier studies of feedback during tests, they report on a study designed to compare the conventional administration (instructions to select a single best answer) of a non-verbal ability test with an AUC administration. AUC scores were found to increase reliability but not validity as measured. (The findings on validity were mixed: correlations with a mathematics examination were unchanged whereas correlations with a verbal ability test were considerably reduced.) More particularly, they found that answer-until-correct administration techniques did not lead to learning during the test.

This is clearly an important finding that bears directly on the viability of measuring learning ability or at least of certain approaches to it. It is imperative for similar studies to be conducted with regard to other approaches to the assessment of learning ability. This will assist both in establishing its credentials for serious use and in refining the techniques for measuring it. Not all approaches to measuring learning ability are equally sound nor, as Whetton and Child demonstrate, can it be assumed that the opportunities for learning which underpin the assessment are always present. Studies of this kind then are essential to establishing the psychometric characteristics of different approaches to learning ability assessment and to ascertaining whether or not the alleged learning is taking place.

A final consideration regarding learning ability assessment concerns its deployment. Assessment is for a purpose, not an end in itself. Much of the stimulus for developing tests of learning ability has come from the deficiencies of other tests, particularly intelligence tests, in respect of minority populations. These deficiencies in turn have been problematic because they have resulted in unsuitable educational provision for individual children, with no differentiation being made between children whose performance is low because of different or restricted learning experiences and those who have more general learning difficulties.

If learning ability assessment is to contribute to improving this situation – which it undoubtedly can do – it is not enough just to differentiate better between children or make more accurate statements about their ability to learn. Real progress will only come when assessment is linked to curriculum reform, when an assessment of a child's learning ability is merely a stage in the process of working out the best educational programme for that child. It is precisely the failure of most uses of SOMPA to date to do just this that has led writers such as Reschly (1979) and Beck (1984) to query its usefulness. If the effect of an assessment is to de-classify children labelled mentally retarded so that they are no longer eligible for special education services *and receive nothing in its place*, then clearly something is wrong. The solution is not to abandon the assessment however but rather to embed it in practice, to direct teaching to the 'zone of next development' identified by accurate assessment of learning ability, and to ensure that the details as well as the global aims of a child's education are informed by a vision of what the child can do rather than being constricted by a static picture of his/her present limitations.

References

Babad, E., Budoff, M. (1974a), 'A Manual for the Series Learning Potential Test', unpublished paper, Cambridge Massachusetts: Research Inst. for Educ. Problems.

Babad, E., Budoff, M. (1974b), 'Sensitivity and validity of learning potential measurement in three levels of ability', *Journal Educ. Psychol.*, **66**, 3, 439–47.

Bailey, D. B., Harbin, G. L. (1980), 'Nondiscriminatory Evaluation', *Exceptional Children*, **46**, 8, 590–6.

Beck, F. W. (1984), 'Another look at the effects of the system of multicultural pluralistic assessment', *Journal of School Psychol.* **22**, 347–52.

Budoff, M. (1969), 'Learning potential: a supplementary procedure for assessing the ability to reason', *Seminars in Psychiatry*, **1**, 278–90.

Budoff, M., Corman, L., Litzinger, S. (1973), 'A manual for the Raven's Learning Potential Test', *Studies in Learning Potential,* **3**, 59.

Figueroa, R. A. (1979), 'The System of Multicultural Pluralistic Assessment', *School Psychology Digest.*, **8**, 1, 28–36.

Guilford, J. P. (1967), *The Nature of Human Intelligence* (New York: McGraw Hill).

Guthke, J. (1982), 'The learning test concept – an alternative to the traditional static intelligence test', *German J. of Psychol*, **6**, 4, 306–24.

Haynes, J. M. (1971), *Educational Assessment of Immigrant Pupils* (Slough: NEFR).

Heese, K. W. (1942), 'A general factor in improvement in practice', *Psychometrika*, 7, 213–23.

Hegarty, S. (1978), *Manual for the NFER Test of Learning Ability* (*individual form*) (Windsor: NFER).

Hegarty, S., Lucas, D. (1978), *Able to Learn? The pursuit of culture-fair assessment* (Windsor: NFER).

Henning, M. H. (1975), *Learning Ability Profile* (Denver: Falcon R & D).

Husband, R. W. (1939), 'Intercorrelations among learning abilities', *J. genet. Psychol.* **55**, 353–64.

Jensen, A. R. (1963), 'Learning ability in retarded, average and gifted children', *Merrill-Palmer Quarterly of Behav. and Dev.*, **9**, 2, 123–40.

Jirsa, J. E. (1983), SOMPA: 'A brief examination of technical considerations, philosophical rationale, and implications for practice', *J. School Psychol*, **21**, 13–21.

Klein, Sandor (1983), 'Intelligence and learning potential theory and practice', *Newsletter of the International Test Commission*, **19**, 3–13.

Mercer, J., Lewis, J. F. (1978), *System of multi-cultural pluralistic assessment: Conceptual and technical manual* (Riverside Ca: Institute for Pluralistic Assessment Research and Training).

Oakland, T. (1979), 'Research on the adaptive behaviour inventory for children and the estimated learning potential', *School Psychology Digest*, **8**, 1, 63–70.

Reschly, D. J. (1979), 'Evaluation of the effects of SOMPA measures on classification of students as mentally retarded', *Amer. Journ. of Mental Deficiency*, **86**, 16–20.

Vygotsky, L. S. (1962, originally published 1934), *Thought and Language* (New York: Wiley).

Whetton, C., Childs, R. (1981), 'The effects of item by item feedback given during an ability test', *Brit. J. Educ. Psychol.* **1,** 51, 336–46.

Woodrow, H. (1938), 'The relation between abilities and improvement with practice', *J. educ. Psychol.*, **29**, 215–30.

Yonge, G. D. (1982), 'Some concerns about the estimation of learning potential from the system of multicultural pluralistic assessment', *Psychology in the Schools*, **19**, 482.

3 Assessment of Learning Ability: A Current Appraisal

Gilbert R. Gredler

INTRODUCTION

The increasing dissatisfaction with the use of conventional intelligence tests has spurred interest in alternative approaches to the measurement of the learning ability of school children. It is stated that the following problems exist with traditional intelligence tests: (a) cultural bias against lower SES children due largely to the use of white standardisation samples and the heavy verbal emphasis of the tests (Carroll and Seely, 1974); (b) assumption of a normal experiential background (Hamilton and Budoff, 1974); and (c) emphasis on being a measure of innate ability rather than reflecting changes in learning (McClelland, (1973).

It is also stated that use of the IQ test in the USA has led to over-representation of the poor and non-white in the educable mentally retarded classifications (EMR) with 85% per cent of the children who are placed in special education in the USA being poor and/or non-white (Budoff and Corman, 1973). It is charged that the IQ test identifies the educationally rather than the mentally retarded since two-thirds to three-quarters or those labelled EMR in the USA become socially and economically independent by adulthood (Budoff, 1967; 1975). Because of these problems it is stated that other approaches are needed as alternatives to the use of the IQ test so as to better assess the learning ability of children in school.

Expediting this concern with traditional measures have been the changes in the political climate in the USA which have occurred over the last twenty years. The prominent civil rights battles of the 1960s sensitised many citizens to various discriminative facets of American society. The American Association of Mental Deficiency as late as 1966 considered as mentally retarded those individuals with IQs up to 85 (Suran and Rizzo, 1983).

HISTORICAL BACKGROUND OF LEARNING ABILITY TESTS

Several research studies are currently underway on methods to measure more effectively the learning potential of children. However, it is necessary to review previous efforts in order to be able to evaluate properly the state of the field today. Unfortunately the impression is given that the use of alternative measures of learning to the IQ test is a recent phenomenon (Meyers, Pfeffer and Erlbaum, 1985). Efforts to discover more effective measures of learning ability have been ongoing for the past fifty years. Important research in this time period has been undertaken with immigrant populations (Ortar, 1960; Haynes, 1971), as well as with children labelled 'brain damaged' (Schubert, 1965; Neilsen, 1966).

Taylor (1959) emphasised the need to provide valid alternative measures of learning ability for brain damaged children. She gives prominent emphasis to Andre Rey's (1935) studies on 'practical intelligence'. She states: 'In many instances it is not easy to decide whether the child has difficulties because he cannot learn or because he has not been taught properly, or whether, owing to other reasons, he cannot profit from what he is exposed to' (p. 11). She adds: 'Rey's approach to learning problems, which separates the study of *how* a child learns from that of *what* he learns or has learned, often allows some insight into the causes of learning defects' (p. 12). One of Rey's graduate students, Feuerstein, later went on to incorporate many of his mentor's tests and ideas into his Learning Potential Assessment Device (1979) with disadvantaged adolescents in Israel.

Thirty-six years ago Scott (1950) emphasised the importance of familiarising Sudanese children with both the IQ test task as well as the examiner before beginning to test. The same points have been made by Zigler, Abelson and Seitz (1973) in their study of the PPVT with Operation Headstart Children. In 1971 Haynes discussed the need to utilise test items for which all children had an equal opportunity to learn the skills which the test required and to become equally familiar with the material which the test employs.

In 1960 Ortar developed test items which were similar to those found on conventional tests and introduced a period of practice or 'coaching' between the initial test and retest in order to improve the predictive validity of the intelligence test. She obtained a substantial increase in the validity coefficients after such a period of instruction. For example, in one school the correlation of teachers' grades and scores on an IQ test increased from 0.25 to 0.54. While a definite increase was obtained the second correlations were still only moderately predictive of academic performance.

That differential familiarity with content has a definite impact on test performance was also seen in the investigation by Covington (1967) of the performance of children of different social class membership on a visual discrimination task. Covington found that increased familiarisation of test content, which he provided by simply increasing exposure time to the type of test item used, resulted in a remarkable improvement in the performance of the lower SES white children used as subjects. Allowing increased familiarity with test content helps (a) the child to become more oriented and accustomed to the content presented; and (b) brings into play various cognitive strategies which middle class children appear to spontaneously utilise (Covington, 1967).

Needed approaches

The suggestion to provide increased familiarity with test content was an important step in further conceptualising different methods for administration of such tasks. Unfortunately, there has been no consensus in the methods utilised to introduce subjects to unfamiliar tasks. What is needed is a structured approach that is standardised as to procedure with the addition of various strategies or learning cues introduced in stages to the child to see what instructional help is needed in order to reach the criterion set. Such an approach has been utilised in assessing the performance of brain-damaged and regular class children as they attempted to reproduce the Bender figures, a visual perceptual task. Smith and Martin (1967) provided a series of 5 'learning cues' to the subject when a rotational error was made in reproducing a Bender figure. Because figure rotations are considered a 'pathological' sign of either brain damage and/or emotional disturbance, it is of interest to note that of the 36 per cent of a group of normal children who produced rotations, *all* corrected their rotation of the figure after presentation of the first learning cue (i.e., the child was simply asked to redraw the design).

The brain damaged sample had to utilise eight times as many cues to correct their figure errors in comparison to the normal children to draw the stimulus figure correctly and not be mislabelled as 'perceptually impaired'. It would seem that a similar approach should be incorporated into assessment work with disadvantaged children. Such an assessment strategy would be helpful in reducing the risk of mislabelling a disadvantaged child as lacking in learning ability. Such an approach has much to recommend it over non-standardised and 'clinical' methods which are so varied as to make meaningless any conclusion drawn (Smith, 1980).

Jensen in 1963 demonstrated that while there was an association between an IQ measure and a learning ability measure some children classified as retarded on an intelligence test obtained as high a score on the learning ability measure as did the gifted children. Budoff (1975) also clearly indicated the usefulness of learning ability scores in differentiating good academic progress among a group of mental retardates.

An important development in assessing the true learning potential of immigrant/minority children was Haynes' study in 1971 of Indian children. However, her battery of five individually administered learning tests required 3 hours for the child to complete. A standardised procedure was developed to assure that the same amount and type of help would be given by the different examiners. Multiple regression analysis indicated the validity of the verbal learning tasks in predicting school achievement. 56 per cent of the variance in predicting reading accuracy was explained by the use of three of the learning abilities subtests in combination with the WISC Picture Arrangement subtest. However, use of the WISC Vocabulary subtest alone was able to account for 40 per cent of the variance when predicting reading accuracy.

Measurement of ability to learn: The rationale

In the evolution of learning ability assessment, emphasis has been placed on providing an opportunity for the child to engage in a learning task. It is maintained that this approach to assessment, a 'process-oriented' method, will predict the child's learning ability more accurately by: 'deemphasizing the effects of differential exposure to previous learning experiences' (Sewell, 1979). Or, as Newland (1963) stated over 23 years ago: 'to the extent that the behavior sampled may be regarded as a *product*, the impact of acculturation upon test performance tends to increase; whereas to the extent that the behavior sampled constitutes *process*, the impact of acculturation on test performance tends to be reduced' (p. 62). Thus, it is theorised that scores obtained from process measures should be more valid indicators of the child's true learning ability.

The construction of measures of learning ability

Several paradigms have been developed for the presentation of learning tasks. One approach used is the test-train-retest paradigm (Ortar, 1960; Budoff, 1975). Children are tested on material presented to them; trained on task-relevant principles and then retested after a specified time period on the original material (Budoff, Meskin and Harrison, 1971).

A second paradigm is called learning screening. Children practice certain specific behaviours or 'pinpoints' of interest. Such behaviours include math facts, spelling or reading (Bailey, 1979). Learning screening as presently structured consists of one minute 'timings' of these behaviours. These timings are undertaken each day for 10 days. The assumption underlying this paradigm is that practice is the most important learning activity. Use of the learning screening model results in two kinds of scores: (a) a performance measure which indicates the child's correctness on a particular skill at the end of the 10-day time period, and (b) a learning index which reflects the change in a child's performance over the screening periods (Kunzelmann and Koenig, 1981).

Specific learning ability measures utilised in studies

Research of the past thirty years with elementary and high school students has utilised a number of different learning ability measures. In one of the first American studies investigators used the Kohs Blocks as the learning ability measure. Objectives of training included assistance in building a design, directing attention to the separateness of the blocks, and increasing familiarity with the procedure through repetition (Hamilton and Budoff, 1974). Subjects were then classified into three groups depending upon their performance on the original test and retest: (1) '*high scorers*' were those who performed well on the original test; (2) '*gainers*' were those who increased their initial poor performance following training; and (3) '*nongainers*' were those whose initially poor performance was not improved by training.

Later, another non-verbal measuring task, the Raven Coloured Progressive Matrices, became popular to use in learning ability research in the USA. The Raven has now become the most frequently used assessment measure in the test-train-retest paradigm. Use of this instrument was prompted by the need to find a measure more suitable for use with younger children (Budoff, 1975).

The Block Design subtest of the WISC has also been utilised in learning ability research (Schubert, 1965; Goodyear, 1979). Schubert administered the Block Design subtest in the usual test-train-retest format. Children were then trained between testing sessions on the Alexander Performance Scale. Objectives of such training sessions were to (1) allow the child to manipulate the blocks; (2) give the child practice on easy problems, and (3) help the child develop problem-solving strategies which would aid him when retested (Goodyear, 1979). It is important to note that while the test-train-retest paradigm has been extensively used in American research, the conditions under which this type of paradigm has been carried out have differed considerably among the various studies completed. There have been differences in the time given for instructional periods; difference in how gain scores have been determined; and a wide number of different ability groups have been utilised.

A number of important dimensions of learning tests have been identified by Kormann and Sporer, 1983. For example, the Raven Learning Potential Test format is generally classified as an approach which requires lengthy training sessions and the goal is to help produce a differential diagnosis and prognosis. Feuerstein's LPAD material (1979) is classified as an 'interval test' with emphasis on curriculum programming, which takes place over a two-year period. An example of a 'short time' learning test is the learning test devised by Roether (cited in Mandl, 1976) for 5–6 year olds. The child is administered a series of 3 problems dealing with shapes, sequences, and colours which reflect the various perceptual modalities. The correct response is given after each answer by the subject and an incorrect answer is followed by a series of standardised prompts. Each series of problems is repeated in a slightly different form three times. Individual learning curves are then plotted to help discern the effects of the various trials.

Results from the administration of Roether's test to a large sample of 6 year olds (N=321) demonstrated that (a) the average child can respond in 20 minutes, while poorer children take up to one hour; (b) learning improvement is the greatest between first and second testing for the poorer group; and (c) all achievement groups showed improvement in their learning scores. Stability of learning effects indicated that the score obtained on the *first* trial of the *retest* four weeks later was equivalent to the child's score on the *third* trial of the *first* test. Subsequent research by Gutjahr *et al.* as discussed by Mandl, demonstrated that normal children showed steep learning increases between the first and third trials and that the learning curve of poor achievers changed hardly at all (Mandl, 1976).

In all of these studies of learning ability the main objective has been to determine the relationship between performance on the various ability measures and the outcomes of school performance. Detailed analysis of these studies follows in a later section.

Another non-verbal reasoning task considered to be of value in learning ability investigations is the Rey Labyrinth Test (Neilsen, 1966). Used extensively in research with brain damaged children because of its effectiveness in pinpointing learning problems in this group of children, the Labyrinth Test currently shares a prominent place in Feuerstein's assessment of the learning potential of disadvantaged adolescent students (1979).

The Rey Labyrinth Test consists of four black boards with several rows of pegs, all of which are loose except one. The child is required to locate the fixed peg on each board and is later asked to recall their location. The procedure is continued until subjects make no errors in three trials or until 20 trials are completed, whichever occurs first. Renamed the Plateaux Test by Feuerstein (1979) that test is similar in design except fixed buttons are substituted for the pegs (Goodyear, 1979).

The child's learning performance on the Rey is assessed through several indices including analysis of number of errors made; number of trials to learn the maze; noting the irregularity of the learning curve; amount of regression (i.e., errors made after initial success); and perseverative behaviour (Neilsen, 1966). Neilsen found that (1) cerebral palsy children learned the labyrinth less efficiently than normal children and (2) their progress on the task was more irregular than that of normal children. Also it was determined that cerebral palsy and normal subjects performed equally well on various auditory memory tasks (a measure of simple verbal learning). However, the results were different when the labyrinth, a more complex learning task, was presented. Neilsen considered such findings helpful in planning the instructional programmes of cerebal palsy children.

OTHER APPROACHES TO MEASURE LEARNING ABILITY

Diagnostic teaching

Another approach to process-oriented assessment has been the use of diagnostic teaching. As used in the assessment of reading performance, the child is taught a series of unfamiliar words . The child's score is the number of words retained after three teaching trials. Contrary to what has been implied by some educators (Hammill, 1971) diagnostic teaching has long been used in the assessment process with American school children.

Witmer, the founder of the first psychological clinic in the USA in 1890 is considered the father of the diagnostic teaching movement in the United States (Levine and Levine, 1970). Witmer worked closely with personnel in the Philadelphia school system in providing educational help for handicapped children. In many of the learning problem cases with which he worked Witmer reported no IQ test results at all. He also believed that no diagnosis could be reached until an attempt had been made to teach the child some academic material.

Despite the fact that he was not certified as a teacher nor a graduate of a special education programme, Witmer provides us with perhaps the most sophisticated discussion of diagnostic teaching that has yet to appear in print. He considered it poor planning to take standardised test items and attempt to vary their administration in order to 'tease' out the child's potential. Instead he emphasised the following procedures: (a) develop educational techniques to test hypotheses about the child's learning difficulties; (b) continue the diagnostic examination over a lengthy period of time; (c) use repeated measurement to validate the correctness of the original diagnosis and the effectiveness of the remedial intervention; (d) continue involvement of the parents and teachers in the work of the clinic with the child; (e) recognise the importance of emotional factors in the learning difficulty; and (f) realise the importance of a positive and hopeful attitude that the child could be helped (Levine and Levine, 1970).

To determine the value of diagnostic teaching as an aid to proper diagnosis of either a disadvantaged or minority group child, it is obvious that data obtained in this way must be the result of the use of a standardised approach in the administration and scoring of the diagnostic teaching task (Ingenkamp, 1979). Such an approach has been followed by Sewell and Severson (1974) and in subsequent investigations of diagnostic teaching by Goodyear (1979) and Goad (1984).

In a stepwise multiple regression analysis Goodyear (1979) found that a combination of the verbal WISC-R IQ, the diagnostic teaching task, and the scores from both the pre-and post-test performance on the Wechsler Block Design subtest accounted for 32 per cent of the variance associated with reading recognition scores. A combination of verbal IQ, the diagnostic teaching task and the pretest Block Design subtest accounted for 44 per cent of the variance in reading comprehension scores.

Contrary to what Budoff (1975) postulated in his studies and the findings of Sewell and Severson (1974) and Sewell (1979) with a first grade population the *pre-test* score of the measure used in the training procedure by Goodyear (1979) was a better predictor of reading achievement than were the post-test scores.

The diagnostic teaching task did exceed the Performance IQ in predicting both reading recognition and comprehension scores and diagnostic teaching also exceed the IQ in predicting reading comprehension performance. However, no single learning ability measure accounted for more variance in predicting reading recognition than did the Verbal IQ (20%). A combination of the diagnostic teaching task and the Block Design pretest score predicted 15 per cent of the reading recognition variance.

Goad (1984) also studied the value of the Diagnostic Teaching task as a measure along with some of the subtests of the Learning Efficiency Test Battery (Gupta and Coxhead, 1983). Her subjects were 52 black males aged 6 to 10 whose measured IQs ranged from 40 to 110. Mean full scale IQ was 78. The diagnostic teaching task was similar to the one used by Goodyear (1979) and Sewell (1979). Goad also used four subtests of the Learning Efficiency Test Battery: 1. Seriation A; 2. Seriation B; 3. and Word Object Picture Association Test and 4. Object-Picture Association Test (Gupta and Coxhead, 1983). The first two tests mentioned are based on Piagetian principles and the last two are based on associative learning principles.

The results obtained indicate once again the importance of the diagnostic teaching task in predicting reading achievement scores. Diagnostic teaching alone exceeded the verbal and performance IQ in predicting reading comprehension scores and diagnostic teaching and Seriation A also exceeded the verbal and performance IQs in predicting reading recognition. But no combination of learning ability variables surpassed the full scale IQ in predicting reading recognition.

The results of these two studies indicate the value of adding a diagnostic teaching task to the assessment process.

Mastery learning and time to learn measures

A variety of cognitive and non-cognitive learner characteristics in addition to instructional variables are considered responsible for the variability in learning (Gettinger, 1978). Reorganising the school curriculum into such components so as to provide for the mastery of specific subunits before new material is introduced has been described by Bloom (1976). Gettinger (1978) suggests that attempting to assess 'time to criterion' with actual instructional material may be helpful in better predicting school achievement and might improve teaching practices by identifying those children who need more time to master curriculum material (Gettinger, 1978). Results of her study effectively demonstrated a 1:3 learning rate ratio between the slowest and fastest learners. While time to learn is an important variable for children referred for learning difficulties, such assessment is probably best used as a screening variable to be followed up by more specific diagnostic measures such as learning ability tests as well as sophisticated standardised diagnostic tests such as the Stanford Diagnostic Reading Test (1984) in order to tease out specific areas of difficulty in learning.

Paired associate learning

Use of paired associate tasks has also been popular as an alternative measure of learning ability. While Lambert, Wilcox and Gleason (1974) champion the use of such tasks as an effective measure of learning ability, recent research (Sewell, 1974; Goodyear, 1979) indicates that such measures correlate poorly with academic learning and would appear to be of little value as an assessment tool.

Testing the limits

This approach to ascertaining a child's 'true potential' has been discussed at length by Sattler (1981). As he states: 'There are times at which examiners desire to go beyond the standard test procedures in order to gain additional information about the child's abilities' (p. 92). While Sattler emphasises such techniques should be used *only* after the test has been adminstered according to standard procedures, use of this alternative method is questionable. This is so because *no specific standardised guidelines* are available to the examiner. While Sattler points out that the examiner can provide a series of 'cues' to the child to help him in solving a problem, the nature of learning cues to be utilised is left completely up to the examiner. Thus we introduce to the assessment process wide variability in the administration of intervention strategies and as a result conclusions arrived at are of questionable validity.

Sattler also suggests the use of alternate scoring schemes (i.e., determining the IQ after 'help' has been given). He states that such scores *may* be related to learning potential. Non-standardised methods are championed by Smith (1980) who makes the startling statement: ' "To ruin the test" for readministration in the near future is a must if we sincerely believe that understanding of the interaction between specific unique child and task characteristics is far more important than preserving the test's reliability.' (p. 51)

A cognitive curriculum programme and the test-practice-retest paradigm

An innovative curriculum programme organised by Burkholder (1968) in an attempt to improve second and third graders' performance in reading was shown to be effective. Not only did these students demonstrate improvement in various facets of reading ability but most importantly their WISC IQ scores also rose.

The emphasis in this investigation was on the development of curriculum materials which emphasised those aspects of cognition found deficient in the lower SES children chosen for this study. Cognitive tasks and exercises were prepared with the goal to improve the student's visual and auditory memory; automatic language skills; visual and auditory closures; sound blending; visual discrimination; and classification skills. This latter area involved the ability to organise perceptions and concepts both visually and verbally.

Burkholder's study can be thought of as another version of the test-practice and retest format as originally practiced by Ortar (1960) and later carried out by Budoff (1975), Roether (Mandl, 1976) and Goodyear (1979). Only in this case, the 'practice' period was a longer one, being three months in length.

While Burkholder developed her curriculum materials from the ITPA model, Pumfrey and Naylor (1983) suggest a careful review of such materials really reflects the use of a multimodal cognitive approach. Such a programme touches the many perceptual and conceptual bases which will be found in any rigorously built cognitive curriculum. Not only did Burkholder's subjects improve their psycholinguistic functioning but as previously stated also increased their WISC scores as well as their reading performance. Average gains found in intelligence scores were as follows: (V) 12 points; (P) 8 points and (FS) 12 points.

Even more importantly, many of the gains on reading measures as well as IQ measures continued to be present in a followup six months later.

Children attended 40 minute sessions over a period of three months. Thus a total of 20 hours of instructional time was involved. Burkholder also points out other features of her study which helped contribute to the children's significant gains: use of attractive special materials; well programmed curriculum subunits; presence of a different teaching personality; and small group teaching, all of which led to a more positively reinforcing environment. The motivational aspects of this curriculum approach should not be underestimated. Previous research has demonstrated this factor to be an important one for improved academic performance (Gredler, 1978).

Analysis of the Raven test-practice-retest paradigm

In reviewing learning potential assessment studies which use the test-train-retest paradigm with the Raven as developed by Budoff (1975) three types of data are obtained: (a) pretraining scores which are considered to reflect the current level of functioning of the child; (b) post training scores which represent '. . . the child's optimal level of performance following an optimizing procedure' (Budoff, 1973, p. 32), and (c) gain scores from pre- to post-test which also reflect the child's ability to profit from instruction.

If the post-test Raven score shows an increased correlation with various achievement measures it is considered that such correlation reflects the child's 'optimal' level of performance. Gain scores have been used in a number of studies when categorising the subject's learning status, i.e., is he a gainer; non-gainer or high scorer. While Budoff found that 'gainers' in his mentally retarded populations performed at a higher level on various educational tasks and thus were possibly misclassified as mentally retarded, other studies have not found the 'gainer' vs. 'non-gainer' status to be a meaningful one. Use of gain scores raises difficult methodological issues (Cook and Campbell, 1979). The current use of the 50th percentile cut-off to categorise students as gainers or non-gainers in many studies appears to be too insensitive to identify all the children who actually make significant gains. For example, Wolf (1984) had to categorise a student as a 'non-gainer' because he did not reach the 50th percentile cut-off on the post-test even though he improved his score by 22 points! Another of Wolf's subjects gained four points and was judged a 'gainer' because his post-test score was just over the 50th percentile. However, another subject made a three point gain but was classified a non-gainer. It would be preferable to change all raw scores to a standardised metric such as standard deviation units and then categorise the various subjects' gain status. Surely a student who increased his Raven score by 22 points has learned some important conceptual principles from the coaching session and when such a student is placed in a category of 'non-gainer' it would seem to indicate the use of inappropriate classification criteria.

Wolf (1984) dealt with the learning ability of learning diabled adolescents in the seventh through the ninth grades. His objective was to ascertain the relationship between the student's status as a gainer, non-gainer or high scorer and mathematical achievement outcomes. Correlation between IQ and math achievement test performance was 0.63 while that between learning ability status (post-test Raven score) and math achievement outcome was 0.66. Because learning ability status was highly related to other measures of general ability (0.62) Wolf concludes it was no more effective in identifying trait-treatment interactions than other measures (p. 92). Although high scorers and 'gainers' obtained higher scores on math achievement measures Wolf stated that these differences were probably related to differences in the IQs of the groups involved.

Platt (1976) investigated the effect of Raven 'Learning Potential' coaching procedures on Raven post-test scores and their correlations with certain predictive variables obtained from learning disabled students. Forty children between the ages of 6 and 10 years and of average intelligence were the subjects; and all children were receiving resource room help.

Platt's analysis indicated no correlation in this group between post-test Raven score and academic performance measures. In fact, he obtained correlations of —0.03 between the Raven and reading achievement, and +0.05 with math achievement. In contrast correlation coefficients of 0.37 between IQ and reading achievement and 0.60 between IQ and math achievement were found. Furthermore, Platt was unable to predict learning ability level (i.e., gainer' vs. 'non-gainer' status) from any of the variables utilised.

Popoff-Walker (1980) also attempted to determine whether performance on a learning ability measure (the Raven) could be significantly improved by utilising a training procedure. She studied 8–9 year old children, one group of whom were mentally retarded (Mean IQ = 61) and one group of normal IQ (Mean IQ = 106). Popoff-Walker also utilised two control groups: a 'pure' control and a 'practice' control group. This latter group was given test-analogous training problems twice in between the pre- and post-test sessions.

The average score gain on the Raven for the EMR group was found to be 1.57 points; for the non EMR group 6.57; that of the practice EMR group 1.80 points; and of the EMR training group 2.60 points. The 'pure' control group composed of EMR subjects showed a 0.30 point gain and that of the 'pure non-retarded control group' a gain of 4.20 points. The non-EMR practice group showed a gain of 6.70 points and the non-EMR training group an 8.80 point gain. No significant correlations were obtained between SES and post-test scores in either the EMR or non-EMR samples.

Popoff-Walker points out that training on a problem solving task did indeed improve performance on the Raven tasks. However, as stated above, the gain for the EMR sample was quite small. It is suggested that the smaller gains found in this study were due to the lower mean IQ of the sample (Mean IQ = 61). Popoff-Walker also found that only 40 per cent of her subjects had age-appropriate adaptive behaviour, while 80 per cent of the EMR sample in Mercer's (1973) study demonstrated adequate social behaviour.

It is important to note that all of the children in Popoff-Walker's study were able to profit from practice in problem-solving even *without* instruction. While training did improve performance on a conceptual task (i.e. Raven material) for both EMR and non-EMR children, practice was found to be almost as effective as the training sessions for the subjects of both ability levels. Popoff-Walker (1982) followed Budoff's time parameter for training by planning two such sessions of 45 minutes each. However, she does raise the issue of whether more time for support building and familiarisation with the testing and training should have been allowed for her EMR subjects. Because it is common knowledge that motivational and attention skill deficiencies may be more prominent to EMR children it would probably be wise to attend to such variables more specifically in future studies of this type.

Bardsley (1979) investigated the use of learning ability assessment with learning disabled children. Utilising the training procedures developed by Budoff and Corman (1973) he tested 33 self contained and resource room students. His subjects ranged in age from 7–11 to 10–11; the average IQ was 84 for the self-contained group and 87 for the resource room group.

Bardsley also found no significant correlations between Raven gain status and any of his academic measures. Both pre- and post-test Raven scores correlated in the range of 0.02 to 0.12 with a reading achievement measure. However, *both* pre- and post-test Raven scores were significantly correlated with math achievement and were better predictors of mathematic status than the IQ measures.

Learning ability assessment with young children

In a study of kindergarten children, Bailey (1979) investigated a number of different approaches to learning ability assessment. He utilised both the learning ability assessment approach of Budoff (1975) and the Learning Screening approach to assessment developed by Kunzelmann and Koenig (1981). The assumption behind this latter approach is that practice is the basic learning activity.

Bailey was interested in the value of the two assessment procedures in predicting those children who would be 'at risk' for first grade. Four experimental conditions were established: (a) a 'practice' group which followed learning screening procedures for a period of 10 days. Activities included touching body parts, writing continuous 'e's' and counting from 1 to 10; (b) a 'training' group which was taught how to complete these various activities; (c) a group who practised the Raven Progressive Matrices each day for 10 days; and (d) a group who were given training procedures on how to complete the Raven (i.e., the usual 'learning potential' coaching approach). The Raven training format reflected the procedures used in previous investigations by Budoff (1975); however, the amount of instructional time was reduced.

Although Bailey utilised a number of different criterion measures in his study, what will be discussed here is the relationship of the various predictors to a curriculum reference measure (CRM) administered in April of the school year. The CRM was a locally developed curriculum measure of kindergarten objectives. Children's scores from the first-day administration of the predictor measures were correlated with the scores from the curriculum referenced measure given in April and then compared with the correlations obtained from the same variables after the practice and training periods were completed.

What stands out in this study is the substantial improvement of the low income children whether practising or being trained in the skills of the 'learning screening' procedure. However, when using the Raven learning ability assessment procedures neither practising with the Raven material nor undergoing a training period with Raven material produced any increase in correlations with the academic outcome measure utilised. With middle income students post practice and training periods did result in an increase in the correlations between the Raven test scores and the curriculum measure did increase. However, the post-test Raven CRM correlation was substantially higher in the *practice* mode rather than in the training mode.

These results first indicate that the use of the learning ability procedure with kindergarten age students is questionable. However, it should be noted that the number of children involved in many of the statistical comparisons was quite small which in turn raises questions as to their significance. Also training procedures used with the Raven were shortened and this may have been a factor in lowering the resultant correlations obtained.

Bailey raises important conceptual issues about early school screening stating that children are 'at risk' for different reasons, i.e. poor skills, poor attention span, slow learner, or emotional problems. It would appear that we may need different types of screening measures to be able to identify correctly various school problems in specific children. Thus the Raven 'learning ability' assessment may be inadequate to identify correctly a disadvantaged child who also has emotional problems.

The fact that the January administration of the curriculum measure correlated 0.82 with the April administration would also suggest that the criterion measure itself might be used as the initial screening measure.

Structured testing: the Carlson approach

Another approach to testing the limits has been advocated by Carlson (1979). Using the Raven Progressive Matrices Test, Carlson demonstrated that 'testing-the-limits' procedures which involved verbalisation and feedback were quite effective in improving performance on the Raven.

Carlson's sample consisted of second to fourth grade children whose average age ranged from 7 years 6 months to 9 years 8 months. The Raven was administered using six different testing procedures. These included the standard method and alternative approaches involving various combinations of verbalisation and feedback strategies. Carlson found that the conditions of elaborated feedback (i.e. the subject was informed of correctness of his choice and given an elaboration of why it was correct) and verbalisation and elaborated feedback (i.e. the subject was asked to describe the pattern used, give an explanation for the reason for his choice; was informed of the correctness of his response; also the principles involved were explained to him). Considerable improvement in scores over standard instruction conditions were obtained for both grade groups. Additionally when a puzzle version was substituted for the standard booklet version, scores increased again for the second grade subjects. Correlations between Raven score and math and language performance as determined by teacher ratings for second graders increased from 0.35 with use of the standard administration to 0.81 under administration conditions which involved elaborated feedback.

In a study of third grade children, Bethge, Carlson and Wiedl (1982) investigated not only the effects of type of test administration (i.e. standard, elaborated feedback, and verbalisation) but also the influence of test anxiety and the type of visual administrative scanning procedures involved. They found once again that verbalisation and elaborated feedback yielded higher levels of performance on the Raven than did testing under standard 'static' conditions. Achievement anxiety was significantly reduced under the alternative test administration conditions. Measurement of visual scanning through eye movement analysis indicated that time spent on and number of fixations made to the stimulus patterns and answer alternatives increased under the 'dynamic' assessment conditions. The authors hypothesise that the children had thus modified their problem solving procedures to some extent.

Dillon and Carlson (1978) were also able to demonstrate reduced performance differences between Anglos, Mexican Americans and Blacks when testing procedures provided for verbalisation and elaborated feedback. In a later research study using the Raven and the Cattell Culture Fair Test with learning disabled pupils Carlson (1983) again was able to demonstrate that an individual's performance on complex cognitive tasks improved when the subject overtly described the task at hand and how he determined the solution. This increase was noted for both learning disabled and non-learning disabled groups.

While test scores of these subjects did increase under test administration conditions of verbalisation and elaborated feedback the Raven and Cattell correlations with achievement measures remained low despite the use of alternative testing conditions. Correlations between these tests and achievement measures ranged from — 0.11 to +0.29 regardless of test administration conditions used. However, for non-learning disabled subjects correlations showed a considerable increase under verbalisation and elaborated feedback conditions (from 0.33 to 0.52).

Carlson attempts to explain this anomalous condition as being due to the learning disabled group's long history of academic difficulties. While demonstrating improved performance on the cognitive tests an important finding in its own right, non-cognitive factors appear to affect the group's response on a traditional achievement test.

CONCLUSIONS

How are we to assess the large body of research studies to date on the use of alternative approaches to the assessment of learning ability? One inescapable conclusion is that such research has demonstrated that a number of disadvantaged and/or borderline retarded children do show improved performance and thus their original classification label may indeed be incorrect.

As has been previously indicated the use of structured learning cues with regular class and brain damaged children has been a definite aid in reducing the number of children diagnosed as having visual perceptual problems when none indeed exist. The use of such test 'prompts' is somewhat similar to procedures Russian psychologists have used to assess a child's 'zone of proximal development' (Brown and French, 1979; Cronbach, 1984). The use of multiple regression analysis techniques has demonstrated that the addition of the diagnostic teaching task scores to intelligence test results accounts for significantly more variance in predicting reading comprehension scores (Goodyear, 1979; Goad, 1984). Also the value of diagnostic testing as a single predicator of reading comprehension scores has been effectively demonstrated (Sewell, 1974; Goodyear, 1979; Goad, 1984).

While the Raven 'Learning Potential' assessment within the test-practice-retest paradigm has been shown to be of value (Budoff, 1975), recent research studies of this model have produced inconsistent results. It would appear that the variability of Raven test results may be due in part to the small samples utilised as well as changes in the training methodology employed. However, Popoff-Walker's (1982) rigorous study indicated that use of the Raven learning potential assessment model definitely did not indicate any inaccuracy in the IQ assessment of children of lower SES and retarded ability.

The Raven status groups of 'gainer,' 'non-gainer' and 'high scorer' as presently defined do not appear to hold up as meaningful categorisations for use with children who have special learning problems whether they are labeled EMR or LD. There are a number of technical problems of measurement involved in the Raven test-retest paradigm. Subjects who have made large increases in performance are not accorded 'gainer' status which suggests that such a categorisation is not a sensitive enough measure of improved performance. It is recommended that such a classification be dropped.

Enough studies have shown increased correlations between ability test scores and academic performance measures following a training or practice period to warrant continued research in this area. However, the present research results cannot justify the automatic substitution of these learning potential assessment measures for individual ability tests within the public schools.

Another area of concern is the lack of reliability studies of learning ability measures. If a specific measure lacks a sufficiently high reliability coefficient it is obvious that the resultant scores can be considered suspect. Griffin (1976) concluded that 'learning potential' status was not a stable measure over a six month period of time.

As has been stated, while a number of studies of learning ability status do indicate improved performance of lower class and disadvantaged students, many of these studies indicate that middle class children also profit from the use of the test-practice-retest paradigm. For example, the Raven post-test scores of middle class students in Sewell's (1979) study correlated more highly with math performance measures than did the scores of low SES children (0.63 vs. 0.04). It can easily be argued that various learning ability measures should be utilised with all children referred for learning problems regardless of socio-economic status.

Many American studies have centered only on the use of the Raven test-practice-retest paradigm as outlined by Budoff (1975). It would appear that other approaches such as Roether's (1971) short-time learning test would be of aid in diagnosis of learning problems. Bailey (1979) has also indicated that when there is opportunity for practice, a number of children can substantially improve their performance on ability measures.

Carlson (1978, 1981, 1983) has introduced important standardisation procedures into his use of alternative administrative procedures with the Raven. While his approach can be called a version of 'testing the limits' his studies indicate the value of offering an additional structured approach when testing disadvantaged children with a cognitive test.

Additional published instructions are needed in order to make sure that Carlson's various alternative methods of test administration are strictly followed. A definite advantage of Carlson's approach is that the training practice period can be eliminated and thus time can be saved when working with an individual child.

Burkholder's (1968) cognitive curriculum approach shows much promise and should be considered a viable intervention programme which should be used more frequently. Analysis of her study definitely indicates the value of her approach. Her cognitive training exercises, are in actuality reflective of a sophisticated cognitive curriculum approach. As has been stated not only did the children demonstrate improved performance on reading measures but there was a significant improvement noted in Wechsler IQs. Equally impressive was the short amount of time invested in the 'payoff': 20 hours of class time over one semester.

The value of alternative structured approaches to test administration have been demonstrated already, when administering perceptual tests to children (Smith and Martin, 1967). For the past thirty years, use of alternative ability tests has been shown to be of value with brain damaged children (Taylor, 1959; Neilsen, 1966; Schubert, 1965).

There is an increased emphasis on the use of Feuerstein's model of process assessment. His approach appears to hold considerable promise, but further analysis is needed before we can speak confidently of the results obtained (Pumfrey, 1985; Cronbach, 1984).

As has been stated, legitimate criticism can be made of the process assessment approach. A main question, however, would appear to be what currently constitutes an adequate assessment of a child. The answer would be that any adequate assessment will require the use of a variety of approaches, i.e. standardised tests both of achievement and ability, diagnostic teaching, various measures of learning ability as well as observational procedures.

Concern about the misuse of intelligence tests in the USA was one factor leading to the passage of federal legislation (PL94–142) in 1974. The aim was to help control the flow of misclassified children into EMR classes. Inaction on the part of school psychologists and the educational profession in the USA thus was met with legal regulations. Rivalries among the professional groups of school psychology and special education have also led each group to trumpet their own idiosyncratic approach to the plight of the special education student and has certainly led to confusion among the public as to what constitutes an adequate psychological examination for use within the school system.

It can be pointed out in defence of intelligence tests that when children perform poorly in school and it is ascertained they have IQs within the normal range, such a discrepancy between school performance and ability probably then reflects undetected problems which need to be diagnosed. Such problems may well include various processing difficulties such as poor auditory sequential memory, visual memory, emotional problem, poor teacher–child relationships, and inadequate instruction. Obviously intelligence tests can be of value in such cases and an indepth assessment of the child's difficulties must be undertaken.

One of the main problems in education today in the USA is that various regulations call for the continued and frequent use of IQ tests.

Less routine assessment will result if access to special educational intervention does not necessarily hinge on intellectual test results. For example, to be currently classified as 'learning disabled' in the USA a child must be given an IQ test to 'prove' that the resultant discrepancy between ability and achievement is found in a child of 'normal' intelligence.

Available today are an extraordinary number of standardised tests of various kinds which can be utilised to help in planning effective instruction for children. For example, the educational battery CIRCUS (1979) is a standardised test which offers useful educational information about a first grade child's processing skills as well as his use of problem solving strategies.

Cronbach (1984) strongly recommends the use of such a test battery because the 'concept of information processing abilities and habits as being plural and developable' is made manifest by the use of such a test. As mentioned earlier the same approach is seen in the use of the cognitive curriculum materials in Burkholder's (1968) study. The Stanford Diagnostic Reading Test (1984) is a good example of standardised test which can provide detailed analysis of a child's deficiencies in reading skills. In addition to offering normative data it can also be utilised as a criterion reference measure.

The continued overuse of IQ tests can certainly be called into question. In fact, the continued use of IQ tests with all students has been sharply criticised both by Jensen (1981) and Cronbach (1984). Jensen goes so far as to say that the school psychologist should not be called upon to explain to anyone the basic causes of any child's level of performance. Rather emphasis should be laid on the child's performance on the various achievement 'tests'. 'The IQ is not so directly helpful as is information about the pupil's actual achievement in what he or she has presently been taught' (Jensen, 1981, p. 723). And further: 'a well designed achievement test, administered after a unit of instruction, provides the teacher with the most essential information – the pupil's actual achievement' (Jensen, 1981, p. 235).

Jensen emphasises that achievement testing should become an integral part of instruction. 'Such tests would provide both the teacher and pupil with information as to what skills have or have not been mastered' (Jensen, 1981 p. 236). Jensen also argues for more use of teacher-made tests for small instructional units.

Cronbach (1984) clearly details the importance of achievement tests in today's schools. Since self-contained placements are fewer today in American schools more regrouping is (or should be) practiced within the classroom. Such practices do not need the results of IQ testing, but rather the use of diagnostic instructional tests as well as shorter learning tests such as described earlier in this chapter (Mandl, 1976). School psychologists can be a valuable resource in aiding teachers in organising and carrying out such a classroom testing programme.

When questions legitimately arise, as to a child's continued learning problems and/or possible retardation, then, in addition to use of an appropriate individual ability test, the school psychologist would also utilise structured alternative approaches to such tests as the Raven or Cattell to see if the child improves his score when additional cognitive problem solving strategies are introduced (Carlson, 1983). Diagnostic teaching which is structured and given in a standardised manner (Goodyear, 1979; Goad, 1984) would also be included.

The real importance of the introduction of learning ability assessment procedures is that many children can be found to benefit from the additional structure provided within the testing situation and the use of elaborated feedback and learning cues which is part of such an assessment approach. Since more informed decisions can be made in many cases with the use of such procedures they certainly should become part of the regular examination of the school referred for learning problems.

References

Bailey, D. B. (1979), *A comparison of nonbiased screening procedures to identify high-risk kindergarten children* (Ann Arbor: University Microfilms).

Bardsley, J. R. (1979), *An exploration of learning potential assessment with learning disabled students* (Ann Arbor: University Microfilms).

Bethge, H. G., Carlson, J. S., Wiedl, K. H. (1982), 'The effects of dynamic assessment procedures on Raven matrices performance, visual search behavior, test anxiety and test orientation', *Intelligence,* **6**, 89–97.

Bloom, B. S. (1976), *Human characteristics and school learning* (New York: McGraw-Hill).

Brown, A. L., French, L. A. (1979), 'The zone of potential development: Implications for intelligence testing in the year 2000', *Intelligence*, **3**, 255–73.

Budoff, M. (1967), 'Learning potential among institutionalized young adult retardates', *American Journal of Mental Deficiency*, **72**, 404–11.

Budoff, M. (1973), 'Learning potential and educability among the educable mentally retarded' (progress report on grant NE.G-00-3-0016 submitted to the National Institute of Education).

Budoff, M. (1975), 'Measuring learning potential' in Gredler, G. R. (ed.), *Ethical and legal factors in the practice of school psychology* (Harrisburg: Commonwealth of Pennsylvania).

Budoff, M., Corman, L. (1973), 'The effectiveness of group training procedures on the Raven learning potential measure with children from diverse racial and economic backgrounds', *Studies in Learning Potential*, **3**, no. 58.

Budoff, M., Hamilton, J. L. (1976), 'Optimizing test performance of moderately and severely retarded adolescents and adults', *American Journal of Mental Deficiency*, **81**, 49–57.

Budoff, M., Meskin, J., Harrison, R. (1971), 'Educational test of the learning-potential hypothesis', *American Journal of Mental Deficiency*, **76**, 159–69.

Burkholder, R. B. (1968), *The improvement in reading ability through the development of specific underlying or associated mental abilities* (Ann Arbor: University Microfilms).

Carlson, J. S. (1979), 'Towards a differential testing approach: *Testing-the-limits employing the Raven matrices*', *Intelligence*, **4**, 323–44.

Carlson, J. S. (1981), 'Reliability of the Raven colored progressive matrices test: Age and ethnic group comparisons', *Journal of Consulting and Clinical Psychology*, **49**, 320–2.

Carlson, J. S. (1983), 'Applications of dynamic assessment to cognitive and perceptual functioning of three ethnic groups' (Washington, D. C.: Report to National Institute of Education).

Carroll, H. W., Seely, K. (1974), 'Historical review of intelligence testing and the handicapped', *Academic Therapy*, **10**, 141–9.

CIRCUS (1979), *Manual*. Reading: Addison-Wesley.

Cook, T. D., Campbell, D. T. (1979), *Quasi-experimentation: Design and analysis for field settings*, (Chicago: Rand McNally).

Covington, M. V. (1967), 'Stimulus discrimination as a function of social class membership', *Child Development*, **38**, 607–13.

Cronbach, L. J. (1984), *Essentials of psychological testing*, 4th edn (New York: Harper & Row).

Dillon, R., Carlson, J. S. (1978), 'Testing for competence in three ethnic groups', *Educational and Psychological Measurement*, **38**, 437–43.

Feuerstein, R. (1979), *The dynamic assessment of retarded performers: The learning potential assessment device, theory, instruments, and techniques*, (Baltimore: University Park Press).

Feuerstein, R. (1980), *Instrumental enrichment* (Baltimore: University Park, 1980).

Gettinger, M. (1978), *Is time to-learn or measured intelligence a stronger correlate of school learning*? (Ann Arbor: University Microfilm).

Goad, T. L. (1984), 'A comparison of learning potential and intelligence measures in predicting reading achievement', unpublished master's thesis (Columbia: University of South Carolina).

Goodyear, P. R., (1979), 'The prediction of reading achievement from learning potential and intelligence measures', unpublished master's thesis (Columbia: University of South Carolina).

Gredler, G. R. (1978), 'Learning disabilities and reading disorders: A current assessment', *Psychology in the Schools*, **15**, 226–38.

Griffin, M. (1976), 'Learning potential stability in relationship to achievement and IQ of learning disabled secondary level students', unpublished master's thesis (Lawrence: University of Kansas).

Gupta, R. M., Coxhead, P. (1983), 'The assessment of the learning efficiency of Asian children', *Collected Original Resources in Education*, **7**, 3, Fiche 1 A4.

Hamilton, J. L., Budoff, M. (1974), 'Learning potential among the moderately and severely retarded', *Mental Retardation*, **12**, 33–6.
Hamill, D. D. (1971), 'Evaluating children for instructional purposes', *Academic Therapy*, VI, 341–53.
Haynes, J. M. (1971), *Educational assessment of immigrant pupils* (Windsor: National Foundation for Educational Research).
Hennessey, J. J. (1981). Clinical and diagnostic assessment of children's abilities: Traditional and innovative models. In Merrifield, P. (ed.), *Measuring human abilities*, (San Francisco: Jossey-Bass).
Ingenkamp, K. (1977), *Educational assessment*, (Windsor: NFER).
Jensen, A. (1963), 'Learning ability in retarded, average, and gifted children', *Merrill-Palmer Quarterly of Behavior and Development*, **9**, 123–40.
Jensen, A. R. (1981), *Straight talk about mental tests*, (New York: The Free Press).
Kenney, M. V. (1984), *Effects of Feuerstein's instrumental enrichment on the reasoning, non-verbal intelligence, and the locus of control of 12 to 15 year old educable mentally retarded handicapped and learning disabled students*, (Ann Arbor: University Microfilms, 1984).
Korman, A., Sporer, S. L. (1983), 'Learning tests – concepts and critical evaluation', *Studies in Educational Evaluation*, **9**, 169–84.
Kunzelmann, H. P., Koenig, C. H. (1981), *Manual for refer and learning screening*, (Columbus: Charles E. Merrill).
Lambert, N. M., Wilcox, M. R., Gleason, W. P. (1974), *The educationally retarded child* (New York: Grune & Stratton).
Levine, M., Levine, A. (1970), *A social history of helping services*, (New York: Appleton-Century-Crofts).
Mandl, H. (1976), 'Current views about school readiness tests in Germany with specific reference to their predictive value for identifying potential failure in school' in Wedell, K., Raybould, E. C., (eds), *The early identification of educationally 'at risk' children*, (Birmingham: Education Review).
McClelland, D. C. (1973), 'Testing for competence rather than for intelligence', *American Psychologist*, **28**, 1–14.
Mercer, J. (1973), *Labelling the mentally retarded*, (Berkeley: University of California Press).
Meyers, J., Pfeffer, J., Erlbaum, V. (1985), 'Process assessment: A model for broadening assessment', *Journal of Special Education*, **19**, 73–89.
Neilsen, H. H. (1966), *A psychological study of cerebral palsied children*, (Copenhagen: Munksgaard).
Newland, E. (1963), 'Psychological assessment of exceptional children and youth' in Cruikshank, W. M. (ed.), *Psychology of exceptional children and youth*, (Englewood Cliffs: Prentice-Hall).
Ortar, G. R. (1960), 'Improving test validity by coaching', *Educational Research*, **2**, 137–42.
Platt, J. S. (1976), *The effect of the modified Raven's progressive matrices learning potential coaching procedure on Raven's post-test scores and their correlation*, (Ann Arbor: University Microfilms).
Popoff-Walker, L. E. (1980), *The relationship between IQ, SES, adaptive behavior, and performance on a measure of learning potential*, (Ann Arbor: University Microfilms).

Popoff-Walker, L. E. (1982), 'IQ, SES, adaptive behavior and performance on a learning potential measure', *Journal of School Psychology*, **20**, 222–31.

Pumfrey, P. D. (1985), 'Just a minute – let me think', *Trainer's Forum*, **5**, 1–3.

Pumfrey, P. D., Naylor, J. G. (1983), 'The alleviation of psycholinguistic deficits and some effects on the reading attainments of poor readers: A sequel', *Journal of Research in Reading*, **6**, 129–53.

Rey, A. (1935), *l'intelligence practique chez l'enfant*, (Paris: Alcan).

Sattler, J. (1981), *Assessment of Children's Intelligence*, (Newton: Allyn & Bacon).

Schubert, J. (1965), 'Retest scores on intelligence tests as diagnostic indicators' in J. Loring (ed.), *Teaching the cerebral palsied child*, (London: William Heinemann).

Scott, G. C. (1950), 'Measuring Sudanese intelligence', *British Journal of Educational Psychology*, **20**, 43–54.

Sewell, T. E. (1979), 'Intelligence and learning tasks as predictors of scholastic achievement in black and white first grade children', *Journal of School Psychology*, **17**, 325–32.

Sewell, T. E., Severson, R. A. (1974), 'Learning ability and intelligence as cognitive predictors of achievement in first grade black children', *Journal of Educational Psychology*, **66**, 948–55.

Smith, C. R. (1980), 'Assessment alternatives: Non-standardized procedures', *School Psychology Review*, **9**, 46–57.

Smith, D. C., Martin, R. A. (1967), 'Use of learning cues with the Bender visual motor gestalt test in screening children for neurological impairment', *Journal of Consulting Psychology*, **31**, 205–9.

Stanford Diagnostic Reading Test Manual (1984), (San Antonio: Psychological Corporation).

Suran, B. G., Rizzo, J. V. (1983), *Special education: An integrative approach* (Glenview: Scott, Foresman).

Taylor, E. (1959) *Psychological appraisal of children with cerebral defects*, (Cambridge: Harvard University).

Wolf, R. K. (1984), *Learning potential and its relationship to success on a math problem-solving strategy with junior high learning disabled adolescents*, (Ann Arbor: University Microfilms).

Zigler, E., Abelson, W. D., Seitz, V. (1973) 'Motivational factors of economically disadvantaged children on the Peabody picture vocabulary test', *Child Development*, **44**, 294–300.

4 Cultural Difference and Cultural Deprivation: A Theoretical Framework for Differential Intervention

Mogens R. Jensen, Reuven Feuerstein, Yaacov Rand, Shlomo Kaniel and David Tzuriel

The theory of Structural Cognitive Modifiability (SCM) (Feuerstein, 1977; 1979, 1980; Feuerstein and Jensen, 1980; Feuerstein, Jensen, Hoffman and Rand, 1985) identifies as 'culturally different' individuals or groups who have benefitted from learning experiences whereby their culture was mediated to them. It identifies as 'culturally deprived' those who have not been inducted into their *own* culture due to the inadequate provision of such learning experiences. Drawing on the paradigm of the Mediated Learning Experience (MLE) this chapter analyses the etiology of cultural difference and cultural deprivation and examines the implications of this distinction for the development of differential approaches to the educational intervention required for the individual confronting the need to adapt and change.

CONFRONTATION WITH THE NEED TO CHANGE: ADAPTATION OR DYSFUNCTION

In our era large masses of people with widely different backgrounds are confronted with the need to adapt to a modern technological society characterised by *rapid and discontinuous change*. To meet this need education has become increasingly democratised with rich and diverse opportunities for learning through both formal and informal frameworks including the mass media. Despite these efforts cognitive dysfunction has become pervasive and large numbers of people are unable to cope with the unfamiliar and complex requirements of this type of society.

To guide the formulation of educational policy, efforts must now be devoted to discover why some individuals are able to take advantage and benefit from encounters with the new while others, who may function more or less adequately in familiar environments and routine situations, manifest little propensity and capacity to do so. For the former, such encounters produce a widening of the schemata of their thought processes while for the latter the encounter with the new and unfamiliar produces evidence of dysfunction and inability to cope. We believe that the difference in modifiability between these two groups derives from a crucial difference in the etiology of their cognitive development and that this difference becomes obvious precisely when the individual is confronted with novelty and change. The pivotal etiological factor is the presence or absence of adequately mediated learning experiences (MLE).

The proposed learning paradigm: the mediated learning experience

The theory of structural cognitive modifiability holds that the individual learns through two distinct modalities. The first and most universal of these is through Direct Exposure (DE). In this modality stimuli impinge on the organism in disassociated, fragmented and even random ways. Biological drives and need reduction will ensure the development of stimulus-response (S-R) contingencies producing stable changes over time in the organism's behavioural repertoire. Additional forms of learning can be accounted for by the processes of assimilation and accomodation outlined by Piaget in the stimulus-organism-response (S-O-R) paradigm. However, direct exposure learning even when defined as a creative, operational organism-stimuli interaction leaves us with a number of unanswered questions.

1. Can we really consider the development of higher mental processes as the epiphenomena of the sole exposure to stimuli?
2. A second question which follows from the first is how can we then explain differential cognitive development under equal conditions of exposure to stimuli? Such difficulties are already evident from the fact that only a relatively small proportion of individuals reach to the level of formal operations even though nobody can claim that they have not been exposed to the stimuli which one claims leads to such a development.
3. Furthermore, how will we explain different cognitive styles as prevalent in different cultures? No less of a difficulty is to explain the

great differences existing between individuals as to their capacity to benefit from their exposure to stimuli in the direction of developing the required conditions of adaptability. Viewed as such, direct exposure to stimuli cannot be considered more than one of the two modalities of interaction necessary in order to explain the characteristics of human modifiability, of the flexibility of the schemata which will insure the processes of assimilation and modification.

In order to account for these observations we believe it is necessary to consider the learning paradigm presented in Figure 4.1. Derived from the theory of Structural Cognitive Modifiability, the paradigm encompasses also the S-R and S-O-R paradigms associated with Direct Exposure. The proposed paradigm considers that learning takes place also through a second modality, the Mediated Learning Experience (MLE). In this modality of learning the organism (O) is no longer exposed directly to sources of stimuli (S). The mediator (H) – an intentioned, initiated and affectionate human – selects stimuli from the environment (S) transforming them according to purposes and goals before they reach the systems of the learner (O). Using the stimuli, the mediator instills a series of cognitive functions and mental operations within the learner, selecting responses offered by the learner (O), shaping them and imposing latencies to produce appropriate response modalities (R). The mediation establishes within the organism the cognitive functions, mental operations, learning sets and need systems which permit the learner to reach higher levels of cognitive modifiability and to benefit from Direct Exposure (S-O-R) to both formal and informal learning opportunities.

Some universal characteristics of the mediated learning experience

The formative value of Mediated Learning Experience is neither related to the context in which it is carried out nor is it contingent upon the language used (gestural, verbal, iconic). The MLE represents purely the *quality* of the interaction and, as such, can be observed in all possible interactions, in all environments, in all cultures, and across very different levels of functioning.

The MLE is characterised by the *intentionality* of the mediator to interact in a meaningful way with the mediatee. Intentionality produces a goal for the interaction which in turn permits the mediator to select some stimuli as relevant and reject others as unimportant. The presence

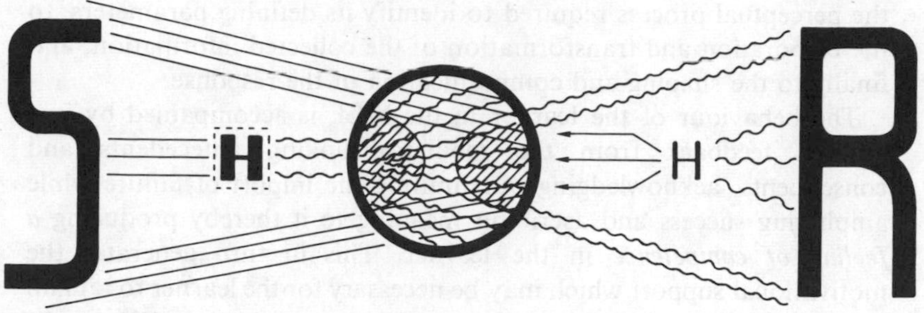

Figure 4.1 The mediated learning experience model
The mediator (*H*) selects stimuli from the environment (*S*) transforming them according to purposes and goals before they reach the systems of the learner (*O*). The mediator (*H*) selects responses produced by the learner (*O*) shaping and transforming them to develop response modalities (*R*). *MLE* establishes prerequisites and instills need systems required for higher levels of modifiability. Following mediation the learner (*O*) is able to interact effectively with the environment (*S–O–R*) without mediation and adapt to needs to change.

of a goal enables the mediator to frame stimuli, to organise them by purpose and attribute, to sequence and schedule their appearance for the mediatee and to imbue them with meaning. Intentionality animates the mediator, making the use of both eyes and gestures conspicuous and creating within the mediatee a state of vigilance and reciprocity leading to the formation of a bond between the learner and the mediator. The mediator adjusts the rhythm of the interaction to suit the needs of the learner, slows down, models behaviour, ensures repetition, and provokes anticipatory behaviours in the mediatee to disconnect between stimuli improperly joined and connect between others.

The MLE is characterised by a quality of *transcendence*. This quality places the goal of the mediated interaction above the requirements, needs, and resolution of the specific context through which the mediation takes place. The goals, instead, are to identify, amplify, and strengthen new or fragile components of the learner's functioning and, through the mediation of *meaning*, turn the learner's functioning into a point of departure for the establishment of broader need systems and propensities of functioning. The mediation of meaning supports the learner's acquisitions with insight to render them applicable also to situations very different from the one employed for mediation.

The mediator *regulates the behaviour* of the learner creating rhythm in the mental act to ensure its orderly flow from the initial perception of a disequilibrium, or problem, to the focused and systematic investment in the perceptual process required to identify its defining parameters, to the elaboration and transformation of the collected information, and finally to the shaping and communication of the response.

The behaviour of the learner in the MLE is accompanied by fine grained feedback from the mediator linking antecedents and consequents, acknowledging but limiting the import of failure while amplifying success and ascribing meaning to it thereby producing *a feeling of competence* in the learner. This in turn generates the motivational support which may be necessary for the learner to remain or become involved with tasks previously considered difficult or inaccessible. The mediation of a feeling of competence creates needs for mastery and shapes expectancies of success following autonomous, independent effort.

Enlisting and developing the social impulse, the mediator instills within the mediatee the propensity to share feelings and products of cognition and, in so doing, to search for the tempo and response modalities which will overcome egocentricity in the learner's communications with others. As such the *mediation of sharing* shapes the energetic component of social behaviour.

Mediated learning experience and cognitive development

Mediated Learning Experience is conceived of as the determinant of the autoplasticity of the cognitive structure. It is this autoplasticity which is responsible for the individual's capacity to enrich the repertoire of functioning with new modalities required to match the discontinuities and changes in his environment.

Although the organism develops and learns through both DE and MLE, the Mediated Learning Experience is considered responsible for the cognitive development most related to the unique characteristic of the human being namely his modifiability. This modifiability, or capacity to modify oneself not only in response to external eco-systems but also as an outcome of an internal decision, is no less important for the individual than it is for humanity in general as it constantly expands and transforms its needs.

The MLE should be considered at once as both complementary with and as departing from Piaget's conception of the S-O-R since it identifies the mediator as playing a role in the development of cognitive processes which goes far beyond the role played by an object creating incongruities within the schemata of the perceiver.

Cognitive development postulated as the outcome of the double process of direct exposure provoking assimulation and accommodation and MLE ensuring the flexibility of the schemata, which enables the process of assimilation-accommodation to take place, must be considered both for its explicit programmatic value and for its meaning as applied to a very large range of human endeavours.

One of the most important questions addressed by the theory of MLE is precisely the question of differential cognitive development, which we raised at the beginning of this paper. To the extent that differential cognitive development is related to environmental conditions, we would like to propose that it depends upon Mediated Learning Experience as its proximal determinant: The more adequately learning experiences have been mediated to the child, the better the cognitive development and the higher the level of functioning.

Cultural deprivation and cultural difference

From a programmatic point of view the concept of the Mediated Learning Experience has important implications both for assessment and intervention (see below) but MLE is actually present whenever groups or individuals transmit to their progenies their own past, culture and self. Both implicitly and explicitly the goal of cultural transmission is to ensure the continuity of the existence of the group or individual beyond the biological limitations of life.

The process of cultural transmission affects the progenies in two ways. The first, and more obvious, equips the child with a repertoire of information and experiences which he/she would not have access to without the act of mediation. However, the role which seems more important to us is the development, resulting from MLE, of the unique human characteristic of modifiability.

The development of modifiability can be accomplished with MLE regardless of the specific cultural transmission offered. In other words, no cultural process entailing transmission is without effect on the individual's capacity to learn from and be affected by new experience. The development of modifiability depends neither upon the nature of the culture, its language, and its content nor upon the specific institutions involved in its transmission. The universal elements of mediated learning (intentionality, transcendence, mediation of meaning, regulation of behaviour, mediation of a feeling of competence, and mediation of sharing) are found in all cultures and may even be considered to constitute a necessary basis for their existence. Cultures differ widely in the stimuli selected, the specific ways in which they are combined and the meaning attributed to them. The development of modifiability, however, is produced by the quality of the mediated interaction which can shape whatever content or language may be used in the cultural transmission. The specific content or language of any culture therefore has nothing to do either with the development or the lack of development of modifiability.

Modifiability and cultural difference develops when the individual is exposed to processes of transmission within his/her own culture whereas cultural deprivation and a lack of modifiability results when the individual is deprived of such processes within his/her own culture. Cultural difference is the antonym of cultural deprivation inasmuch as cultural difference is a direct function of exposure to one's own and uniquely different culture.[1] The greater the exposure the greater the difference. Individuals who have been exposed to their own culture, and have internalised its values, have learned to integrate these values and to be affected by them. The culturally or MLE deprived individual is seldom different in this sense. Of course, there are culturally deprived individuals who come from an environment where content or language is different compared to their present environment, but these individuals are not really *culturally* different.

Now our previous proposition will be better understood: When exposed to a new environment, and confronting a need to change, the culturally different individual will of necessity show a higher level of adaptability and capacity to be affected by and learn from the new than will the culturally deprived. The difference is due to the difference in modifiability which in turn is due to the development among the culturally different of the prerequisites of higher levels of functioning as a result of the mediation offered to them through cultural transmission.

The difference in adaptability to new and unfamiliar environments can be seen despite what might be considered more probable, namely that the person with the stronger and more articulated cultural profile has to unlearn previous cultural habits and give up linguistic behaviour, and other typical modalities of interaction in order to accept new language, new perspectives and new mores. In their classic study Stodolsky and Lesser (1967) showed that students whose performance was relatively unlike the profile typical for their ethnic group also were more likely to be lower functioning within that group. Moreover, among those who performed at higher levels within each ethnic group there were more individuals who exhibited the profile characteristic for that group than there were among those who performed at lower levels. Consistent with the theory of MLE closer resemblance with the profile unique for the culture was associated with *higher levels of cognitive functioning*.

The syndrome of cultural deprivation

Lack of MLE produces the syndrome of cultural deprivation whose primary manifestations are the rigidity and inflexibility of the cognitive system and the inability to widen schemata as a function of the encounter with the new, incongruous and unfamiliar.

The rigidity of the system of the culturally deprived is strongly related to a set of deficient cognitive functions, mental operations and need systems whose impairment, or underdevelopment, is due to the lack of MLE (Feuerstein, 1979).

The individual who has been deprived of adequately mediated learning experiences is characterised by an episodic grasp of reality which is responsible for the fact that relationships are not created between experienced events. Instead, each experience is left as an isolated, fragmented and dissociated episode with little or no relationship to what preceded it and even less with what followed. Among other deficient functions likely to be seen are the following: inability to experience the existence of an actual problem, inability to select relevant cues, impulsive and unsystematic explorative behaviour, impaired receptive verbal tools, impaired spatial and temporal orientation, impaired conservation of constancies, impaired capacity for considering two, or more, sources of information at once, lack of spontaneous comparative behaviour, narrowness of the mental field, lack of planning behaviour, impaired need for summative behaviour, impaired need for logical evidence, restricted interiorisation, lack of inferential-hypothetical thinking, impaired strategies for hypothesis testing, egocentric communicational modalities, blocking, trial and error responses, impaired verbal tools for communicating even adequately elaborated responses, impaired visual transport and a general lack of need for precision affecting all three phases of the mental act – the collection of information (input), the transformation of information (elaboration), and the communication of the response (output).

The syndrome of cultural deprivation is characterised also by attitudinal and motivational deficits which include, among others, the perception of the self as a passive recipient of information, lack of need for mastery, lack of curiosity, expectancies of failure, and external locus of control.

IMPLICATIONS FOR INTERVENTION: AN ACTIVE MODIFICATION APPROACH

In conventional approaches to the human organism cognitive, emotional and behavioural differences are considered to be a direct function of hereditary conditions, acquired traumata, constitution, or early experience. Since these factors are all associated with high degrees of immutability, the conventional models tend to view the individual experiencing dysfunction as a *closed system* inaccessible to meaningful change. Reflecting the passive acceptant approach these models advocate the creation of low-expectation environments designed to suit the individual's irreversible level of functioning.

As is apparent from the discussion of MLE, our theoretical framework is guided by a philosophy which assumes that the human organism is an *open system* accessible to structural change through environmental influences designed to modify the ways by which the individual registers, elaborates, and communicates information. Embodied in the theory of structural cognitive modifiability this view certainly recognises individual differences in heredity, constitution, and early experience but it challenges the assumption that these factors are linked to cognitive-emotional functioning through direct and unavoidable relationships.

Considered along with exogenous conditions such as low SES, parental apathy and emotional disturbance to represent *distal* etiological factors we contend that these variables in and of themselves do not determine the cognitive development of the individual. We believe the *proximal etiology* of far greater consequence is the adequate or inadequate provision of MLE. It is only when distal etiological factors succeed in preventing or disrupting the provision of MLE that the inadequate development occurs. Alternatively, if ways can be found to overcome or bypass the effects of distal etiologies and provide the requisite MLE our theory predicts that higher levels of functioning can be reached across such variables as age, etiology, and level of impairment which traditionally have been seen to impose firm upper limits for structural change.

This distinction between distal and proximal etiologies removes the basis for maintaining a passive acceptant approach to the low functioning individual. The active modification approach directs intervention away from the creation of low-expectation environments in favour of the determination and provision of the specific nature, intensity and amount of investment in the individual which may be required to produce higher levels of functioning.

Programmatic implications

Implications for assessment: the learning potential assessment device (LPAD)

Identifying Mediated Learning Experience as the proximal determinant of cognitive development produces an agenda for assessment which differs radically from conventional testing in terms of purpose, goals, instruments, techniques and interpretation of results (see also Feuerstein, Miller, Rand and Jensen, 1981; Jensen and Feuerstein, in press).

Whereas the purpose of traditional testing is to classify the individual's presumed stable and irreversible level of functioning with the goal of placement in a suitable low-expectation environment, the purpose of the Learning Potential Assessment Device (LPAD) is to determine how the modifiability of the examinee can best be enhanced with the goal of reaching higher levels of cognitive functioning.

In order to classify respondents, traditional approaches rely upon tests which typically have been developed following careful and precise psychometric criteria, norm referencing and standard administration procedures to permit a comparison between the specific individual's performance and that of same aged peers. Rejecting the concept of comparability as the basis for decision-making, the materials and techniques of the LPAD represent a radical shift away from the psychometric approach. The LPAD employs tools, or instruments, rather than tests. The instruments are designed to permit the examiner to access the cognitive structure, identify deficient cognitive functions, mental operations and attitudinal-motivational learning sets, provide an intensive, focused MLE and subsequently ascertain the extent to which this mediation has enhanced performance on tasks progressively more remote from the one utilised for the remediation.

The LPAD tasks are specially constructed to permit the form of learning to occur which may affect the enhancement of learning capacity. The tasks neither tap nor offer specific content knowledge but instead permit the examiner to single out and address those aspects of functioning which may relate to such enhancement. The instruments of the LPAD are constructed to be sensitive to change through carefully controlled variation of such task parameters as complexity and abstractness. The examiner is able to observe even small changes in the examinee's functioning, to amplify them further and ascribe to them their proper meaning for the modifiability of the individual. Careful attention has also been given in the construction of materials to enlist the support of attitudinal and motivational factors by offering opportunities for successful interaction and experiences of growing competence. To achieve this, LPAD materials carefully balance familiarity with complexity to produce appropriate challenges enabling mastery to occur and to make transfer possible.

The rejection of comparability as the criterion sine-qua-non for decision-making frees the LPAD examiner-examinee relationship from the severe constraints which in the standardised testing prevent the examiner from exploring the sources of failure and provide feedback to the examinee. In the LPAD the examiner – guided by the qualities of the mediated learning experience – establishes a partnership with the examinee imbued by genuine readiness to seek and produce the removal of the obstacles which prevent the examinee from functioning at higher levels.

The dynamic assessment technique is guided by an orientation which seeks to affect the *processes* of the examinee's functioning. Using both highly dysfunctional and exceptionally successful responses for diagnostic purposes the LPAD examiner derives working hypotheses both for the areas in greatest need of remediation and for the best ways to provide it. Rather than attributing failure as necessarily due to lack of capacity the examiner assesses the possibility that failure might be due to such factors as unfamiliarity with the particular contents of the task, the language of its presentation (e.g. figural, verbal, numerical), the absence or fragility of cognitive functions and mental operations required to solve it, the possibility that task-complexity exceeds the examinee's present capacity to process information, that the level of abstraction required is too high or the possibility that failure might be due merely to underdeveloped efficiency of prerequisite components already available in the learner's system.

Figure 4.2 provides an example of tasks from the LPAD which can be used to provide mediation and subsequently assess modifiability. The mediated interaction utilises a specific task but seeks to equip the learner with awareness of principles and modalities of functioning which transcend this particular task to establish within the learner the prerequisites which will enable a successful approach to similar and progressively more different tasks.

The LPAD has been developed both as an assessment device for individuals and as a screening device for groups (Feuerstein, Haywood, Rand, Hoffman and Jensen, 1985). Although the group version is accompanied by a reduction in the precision of the mediational interaction the conditions of mediation in that format are much more similar to the types of mediation which typically can be offered in a classroom. Evidence of modifiability obtained under these conditions therefore points to changes which can be reached with limited amounts of investment. The LPAD group test can be utilised to screen large masses and groups of people for modifiability for purposes of structuring educational environments based upon their capacity to change rather than upon their manifest level of functioning (Feuerstein, Rand, Jensen, Kaniel, Tzuriel, Ben Schachar-Segev and Mintzker, in press). Individuals who do not benefit from the mediation offered in the group format may require more specialised forms of intervention which the examiner may be able to describe following assessment in the individual format.

Implications for intervention: the instrumental enrichment (*IE*) *programme*

Instrumental Enrichment is, like the LPAD, based upon the open systems philosophy and the theory of Structural Cognitive Modifiability. The purpose of the LPAD is to diagnose the modifiability of the examinee through a direct attempt to enhance it. This attempt produces information about the nature, type, amount, and intensity of the investment which may be required to overcome deficiencies identified in the examinee's cognitive structure. Although it charts the course which remediation might follow, the LPAD itself is too brief to be counted on to produce a lasting remediation although it occasionally suffices to bring it about. Typically – over months or even two to three years – a much more extensive and long-lasting attack on the deficient functions, mental operations, and inadequate learning sets is necessary to permit habit formation to occur and to accomplish the crucial transformation in the self-perception of the MLE deprived individual from that of a passive recipient of information to that of an active generator of information.

The Instrumental Enrichment programme was developed as a tool to bring about the actual and lasting enhancement of modifiability. The purpose of the programme is to provide both an age appropriate and a phase-specific substitute for mediational processes which for a great variety of reasons may not have been sufficiently or adequately provided to the low functioning individual. Utilising materials and techniques

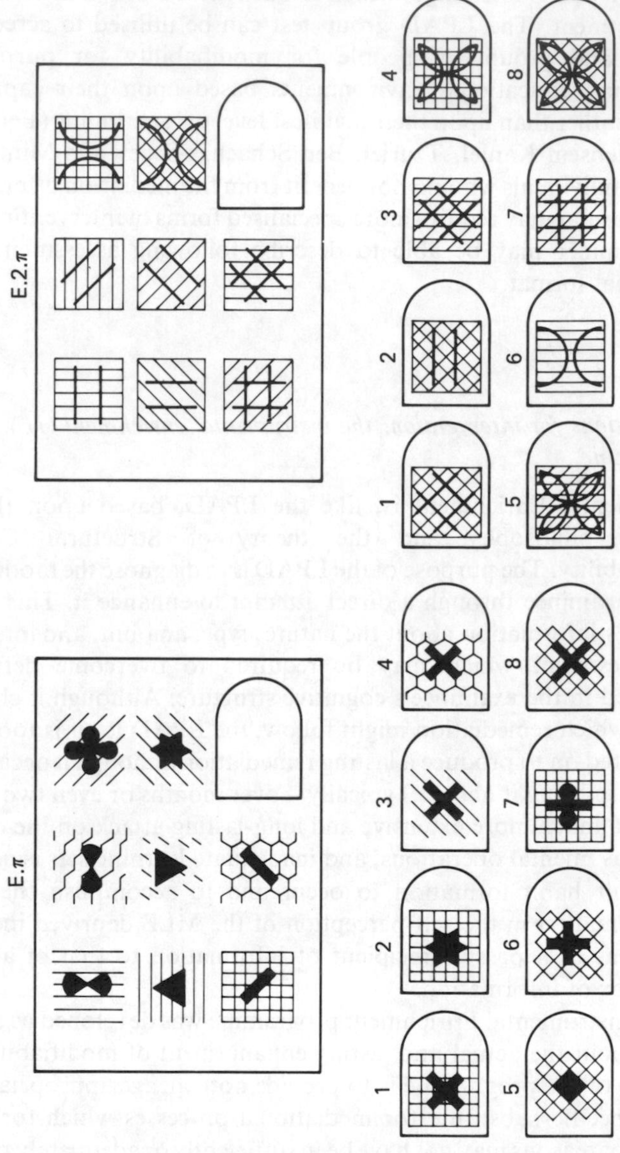
E.2.π
E.π
1
2
3
4
5
6
7
8

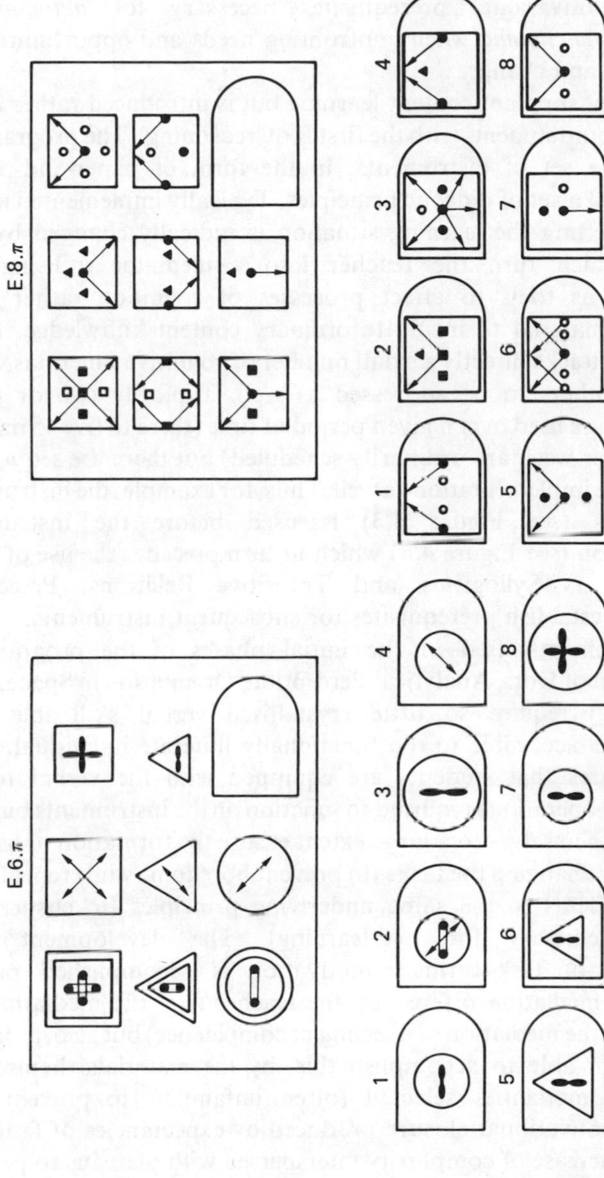

Figure 4.2 LPAD set-variations

Examples of tasks from the LPAD which can be utilised to assess the modifiability of the capacity to learn. The mediated interaction seeks to equip the learner with the prerequisites of functioning which will enable a successful approach to tasks and situations that may differ from those initially employed for mediation.

commensurate with age and level of development the goal of the programme is to equip the learner with both the intellective and the attitudinal-motivational prerequisites necessary for *autonomous-independent functioning* when confronting needs and opportunities to learn, adapt and change.

IE does not supplant content learning but is introduced rather as an adjunct to equip students with the first R of 'reasoning'. The programme consists of a set of instruments, in the form of paper-and-pencil exercises, and a set of didactic principles. Typically implemented in the classroom setting the learning situation is radically changed by the didactics which turn the teacher into a mediator utilising the instruments as tools to affect processes of cognition rather than curriculum material to inculcate ordinary content knowledge. Each instrument attacks directly a small number of cognitive functions while permitting others to be addressed as well. Typically two or three instruments are used over a given period of time (three to five 45 minute IE lessons per week are ordinarily scheduled) but there are sequential aspects of the implementation as well. Thus, for example, the instrument Comparisons (see Figure 4.3) is used before the instrument Categorisation (see Figure 4.4) which in turn precedes the use of such instruments as Syllogisms and Transitive Relations. Preceding instruments establish prerequisites for subsequent instruments.

The instruments used in the initial phases of the programme (Organisation of Dots, Analytical Perception, Orientation in Space, and Comparisons) require so little crystallised verbal skill that the programme is accessible to the functionally illiterate individual. The teacher ensures that students are equipped with the verbal tools, concepts and operations required to function on the instruments but the instruments themselves to a large extent ensure the formation of habits by constantly changing the tasks (to prevent boredom) while repeatedly exposing students to the same underlying principles (to ensure the repetition necessary for overlearning). The development and maintenance of task-intrinsic motivation is accomplished partly through the mediation offered by the teacher (e.g. the mediation of meaning and the mediation of a feeling of competence) but also, as far as we have been able to accomplish this, by the materials themselves through the modalities selected (often unfamiliar to prevent the premature motivational closure produced by expectancies of failure), the careful increase of complexity interspersed with plateaus to permit consolidation and mastery, and by the great care which has been given to make the materials attractive and appealing.

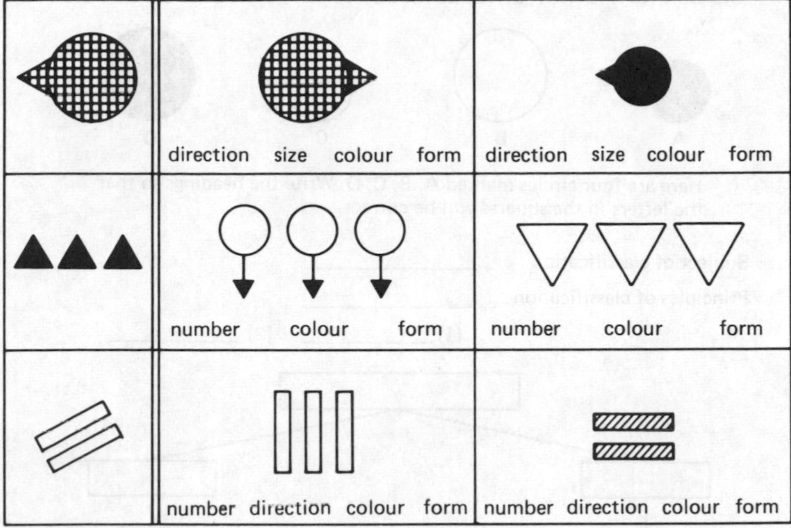

Figure 4.3 Comparisons
Circle that which is common between the sample picture on the left and each of the pictures in the same row.

Sample

To automatise the act of comparison, to provide the basis for classification and to correct episodic grasp of reality the student learns to find similarities and differences between objects, events and ideas. The student learns to use concepts in the identification of the most essential or characteristic dimensions and to ignore the irrelevant. Among the deficient cognitive functions treated are: Blurred and sweeping perception, unplanned and unsystematic exploratory behaviour, lack of verbal tools, inability to relate to two or more sources of information, narrowness of the mental field and trial and error responses.

The goal of the mediated learning experience is to increase the autoplasticity of the learner. The instruments are therefore never used merely for their own sake but rather as opportunities, or points of departure, for the development of larger need systems sustained by insight. To accomplish this an important feature of the IE programme is the constant endeavour of teacher and students to identify precise applications of the learned principles in both academic and non-academic content areas. Students often become very adept at such bridging both from IE to content and from their regular curriculum to IE.

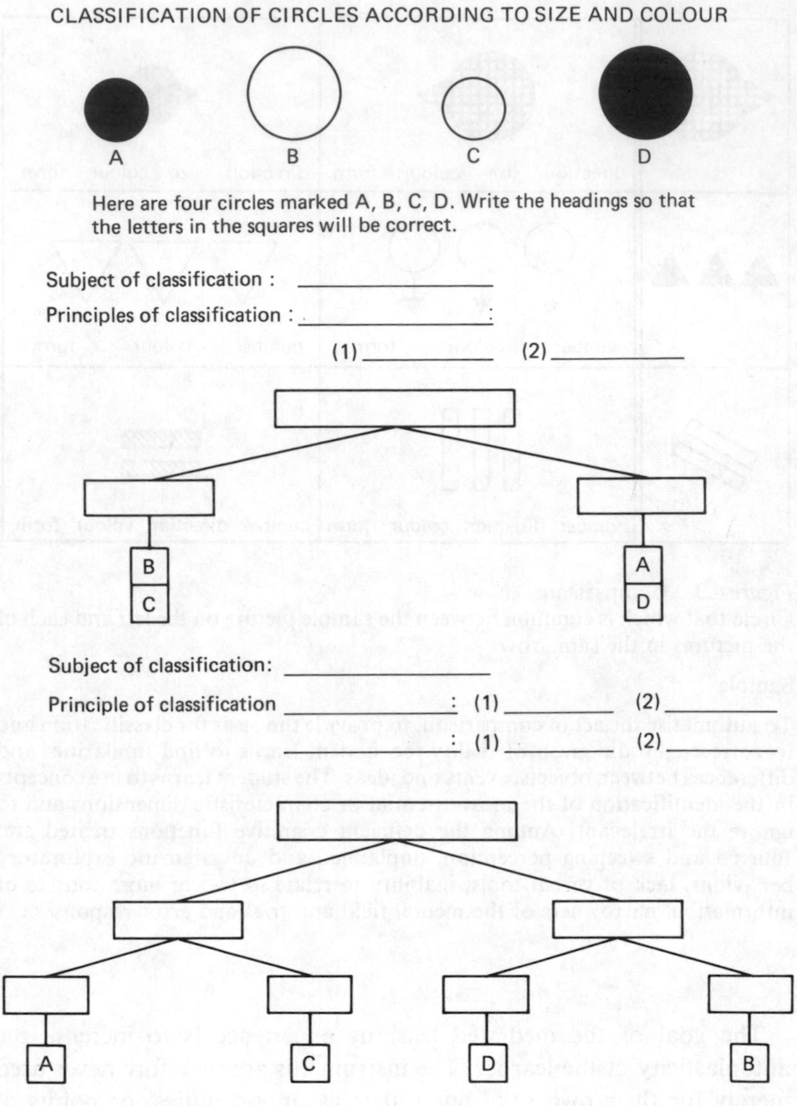

CLASSIFICATION OF CIRCLES ACCORDING TO SIZE AND COLOUR

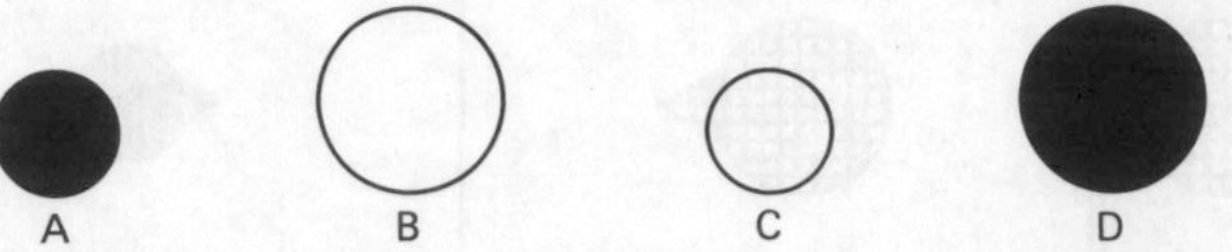

Here are four circles marked A, B, C, D. Write the headings so that the letters in the squares will be correct.

Subject of classification : ____________

Principles of classification : ____________ :

(1) ____________ (2) ____________

B
C

A
D

Subject of classification: ____________

Principle of classification ____________ : (1) ____________ (2) ____________

: (1) ____________ (2) ____________

A C D B

Figure 4.4 Categorisation

In order to group objects according to underlying principles, and to subsume them into appropriate sets, the learner must become familiar with hierarchially ordered mental processes for the organisation of data into superordinate categories. Through comparison, differentiation, discrimination, analytical perception and projection of relationships the learner becomes aware of the invariant attributes of group categories and, by encoding of operations, discovers the possibility of grouping and regrouping according to objectives and needs.

Throughout the programme the mediation echoes the learner's right to seek a dualistic relationship with the world. Along with the regulation of the learner's behaviour and the mediation of a feeling of competence the teacher seeks to establish an internal locus of control, to foster a sense of individuation and psychological differentiation and to create both the cognitive basis and the attitudinal support for autonomous independent functioning. Focusing upon a decentration from egocentric modalities of functioning the IE programme continually encourages the learner to seek to produce and formulate his/her own point of view. In this way the programme invests directly in shaping the self-perception of the learner to overcome the attitudinal basis for passivity which often accompanies cultural deprivation.

The Instrumental Enrichment programme represents a so-called content free approach to the remediation of cognitive deficiencies. The programme's content-free nature is not due merely to its intended use as a tool to reach cognitive goals that transcend particular circumstances. The rejection of ordinary content for purposes of cognitive redevelopment also derives from the resistance shown by students whenever 'deviations' are made from materials which have their own rhythm and purpose (e.g. geography, mathematics home economics). Such materials are not easily bent to suit the needs to redevelop cognitive functions and mental operations. Moreover, some students – and especially those who have experienced failure in the past – will reject the familiar content which has become associated with their failure. A specially designed, content-free, and planned programme was developed, finally, to free the teacher from the burden of constructing or adapting materials and to avoid entanglements of content with the teacher's own fragilities in cognitive functioning.

Implications for systems: the structure of powerful environments

After modifiability has been unveiled (e.g. with the LPAD) and enhanced (e.g. with the IE programme) the most important condition for its development is a *powerful environment* whose most important characteristic is the demand that one uses modifiability to cope. In order to produce environments which can generate a demand for modifiability it is necessary to create the conditions which will permit larger service-delivery systems to be changed from closed to open systems.

School and other systems that consider those they serve as closed systems tend to be no less closed themselves. Often such a system perceives itself to embody the stable and unchangeable values of the society which erected it. The rationale for the passive acceptant approach to the low functioning individual is rooted no less in the lack of such a system's readiness to change itself as it is grounded in the perception of the student's lack of capability to benefit from such changes. Closed systems organise themselves so that change is neither expected nor promoted. Individuals within them are exposed to little novelty, homogeneous groupings are created, the level of requirements stay constant and the message communicated is that the individual is not meant to become anything except what he/she already is.

In school systems of this kind the emphasis of assessment is not on the identification of changes which the individual has – and eventually may be able – to undergo. The emphasis, instead, is on the existent IQ, the existent motivation, the existent repertoire of behaviour and on current knowledge of school skills.

The powerful environment creates new structures to produce new capacities in the individual. Increasingly a necessity due to the rapid and discontinous changes in society, this environment focuses less upon the inculcation of the present body of knowledge and the way this body of knowledge is gathered, stored, and communicated. All of these are likely to become obsolete requiring that the student must forget both what was learned and how it was learned in favour of new contents and innovative ways to learn it. In this environment modifiability and its enhancement through autoplastic changes in the ways information is collected, stored, retrieved and communication is emphasised. To support the process of autoplastic enhancement the environment constantly imposes new need systems and offers new opportunities and challenges for adaptation. Without such environments even the most modifiable person will not thrive.

Implications for parents: the parent as mediator

A need to recreate oneself not just biologically but also culturally typically provides an energetic impulse for parents to mediate to their progenies. However, the processes of cultural transmission as discussed above may be disrupted for a great variety of reasons. Due to temperamental factors, or other inherited or acquired characteristics, children may vary considerably in their accessibility to mediation. The accessibility of the particular child may deviate from the parent's expectancies of the investment required to reach certain outcomes and while some will search for and find ways to mediate to the child others may give up or argue that the child prefers to be left alone. Conditions of preoccupation, emotional disorder, stress and apathy in the parent may contribute to or themselves be the main cause of inadequate provision of MLE but also socio-economic conditions, cultural difference, educational philosophy and broader changes in society may contribute to such inadequacy.

Socio-economic hardship may compel the parent to invest largely in providing for the immediate physical needs of the child. Cultural difference may disrupt mediation when – often out of concern for the child's adjustment to a predominant culture – parents deliberately withhold mediation, not wanting the child to be like they are. Certain educational philosophies, such as the laissez-faire doctrine, are inherently anti-mediational espousing the belief that deliberate abstention from direction is necessary to avoid tampering with the child's existential rights and best interest. Finally, the extreme cultural, vocational, informational and communicational discontinuities characteristic of modern society may cause parents to curtail processes of transmission feeling that their contribution at best will be irrelevant for the child and at worst may even harm the child's chances for adjustment in the future.

The identification of MLE as the proximal determinant of modifiability reaffirms the significance of the parent–child relationship. The theory of Structural Cognitive Modifiability orients both parents and professionals consulted by them to seek ways to overcome or bypass obstacles produced by either the organism or the environment so as to enable mediation to occur. The significance of mediation for the child's development must be imparted to the parent along with information about the qualitative properties of this modality of interaction.

The involvement of the parent as mediator requires no formal materials nor that any specific set of activities be learned and utilised. Imbued with the qualitative characteristics of MLE (intentionality, transcendence, mediation of meaning, regulation of behaviour, mediation of a feeling of competence, and mediation of sharing) the most accessible and best tool for use by the parent is the parent's own culture.

When the child incurs failure, the parent is oriented to the need to localise the import of the failure and to search for the characteristics which may reveal both the nature of the difficulty and point to ways in which it may be possible to overcome it. The mere possibility that failure might be due to factors other than lack of ability and motivation to achieve will make the parent more likely to search for and create the conditions which may be necessary to overcome it. This may profoundly affect the motivation of the parent to remain involved with the child, producing curiosity about challenges instead of frustration, irritation, and feelings of rejection and failure.

Whereas the LPAD examiner and IE teacher use content-free materials to remediate the prerequisites for modifiability the parent employs MLE for purposes of both cognitive development and child rearing. The parent selects and frames stimuli, schedules their appearance, orders them in time and space, and imbues them with meaning to equip the child with experiences inaccessible except for their provision through mediated learning and to institute modalities of functioning and need systems for which direct exposure provides no perceptual support or guidelines.

Through mediated learning, and beginning shortly after birth, the parent may initiate the establishment of propensities to focus, reciprocate, and imitate and foster the development of a sense of task-completion through association with the re-establishment of equilibrium. The propensity to reciprocate, for example, can be fostered by making eye contact a condition for interaction and by interspersing periods of silence reflecting a readiness to await the child's response.

Also the perception of feelings is normally initiated early through mediation. Making herself conspicuous by the way she uses her eyes, voice and gestures the child learns to focus on the mother and to perceive the changes in her appearance as transformations of a constant figure. This creates a sensitivity to change in appearance as an important cue whereby social interactions may be interpreted. The child becomes oriented to intercepting faces and to interpret changes in their expression as a transfiguration related to circumstances.

Mediated confronting of reality seeks to overcome the perception of reality as a capricious reflection of the choices and actions of others. Perceived transpersonally as a set of limitations and openings, reality becomes an abstract entity which the child none the less can relate to and decide whether to accept or seek to change.

The mediation of individuation/psychological differentiation addresses the child's capacity for and right to a dualistic relationship between the self and the world. Through the mediation of feelings of competence, reinforcement and reward, the parent seeks to establish an internal locus of control and to instill those cognitive and attitudinal components of functioning which may be required to maintain it.

Mediated assuming and sharing of responsibility is based upon the formation of the above components. Making the child accept, understand and fulfil responsibility is directly related to reinforcement and reward once the prerequisites for autonomous functioning exist. The parent selects or creates situations where the child is made to share and participate actively and morally in the outcome.

Mediated transmission of values is accomplished through a combined energetic and cognitive process. The parent endows certain events or their properties with particular, powerful, emotional energy which produces a rank order and a basis for establishing priorities among them. The energetic component is most regnant in the creation of this rank order but cognitive components required for discrimination and mental reconstruction are required for the child to internalise such a rank order and turn it into a set of values, preserving and invoking them as guidelines for behaviour.

Mediated learning is also offered to establish an orientation towards goal seeking, goal setting and goal achievement especially in areas which have no support in the individual's immediate, elementary and cyclic needs. Mediation must be oriented to overcome episodic grasp of reality, establish orientation in time, and develop the capacity to represent and project into the future. Following the establishment of these prerequisites the parent may mediate goal-seeking behaviour by relating it to contingencies of awareness, attitudes and values.

Many additional areas can be targeted with mediation including the need for repetition to ensure consolidation, the constructive principles of short-term memory, the facilitation of storage and retrieval from long-term memory, the propensity to seek out tasks for their novelty and complexity (which may entail a temporary acceptance of incompetence) and the process of change itself which involves the establishment of internalised expectancies of reinforcement and reward as well as revisions of these as new acquisitions become detached from the conditions initially surrounding their emergence.

SUMMARY: MLE, CULTURAL DIFFERENCE AND THE FORMATION OF IDENTITY

The theory of Structural Cognitive Modifiability identifies a close relationship between the provision of Mediated Learning Experience, processes of cultural transmission, cultural difference, the formation of identity and the development of human modifiability. Cultural difference is presumptive of MLE and the transmission to the individual of certain linguistic behaviours, knowledge, experience, values, mores, skills, habits, rules, principles, strategies and other cognitive repertoires.

Cultural difference implies identity and, conversely, identity implies cultural difference. This may neither be seen nor acutely experienced as long as the individual lives in a society where his/her own culture dominates but any move to another culture will make it apparent.

Confronted with a novel culture the culturally different individual will at critical stages have difficulty and be likely to manifest reduced capacity, less knowledge and less skill as compared with initiated members of this culture. At such times the culturally different individual may function at a manifest level very similar to that of the culturally deprived. The danger is that passive acceptant approaches to assessment will identify the culturally different individual as low functioning and recommend wholly inappropriate educational programmes and goals.

Over a period of time the culturally different person will mobilise from the repertoire of learned elements those with affinity to the new culture. Time for adaptation is necessary but the prerequisites for modifiability, already available within the structures of the individual, ensure it can be accomplished. The culturally different individual confronts the need to change while still maintaining his identity but the prerequisites exist to modify himself in those areas where there is a desire or need to adjust while retaining, or even increasing, his difference in others.

One of the most important needs of the modern pluralistic society is to safeguard the right to be different and provide encouragement for the continuation of the diversity of cultures. Cultural difference *vis-à-vis* the dominant culture should not be a source of disadvantage. The more continuity in MLE processes within diverse cultures the greater the chances that the individual will confront the dominant or any other culture in a useful and efficient way. There is a direct relationship between cultural diversity and learning efficiency and in a society where all sectors are exposed to sharp discontinuities, the encouragement of mediated learning is necessary to enable its members to undergo meaningful transformations while retaining their identity. The conception of the human organism as a closed system must be supplanted along with the passive acceptant approach to assessment and education with philosophies, policies and programmes that permit and assist people to undergo such changes.

Note

1. Cultural difference and cultural deprivation do not represent dichotomous categories but are, rather, the opposite end-points of a continuum. The less culturally deprived the individual is the more he/she is culturally different. Many culturally deprived individuals have received some parts of their culture, for example its kinesics and language, while other parts – and usually those required for higher levels of modifiability – are missing.

The authors acknowledge the support of the Hadassah-WIZO Organisation of Canada which has helped us with much of the work which is included in this paper. We also want to express gratefulness for the encouragement of Dr Lore Hartman von Monakow, Chairman of the Freunde des Schweizer Kinderdorfs, Kiryath Jearim in Israel of Zurich. Her support and help were offered to us throughout our work.

References

Feuerstein, R. (1977), 'Mediated Learning Experience: A Theoretical Basis for Cognitive Modifiability During Adolescence' in P. Mittler (ed.), *Research to Practice in Mental Retardation, Education and Training, Volume II,* (University Park Press, Baltimore).

Feuerstein, R. (1979), *Dynamic Assessment of Retarded Performers: The Learning Potential Assessment Device, Theory, Instruments, and Techniques*, (Glenview, Illinois: Scott, Foresman & Company).

Feuerstein, R. (1980), *Instrumental Enrichment: An Intervention Program for Cognitive Modifiability*, (Glenview, Illinois: Scott, Foresman & Company).

Feuerstein, R., Jensen, M. R. (1980), 'Instrumental Enrichment: Theoretical Basis, Goals, and Instruments', *The Educational Forum*, **44**, 401–23.

Feuerstein, R., Miller, R., Rand, Y., Jensen, M. (1981), 'Can Evolving Techniques Better Measure Cognitive Change?' *Journal of Special Education*, **15**, 201–19.

Feuerstein, R., Jensen, M. R., Hoffman, M. B., Rand, Y. (1985), 'Instrumental Enrichment. An Intervention Program for Structural Cognitive Modifiability: Theory and Practice' in J. W. Segal, S. F. Chipman, R. Glaser (eds), *Thinking and Learning Skills, Vol. 1, Relating Instruction to Research*, 43–82 (Hillsdale, New Jersey: Lawrence Erlbaum).

Feuerstein, R., Haywood, H. C., Rand, Y., Hoffman, M. B., Jensen, M. R. (1985), *Learning Potential Assessment Device: Manual* (*Experimental Version*), (Hadassah WIZO Canada Research Institute, Jerusalem, Israel).

Feuerstein, R., Rand, Y., Jensen, M. R., Kaniel, S., Tzuriel, D., Ben Schachar-Segev, N., Mintzker, Y. (in press); 'Learning Potential Assessment' in R. E. Bennett and C. A. Maher (eds), *Emerging Perspectives on Assessment of Exceptional Children*, Journal of Special Services in the Schools, 2 (2).

Jensen, M. R., Feuerstein, R. (in press), 'Dynamic Assessment of Retarded Performers with the Learning Potential Assessment Device: From

Philosophy to Practice' in C. Lidz (ed.), *Dynamic Assessment: Foundations and* Fundamentals, (New York, N.Y.: Guilford Press).

Stodolsky, E., Lesser, G. (1967), 'Learning Patterns in the Disadvantaged', *Harvard Educational Review*, 37, 546–93.

5 L. S. Vygotskii: The Cultural-Historical Theory, National Minorities and the Zone of Next Development*

Andrew Sutton

Lev Semenovich Vygotskii (1896–1934) is widely recognised as one of the greatest thinkers, perhaps *the* greatest, in the field of child psychology. His work, however, has remained virtually unknown to psychologists and educators in the English-speaking West – partly because of the dearth of translated material and partly because of the philosophical gulf that separates his views from those of non-Marxists. Vygotskii's approach to understanding the human mind has proved immensely fruitful in his own country and recent years have seen the beginnings of an attempt to benefit from this in both the United States and Western Europe. Vygotskii's Cultural-Historical Theory of human mental development by its very nature lends itself to questions of the education of children from minority groups, whose backgrounds differ in substantial respects from the host culture. And of course, such circumstances provide an enormous natural experiment in which his Cultural-Historical Theory may be put to the test.

This chapter can offer no more than a brief introduction to the implications of Vygotskii's views for education in a culturally diverse context. In order to find the authentic voice of Vygotskii it is essential to quote direct from the Russian and, because of the exceedingly limited

**A note on transliteration and translation.* Russian names have been transliterated throughout, according to British Standard *BS 2979* (1958), without diacritics, hence Vygotskii and Luriya rather than Vigotsky, Luria, etc. The Russian verb '*sozret*' may be translated into English equally as 'to mature' or 'to ripen'. In the extracts translated from Vygotskii (1934a) the sense of ripening has been used throughout to maintain the force of Vygotskii's parable of the foolish gardener.

(and often unreliable) store of published English-language translation of Vygotskii's writings, there is still comparatively little that the reader can do to follow up any interest engendered – without, again, direct recourse to Russian-language texts. The situation is certainly easier now than it was ten years ago and may continue to improve but the reader should be warned that the growing body of translated material from the Russian contains many sources of potential confusion (Sutton, 1983a). As well as confusions of a linguistic nature, social, cultural and historical differences between Vygotskii's position and our own give the possibility of further misunderstanding. True to the spirit of the Cultural-Historical Theory, therefore, any discussion of Vygotskii's views must begin with an understanding of the context in which they were framed.

THE NATIONAL MINORITIES

Vygotskii himself had grown up as a member of an oppressed minority group, a Jew living in the Jewish Pale of White Russia in the final years of Tsardom. He had his own direct, personal experience of the racialist policies of the anti-Semitic Autocracy for, despite a brilliant academic record, he only gained a university place by lottery in an admissions policy specifically designed to keep down the numbers of bright young Jews at the universities (Dobkin, 1982). After graduating from Moscow university Vygotskii returned home to White Russia and, following the establishment of Soviet power, worked there as a school teacher until he returned to Moscow in 1924 as a psychologist. Vygotskii's years as a school teacher coincided with the first stage of the enormous drive for the elimination of illiteracy (*likvidatsiya bezgramotnosti* – or *likbez*, for short). Until his death in 1934 the cultural development of children and of adults was the central concern of Vygotskii's work, with the word 'development' used very much in its active sense.

The *likbez* campaigns of the 1920s and 1930s were the basic step in raising the cultural level of the Soviet population (McLeish, 1972). In Tsarist times elementary schooling, such as there was, had been located almost entirely in the towns, whilst the bulk of the Russian population were peasants and there was virtually no education at all for the children of non-Russians in the Russian Empire. Right from the start of the new regime, however, enormous mass revolutionary energy was directed not only to establishing elementary education for all children but also to catching up on the huge backlog of adult illiterates. The census of 1920 indicated the enormity of the problem to be overcome out of a total population of over 140 million (see Table 5.1)

Table 5.1 Literacy figure compared: 1897 and 1920

Literates per thousand	*1897*	*1920*
European Russian	229	330
North Caucasus	150	281
West Siberia	108	218

Source: Adapted from McLeish, 1972.

The raising of the cultural level, as particularly manifest in the matter of literacy, promised two national benefits, political and economic. The former was particularly emphasised by Lenin.

> While we have a phenomenon such as illiteracy in our country, it is very difficult to say anything about political education. Literacy is not a political problem but the very foundation without which it is impossible to speak about politics at all. The illiterate remains right outside of politics: to begin with it is necessary to teach him the alphabet. Failing this, it is not possible to have any politics at all; failing this we have rumours, gossip, fairy tales, prejudices but we cannot have politics. (Lenin, as quoted by McLeish, 1972)

Later, Stalin was to express the economic advantages – and to link the specific matter of literacy with wider goals of education and socialisation.

> The cultural development of the working classes and the toiling masses of the peasantry does not only mean the development of literacy, although literacy is the basis of all culture. Besides this, it means the acquisition of habits and the ability to participate in the work of directing the nation. It is the basic level of the betterment of the governmental and all other apparatus. In this lies the significance and meaning of Lenin's slogan on the cultural revolution. (Stalin, as quoted by McLeish, 1972)

Throughout the 1920s and 1930s cultural backwardness in both children and adults was attacked, at times with millenial fervour, by both state and voluntary bodies until, according to the census returns for 1939, the literacy rate for those between 9 and 49 years of age stood at 89.1 per cent.

Throughout this process various groups lagged behind in their progress, for example, women behind men, rural dwellers behind town dwellers. Particularly disadvantaged from the outset were the previously subject people of the old Russian Empire.

> At this period the Soviet Union numbered over 140 000 000 people, of these, 65 000 000 were non-Russian. The policy of Tsarism had been to destroy the political organizations of the subject races, to forbid absolutely, or drastically to restrict, the use of the native language in schools, courts and in the administration. It sought to cripple the native culture and to keep the great majority of the subject people in a state of ignorance. The theses accepted by the Tenth Party Congress in 1921 declared the policy of the Soviet Government to be that each national minority should establish its own Soviet State system, in forms consistent with its own national character. Lenin's slogan was: 'Nationalist in form, socialist in content'. This means that the courts and other administrative and executive organs should function in the native language and be recruited from the local people; that a popular press, schools, theatres, clubs, cultural and educational institutions should be established in the native language. A roll-call of some of the national groupings incorporated in the Soviet Union at this time will give some indication of the magnitude of the task the Soviet Government had assumed: Ukranians, White-Russians, Kirkhiz, Uzbeks, Turkmens, Tadjiks, Azerbaidjanis, Tatars, Bokharans, Khivans, Bashkirs, Armenians, Chechens, Kabardians, Ossetians, Circassians, Ingushes, Karachais, Balkarians, Kalmucks, Karelians, Avarians, Darghis, Kazikumukhians, Kurins, Kumyks, Marsis, Chuvash, Volga Germans, Buryats, Yakuts, and many others. Some of these national groupings were quite small, in some cases less than a thousand. In others, whole nations with a long history and a highly-developed cultural tradition, spread over a vast territory, and including many millions of individuals, were involved. (McLeish, 1972)

By the end of the twenties Vygotskii had already directed his attention broadly within psychology and education. Although from the very start of his career as a psychologist he had been concerned with questions of the nature of psychological science, much of his political work and writing in the mid-1920s was on various aspects of the education and upbringing of handicapped children. His convalescence after a serious bout of tuberculosis in 1927 provided him the opportunity to formalise his thoughts on the cultural development of the child (see Vygotskii, 1929a, for the first – and largely ignored – account of this in English). The year 1928 saw the initiation of the First Five-Year Plan for economic development, which recognised that industrialisation and collectivisation could only be achieved on the basis of a substantial raising of the cultural level of the workers and peasants. The creation of a modern industrial state demanded scientists, technicians, specialists and managers, to be drawn from the ranks of the common people of what a decade or so ago had been one of the most backward states in Europe. This demanded not only universal literacy but also a broad base in technical education. And as the national minorities were to share in this social reconstruction then they too had to share in the cultural revolution.

THE PAEDOLOGY OF THE NATIONAL MINORITIES

One hundred and eighty-six written works have been traced to L. S. Vygotskii (Shakhlevich, 1974), only one of which, published in 1929, refers specifically to the issue of the national minorities. This article appeared in the journal *Pedologiya* at a time when Vygotskii still regarded himself proudly as a 'paedologist'. Paedology was intended as the all-round scientific study of child development in its every aspect, biological, psychological, educational, and was regarded by its proponents as an essential feature of a developed educational system. Also an unashamed paedologist at this time was N. K. Krupskaya, Lenin's widow, who in 1929 became Peoples' Commissar for Enlightenment. In a very few years, however, the paedologists fell under a shadow, especially for continued uncritical use of Western psychometric tests. The journal *Pedologiya* was withdrawn from publication in 1932 and Vygotskii strove hard (and in vain) to dissociate himself from his earlier association. The last trace of this movement was swept away by the Central Committee decree 'On paedological perversions . . .', with firm strictures against uncritical psychological testing which do not look out of place today (Sutton, 1980).

Vygotskii was a committed Marxist and the theory of mental development that he sought to create was a conscious attempt to extend Marx's Historical Materialism to the ontogenetic plane. In doing this he was very influenced by Engels' anthropological views. Vygotskii was not a modern Western liberal and was not troubled by liberal notions of cultural relativism. Opening his discussion, therefore, he found the task ahead to be quite clear.

> The five-year economic plan envisages the rapid economic and cultural elevation of national minorities standing at a lower stage of economic and cultural development. In connection with this, many nationalities in the next five years will have to accomplish a grandoise leap up the ladder of their cultural development, jumping across a whole number of historical stages. The complexity of the economic structure of our Union, expressed in the existence of five different economic levels, from the natural economy to the socialist, demands in its turn a complex structure for the cultural form of development. The stages of cultural development, like the basic economic levels, range from the most primitive to the highest. The involvement of backward nationalities in the general circle of economic and cultural construction must surely be accompanied by a change in the whole cultural level of their life.
>
> The next five years and the years that follow them must therefore be an experiment, unprecedented in history, in the forced cultural development of the abilities of different nationalities. (Vygotskii, 1929b)

Vygotskii considered that this experiment would be unsuccessful without the fullest involvement of paedology, 'without the scientific knowledge of the peculiarities and essences of the material on which we have to work'. Yet, in comparison with the huge educational task that would be undertaken, very little relevant paedological work was being done. Moreover, what there was was scattered and often involved no more than the simple transfer to local centres of approaches worked out in the capital, based in part 'on the false proposition that basically the child from the national minorities must not be distinguished from the Russian child in any essential way'.

What was needed was the organisation of an altogether new branch of Soviet paedology. Vygotskii started by elaborating on two general theses on this work, put forward by the leading paedologist A. B. Zalkind, concerning (in Vygotskii's words) 'the uselessness of the usual tests and standards applied to the child of the national minorities' and 'the task of investigating and studying the cultural-social characteristics of the national environment'.

The testing of minority children that Vygotskii described in his own country in the 1920s may seem remarkably familiar to modern Western readers. Already common in the Soviet Union when Vygotskii wrote his article was the straightforward administration of existing tests to minority children: 'Such research almost always ends in failure, as it usually reveals an almost universal mental backwardness amongst the children of nationalities that are backward in their cultural development or nationalities with a peculiar cultural-social level'. Already, some researchers had begun to see reasons for this in their test material and to adapt this accordingly, translating the test into the local language, changing the pictures used to suit the local culture, etc. But these changes lead to no decisive change in outcome.

> So, for example, the psychological investigation of children of the indigenous population of one of the Union republics, *conducted according to such tests which had been changed and brought nearer to the children's understanding*, revealed the following situation in their mental endowment, in per cent: normally endowed – 16.8%, mildly retarded – 63.4%, severely retarded – 19.8%. Thus, it seems that only one sixth part of the whole child population is normally endowed and that the endowment of the child of the given national minority, in comparison with the Russian child's endowment, is several times less (from 2 to 5 times). (Vygotskii, 1929b, emphasis in original)

The authors of such investigations, Vygotskii granted, accounted for their results by deprivations and inhibitions in the children's cultural-social background but, he argued, 'the way out of the embarrassing position that they have created . . . [is] the presentation of lower demands and the introduction of lower age standards and norms of mental development for the children of backward nationalities'. On the contrary, Vygotskii concluded, such results testified to the uselessness of the whole approach: 'The flaw in these methods is not just that the very *methods* of the tests' construction is taken from a cultural-social environment that is alien to the child . . . the flaw obviously lies deeper'.

Zalkind's second thesis, the study of the local cultural-social environment, Vygotskii regarded as closely linked to this first.

> The difficulty is that cultural development is accomplished in diverse and extremely complex national forms. The child grows and develops in an extremely individual cultural-social and environment which reflects the complex path of the historical development of the given people and the complex system of economic and cultural conditions of its present-day existence.

Hence: the primary task for paedology is the study of the children

> of the national minorities not in an isolated fashion, not cut off from their specific cultural-social forms, but above all against the background of these peculiarities, in connection with them, in vital interaction with them. To put it more simply, there stands before paedology the task of understanding the child as an inseparable part and the natural product of the particular environment in which he is growing and developing. (Vygotskii, 1929b)

The problem, Vygotskii considered, was to establish a completely new and *positive* paedology of the national minorities

> The essence of this radical 180° turn in methodological viewpoint is easy to understand if one brings to attention the fact that till now the huge majority of investigations in this area have been dedicated *towards purely negative goals*. These investigations attempted to establish what the given child lacks in comparison with the more developed child, what sides of his character are depressed, weakened, inhibited, what flaws his mind and behaviour display in comparison with the child from more cultured people. One cannot but say that the negative aim of the investigation is a consequence of the traditional psychological approach to the 'savage' and the little-cultured man. Traditional investigation tries above all to establish the crudest, chiefest, most massive, hit-you-in-the-eyes indices of difference. Above all, it fixes the 'empty spaces', the problems in cultural development. (Vygotskii, 1929b, emphasis in original).

In contrast, the new paedology should 'reveal all the positive particulars of the mind and behaviour of such a child and show how the general laws of child development take specific, concrete expression in a given cultural-social environment, how they are refracted through the given concrete, historical, national form of the existence of the whole people'.

Vygotskii proposed a complex plan for the organisation of such paedological investigation. Firstly, he proposed a major centre, to be sited preferably in Moscow, to concern itself with fundamental research and to overview the general principles of cultural development that should emerge from the study of different minorities. Secondly, the investigation of practical problems, the testing out of principles derived at the centre, must be conducted by local research establishments. Thirdly, there should be 'expeditionary research', organised both centrally and locally: 'The organisation of paedological expeditions must become as constant and necessary a means of scientific investigation as is the "field method" of contemporary ethiography and ethiology'. Only an approach integrating all three features proposed would offer, in Vygotskii's opinion, the full realisation of the tasks then standing before Soviet paedology.

Given such an organisational framework, Vygotskii warned against three prevalent views on how the research should be conducted. Firstly, the view popular in Moscow, was that local innovations should be put aside in favour of the application of general principles, centrally derived, a view that Vygotskii regarded to be especially inappropriate at the very outset of the work and almost guaranteed to lead to absurd results: 'Surely, if it is agreed that the method determines the properties of the object to the study of which it is directed, then one has to anticipate in good time that the methods created for the investigation of children of one cultural level will prove unfit for the investigation of the children of another cultural level.' In practice, this use of ready-made methods and concepts led to 'whole peoples' being located at a level of development corresponding to a 5- or 7-year child. While such a comparison has its relative value within the psychology of the European child, to take this ontogenetic route in a phylogenetic context is quite inappropriate'. Secondly, Vygotskii referred back to the model whereby the tests and methods of investigation remained basically the same – only re-edited and otherwise modified to bring them closer to the children's social experience. As he pointed out, the original spread of Binet's scale to almost every European country had been accompanied by just such modifications. But he had already shown in this context that such simple modifications, showing 'only 16 per cent normally endowed children amongst a whole people', were apparently quite insufficient without knowing how to correct the very basis of the investigation itself. Yet thirdly, the point of view advanced by many in the local research establishments, that the methods of investigation created for the study of the European child were altogether unsuitable for use with children from the minorities, and that all paedological investigation had to be created and worked out anew for each separate nationality – this view Vygotskii dismissed abruptly as 'bankrupt'.

The only way forward would be to move straight on from thoughts of improving test method to a thorough and fundamental investigation 'of the whole problem of the development of the child of the national minorities' – and this problem should cut across every head in the five-year educational plan, pre-school, primary, secondary, vocational, etc.

> The first and commanding feature that determines the section of the plan that interests us is that the study of the environment is advanced to the centre of investigation. The fundamental and central factor determining the specific peculiarities in the development of all aspects of the child is some or other structure of the environment. The paedological study of the national environment, therefore, its structure, its dynamics, its contents, are the paramount task, without the solution of which we cannot even approach a solution to all the different tasks of our plan. It is not the biological difference in human type, not the racial peculiarities, that are brought to the fore, but precisely the formative influence of the environment. (Vygotskii, 1929b)

The second feature follows closely from the first, to bring about the cultural development of psychological functions. Without such investigation 'primitiveness is identified with backwardness, cultural development with the biological'. Instead, paedological research must show that 'the environment is not only a more or less favourable factor for the development of the basic mechanisms of behaviour but also that itself it forms and shapes all the higher forms of behaviour, everything that is built upon the elementary functions in the development of the personality'. And thirdly, a surprising point perhaps, until one recalls that Vygotskii's thinking was dialectical and materialist, and had as little time for naïve environmental reductionism as for its biological counterpart, the final feature should be the elucidation of the 'racial, biological peculiarities which undoubtedly exist and show an influence upon the type of the child's development'.

The article is very typical Vygotskii, polemical in form, rather rambling and superlative in style and, above all, determined to face real practical problems at the level of revolutionary first principles rather than through the convenience of established practice, shifting the focus of psychology from supposed properties or failures in the child to the responsibility of society for bringing about the child's mental development.

EXPEDITIONS – AND AFTERWARDS

The year 1929 seems to have been a great year for paper-plans of how best to organise and co-ordinate the development of educational services. What precisely happened to Vygotskii's proposals for the rational development of paedology of the national minorities has yet to be described. In the immediate years that followed there were major changes in emphasis in the direction of Soviet pedagogy as a whole – and in that of Soviet psychology. The emphases of the works of Vygotskii and his growing band of followers also developed; with Vygotskii's writings concentrating increasingly upon the mechanisms of human mental development, and especially upon its stage structure. Vygotskii wrote no further himself on the children of the national minorities – and sought to distance himself from those, still calling themselves paedologists, who had quite failed to shake themselves free of practices and ways of thinking that he regarded as harmful. One aspect of Vygotskii's programme, however, we do know to have been put into operation – the expeditionary method – though Vygotskii himself was not well enough to take part personally.

In 1931 there appeared an unsigned notice in the 'Scientific events' columns of the journal *Science*, recording the completion that Summer of the first 'Psychological Expedition to Central Asia'. An identical notice appeared in a specialist publication signed by Vygotskii's pupil, friend and close associate, A. R. Luriya. As Vygotskii had recommended, this expedition had been jointly organised by a local institution (the Uzbek Research Institute in Samarkand) and a central one (the Institute of Experimental Psychology in Moscow) and its aims, both general and specific, closely echoed those outlined by Vygotskii in his article.

> The aim of the expedition was to investigate the variations in thought and other psychological processes of people living in a very primitive economic and social environment, and to record changes which develop as a result of the introduction of higher and more complex forms of economic life and the raising of the general cultural level.
>
> One special task of the expedition was to develop new methods for evaluating intellectual status of individuals in very backward communities, because the aural methods of determining intelligence are inapplicable in the very special cultural conditions influencing the intellectual processes of the members of these groups. Another task was the preparation of educational methods which could be applied to these communities, such as the teaching of counting, reading, etc. (Luriya, 1931/2)

The results of all the studies conducted on this expedition were promised for future publication and a similar expedition announced for the next year, with foreign participation invited. Enquiries were to be addressed to Luriya, the leader of both expeditions.

A year later Luriya published a 'Special correspondence' in *Science*, outlining the work of the second psychological expedition, conducted in the Summer of 1932. The first expedition had studied only adults, the second included young people as well and its goals were an ambitious elaboration on the findings of the first.

> The immediate aim of the [second] expedition consisted in the further study of thinking which is characteristic of primitive societies, the development of the psychological functions in their thinking and to point out those changes which this thinking undergoes in social and cultural transformation connected with socialistic growth. In the account of the first expedition it was shown that in the primitive community life one finds a specific system of thinking which is characterised by its own structure and by a different role which speech takes in it. A fact was noted that the main function of this thinking is not the formation of abstract connection and relationships between symbols, but reproduction of whole situations, whole complexes closely connected with specific life experiences; it was pointed out that separate psychological operations, such as memory, comparisons, generalisation and abstraction, are formed in this type of thinking quite differently, and that with the change in economic conditions this situational or complicated thinking very quickly becomes changed, giving place to other more complex forms of thought. It was the aim of the second expedition to study in more detail the characteristics of the structure of the "situational" thinking and its various functions as well as a study of those paths along which the transformation of the situational thinking takes place by the development of thought into concepts under the influence of such new moulding forces as collectivisation, cultural development, literature, etc. (Luriya, 1933)

Amongst those who took part in the expedition was Kurt Koffka, the German gestaltist. No further expeditions were announced but a continuing programme of research was anticipated with a full analysis of the findings of the two expeditions promised during 1934, under the editorship of A. R. Luriya, with more detailed accounts of the second expedition itself promised for both the *Journal of Genetic Psychology* and the *British Journal of Psychology*.

But by 1933 and 1934 the political and intellectual context of Soviet psychology was changing very fast and Vygotskii and his followers were under virulent attack on a variety of counts (see van der Veer, 1984). In 1934 Vygotskii himself died from tubercular complications and Luriya returned to his medical training. Soviet science closed its doors to the West and the promised analysis and reports never appeared, either at home or abroad, till years later. Parts of this unique work are now available to the English-language reader (Luriya, 1971, 1976).

Soviet psychology faced difficult times under Stalin and the name of Vygotskii (publically, at least) was expunged, to emerge again with increasing acclaim from the mid-1950s onwards. Out of the Cultural-Historical Theory, Leont'ev's Activity Theory and the work of other post-Vygotskians, have developed a broad span of psychological theory and practices closely integrated with the task of facilitating the mental development of new generations. Within this, Vygotskii is now of course a distant historical figure but the philosophical paths that he established are regarded as still far from fully explored. Moreover, despite distinct disagreements with specific aspects of his work, the general pattern of the understanding of human development adhered to by leading Soviet psychologists is still quite clearly 'Vygotskian' – and quite different from the dominant traditions in Anglo-Saxon psychology. The modern-day Soviet student teacher is presented with an unequivocally Vygotskian view of the conditions of mental development.

> *Development as the process of the child's mastering social-historical experience*. The mind of man and animals is in a state of continual development. The character and content of the processes of development in the animal world and in man differ, however, qualitatively. The mental functions of man and animals cannot be identified with each other either in origin or in structure. The basic mechanism of the development of the mind of animals is the transmission of *inherited, biologically consolidated experience*. At its basis is the unfolding of the animal's unfolding adaption to its external environment. *The peculiar character of the mental functions of man is that they develop in the process of the child's mastery of social-historical experience*. The child is born and lives in a human world, a world of human objects and human relationships. In these is fixed the experience of social practice. The child's development is the process of mastering this experience. This process is realised in conditions of continual direction on the part of adults, i.e. in teaching (*obuchenie*).
>
> Man's mental activity in its highest forms bears a *mediated character*. Already in antiquity people were using special objects,

conditional representations and signs as a means of fixing and transmitting definite information in the process of labour activity, teaching, etc. Signs and speech mediate people's activity and the process of teaching. Consequently the beginning and development of these means, including the development of culture, characterises above all the process of the historical development of the mind. It is the mastery of these means that is the process of individual development. The child masters the experience in man's history. The child's thinking, memory and perception are brought about essentially by mastering speech, certain modes of activity , learning, etc.

Over the history of humanity there have developed not only the means of accomplishing activity but a *special way of transmitting these means, of social experience to successive generations* also took shape, developed and became more complicated. This specific way is *teaching*. It is *the unswerving and specially organised means of transmitting social experience. Thus teaching plays a definite role in the process of the child's mental development*. (Petrovskii, 1973, pp. 21–2, emphasis in original)

The material base for mental development, in this very obviously Historical-Materialist account, is the human body with its infinite variability in all its functions. These indubitable, lower-order biological variations, cannot, of course, account for the higher-order variations built upon them by the learning and social interactions of childhood through the medium of teaching.

The word 'teaching' presents one of the major specific difficulties in translating Soviet psychological texts into English and, however translated, constitutes a major source of potential confusion for the English-language reader. The Russian word *obuchenie* can be equally correctly translated by both the English words 'teaching' and 'learning', for it refers to both ends of the process. It should be clear that the Vygotskian tradition in psychology, in contradistinction to our own, places an especial emphasis upon the active role of society in determining the outcome of development. Thus the phrase 'the cultural development of the child' implies not merely the passive sense, that the child develops culturally, but also the active sense, that culture develops the child. In the same way that the English word 'development' may be active or passive in its meaning (though Western educational and developmental psychology have tended to assume its passive sense) so too is the Russian word *obuchenie* (with Russian psychology emphasising the active sense). Especially in the past, translators have tended to assume the common Western sense of the word (hence such absurdities as 'learning leads development' – it doesn't, teaching does!). In more recent years a wider recognition of the sense of the Russian texts has shifted the emphasis. Some translators use the English word 'instruction', which seems too specific, too one-sided. Here the word 'teaching' is used and the reader should understand it as referring to the whole linked process of teaching and learning.

And for all this, what has happened to the Uzbeks and all the other diverse peoples of the USSR? There has most certainly been a major transformation in the quality of their life in the last fifty years. Luriya was often asked whether he felt that a follow-up or replication of his earlier studies might not provide an interesting comparison with the findings from his expeditions of the early thirties. He would put the suggestion aside, saying that the changes in Uzbekistan, economic, social, psychological and educational, were self-evident and it did not need specific research to confirm this (Luriya, 1976, p. 164). Nevertheless, in the mid-1960s such a longitudinal comparative study had been mounted, to repeat one of the early psychometric surveys of the sort harshly criticised by Vygotskii in his article. The original survey had been made in the Altai mountains, one of the backward areas visited by Luriya in 1931 and 1932. The expedition had administered the Binet scale to mountain children: the follow-up in 1966 administered the same test to children in the same area (the first publically reported use of a Western standardised test in the Soviet Union since the 1936 Decree 'On paedological perversions . . .'). The results of this follow-up (fortunately also available in English translation, Gurova, 1971) are outlined in Table 5.2.

This is not, of course, to imply that the problem of educating the children of the Soviet national minorities has been completely solved.

Table 5.2 Comparison of children in Altai mountains: 1929 and 1966

Age in years	*Mean Binet IQs 1929*	*Age in years*	*Mean Binet IQs 1966*
—	—	3 to 6	92
8 to 12	69	7 to 10	97
12 to 16	65	11 to 17	99
8 to 16	67	3 to 17	96

Source: Figures extracted from Gurova (1971).

Disadvantages continue to exist compared with children from Russian and certain other more advantaged national or cultural groups (Lane, 1971). The reasons for these continuing differences are complex. Not least amongst them is the continuing problem of language. Whilst every Soviet child has the right to education in the native tongue, in practice a thoroughgoing knowledge of Russian is essential to educational advancement, especially at the higher levels, and bilingualism is a prerequisite to social success for all non-Russian Soviet citizens. In both the more extreme cases of cultural diversity (Dagistan has 1.7 million people, 80 per cent of whom are non-Russians speaking 30 different native languages) and in less diverse settings, such as Uzbekistan, many accommodations are made in practice (Sutherland, 1985). The provision of special schooling outside European Russia continues to lag in its development for a host of economic and cultural reasons (Anderson *et al.*, in press). In this sprawling context the determination of the general principles of the cultural development of the child from the national minorities, as advocated by Vygotskii so enthusiastically half a century ago, does not appear to have re-emerged as a major issue.

THE ZONE OF NEXT DEVELOPMENT

The Marxist position on human mental ability is that it is created out of the social-historical experience of *Homo sapiens*, on the material basis of human brain. Within this metasystem emphases have varied. For Vygotskii, the founder of the Social-Historical Theory, it was particularly speech that plays the essential role in the creation of individual consciousness; for Leont'ev, his pupil and collaboration, it was the internalised practical activity that plays the key role (Leont'ev, 1981). Even in the most neo-Pavlovian days of Soviet psychology the overall view of human potential stood upon the same general philosophical position of the perfectibility of humankind. As for the Marxist psychologist *par excellance*, Vygotskii's theoretical system was a revolutionary one: not only can people be changed, they *should* be – and this will be achieved through changes in their social world. And such revolutionary change can and should be open to all the peoples of the world, no matter how lowly their present level of social, cultural and economic development.

Towards the close of his life Vygotskii advanced a concept whereby the plasticity of child development under the influence of social intercourse could be operationalised in the individual case. Given the spirit of those years and his own personal rejection of crude paedological practices, it seems likely that this approach was offered as much as a direct opposition to the continuing practice of intelligence testing as for its indubitable contribution to the development of his theoretical ideas. He called his concept *zona blizhaishego razvitiya*, a term which has been variously translated in English over the last twenty-odd years ('zone of proximal development', 'zone of potential development', even 'zo-ped'). It is rendered here as 'zone of next development' (ZND), as being the most concise translation consistent with maintaining the sense of the original.

The idea of ZND seems to have been first formulated in print at the very end of Vygotskii's life, appearing in his book *Myshlenie i rech'* (Thinking and Speech) published in the same year as his death (Vygotskii, 1934a). A similar account appeared a year later in a further, posthumous publication 'The problem of teaching and intellectual development at school age' (Vygotskii, 1934b/1963).

> Psychological research connected with the problem of teaching has usually been restricted to establishing a child's level of mental development. But it is not enough to define the state of a child's development by means of this level alone. How is this level usually defined? Problems that the child solves on his own serve as the means to define it. We will learn from these what the child can do and what he knows today, since we pay attention solely to those problems which the child can solve on his own: it is apparent that by this method we can only establish what has already ripened within the child at the present day. We determine only the level of his present development. But the state of development is never defined only by that part of it which is already ripe. Just as a gardener who wants to determine the state of his garden will be wrong if he takes it into his head to evaluate it solely on the basis of the apple trees which have ripened and been picked of fruit, so too the psychologist, when he is evaluating the state of development, must inevitably take account not of the present level but also of *the zone of next development*. How is this to be done?
>
> When we define the level of present development we use problems that require the child to solve them on his own and which are indicative only of functions that have already matured and taken shape. But let us try a new method. Let us suppose that we have determined the mental age of two children and that for both of them it is 8 years. If we do not stop there, but try to show how both children solve problems which are meant for children of the next age level and

which they are in no position to solve on their own, if help comes to them in the form of demonstration, a leading question, the start of the solution, etc, then it turns out that one of them, with help, with cooperation and under instruction, solves tasks up to the 12-year level, the other to the 9-year level. This discrepancy between the mental age, or the level of present development, which is determined by problems that the child has solved on his own, and the level of problem-solving that the child achieves when he is not working on his own but in cooperation, defines the zone of next development. In our example the zone of next development is defined by the figure 4 in the one child, by the figure 1 in the other. Can we then consider that both children stand at an identical mental level, that the state of their development is the same? Clearly we can not. As investigation shows, there prove to be far greater differences between these two children at school, caused by the discrepancy between their zones of next development, than there are similarities arising from the identical level of their present development. This tells above all in the dynamics of their mental development in the course of teaching and in their relative school achievement. Investigation shows that *the zone of next development has more direct significance for the dynamics of mental development and school achievement than does the present level of children's development.*

For the explanation of this fact, which has been established in the investigation, we can refer to the commonly known and indisputable state of affairs that a child can always do more and can solve more difficult problems in cooperation, under supervision and with help, than he can on his own. In the case under consideration we have only a particular instance of this situation. But the explanation must go further. It must uncover the reasons that lie at the basis of this phenomenon. In the old psychology and in the day-to-day way of thinking there has taken root a view of imitation as a purely mechanical activity. From this point of view a solution that the child has not arrived at on his own is not usually regarded as significant, as symptomatic of the development of the child's actual intellect. It is held that anyone can imitate if he wants to. It is held that what I am capable of doing in imitation tells nothing about my real intellect and consequently can in no way characterise the state of its development. But this view is totally false.

It may be considered established in the contemporary psychology of imitation that a child can only imitate what lies in the zone of his own intellectual abilties. So, if I do not know how to play chess, then even if the best of chess players shows me what I have to do to win a game I will not learn how to do it. If I know arithmetic but find difficulty in solving some complicated problem, then showing me how to do it must lead straightaway to my doing it myself: but if I do not know higher mathematics then showing me how to do a differential equation will not advance my own thinking in this direction a single step. In order to imitate I must have some means of crossing from what I know to what I do not know.

Thus we can introduce a new and essential rider to what has been said above about work in cooperation and about imitation. We were saying that the child can always do more in cooperation than he can on his own. But, we must add, not infinitely more but only within certain limits strictly defined by the state of his development and by his intellectual abilities. The child proves to be stronger and cleverer in cooperation than when he is working on his own, he raises himself up higher in terms of the level of the intellectual obstacles that he is able to overcome. But there always exists a certain strictly regulated distance which defines the divergence between his intellect when he works on his own and when he works in cooperation.

Our investigations have shown that the child does not solve by imitation all the problems that remain unsolved. He goes up to a certain limit which is different for different children. In our example this limit lay very low for one of the children and was only one year away from the level of his development. In the other child it was 4 years away. If it were possible to imitate as one pleased irrespective of the state of development then both children would have solved all the problems with equal ease. In actual fact not only does this not happen but it also turns out that even in cooperation the child more easily solves the problems which lie nearest to his level of development, further on it becomes harder to reach a solution, and finally it becomes insuperable even for a solution in cooperation. The greater or lesser the child's ability to transfer from what he knows how to do on his own to what he can do in cooperation proves to be the most sensitive symptom that characterises the dynamics of the child's development and school progress. It wholly coincides with the zone of his next development. (Vygotskii, 1934a, 246–8, emphasis in original)

Vygotskii went on to contrast this specifically human learning with that of apes, distinguishing teaching from mere training, and insisting upon the qualitative uniqueness of human learning.

Investigation shows unquestionably that what lies within the zone of next development at one stage of a given age level is realised and transfers into the level of present development at the subsequent stage. In other words, what the child can do in cooperation today, tomorrow he will be able to do on his own. The likely thought therefore presents itself, that teaching and development at school are related to each other in the same way as are the zone of next development and the level of present development. The only good teaching at school age is that which runs ahead of development and draws development after it. But it is only possible to teach the child what he is already capable of learning. Teaching is possible where there is the possibility of imitation. This means that teaching must be oriented towards cycles of development that have already been passed, towards teaching's lower threshold: it is based, however, not so much on ripe as upon reopening functions. It always begins from what has still not ripened within the child. Teaching's possibilities are defined by the zone of the child's next development. Returning to our example we could have said that the two children that took part in the experiment would have different abilities for teaching despite the fact that their mental ages were identical, since their zones of next development diverge so sharply. The research mentioned above has shown that every subject of teaching at school is always built upon still unripened ground.

What must we conclude from this? One may reason: if written speech requires volition, abstractions and other functions that have not as yet ripened in the pupil, then one has to put aside teaching it until such time as these functions ripen. Yet world-wide experience has shown that the teaching of reading is one of the most important subjects of school teaching at the very start of school and that it calls to life the development of all those functions that have still not ripened within the child. So, when we say that teaching must depend upon the zone of next development, upon functions that have still not ripened, we are not writing out the school a new prescription, but simply freeing ourselves from the old error that development must go through its cycles and totally prepare the ground upon which reading builds its edifice. Connected with this there is also a change in the principle of drawing educational conclusions from psychological investigations. Formerly it used to be asked: has the child matured enough to teach him reading, arithmetic etc.? The question of ripened functions continue in force. We must always define the lower threshold of teaching. But the business is not settled by this. We must also know how to define the upper threshold of teaching. Only at the

> boundaries between both these thresholds can teaching prove fruitful. Only between them is there contained the optimal period for teaching a given subject. *Education must be oriented not towards the yesterday of child development but towards its tomorrow*. Only then will it learn how to call to life in the process of teaching those processes which at present lie within the zone of next development. (Vygotskii, 1934a, 250–1, emphasis in original)

By the time that Vygotskii wrote these words his emerging though still unformulated theoretical system ranged across a huge span of psychological endeavour. It was, moreover, more than simply 'a psychology': it was a conscious part of a philosophical system that sought to implement momentous changes upon society, people and nature. In short, Vygotskii was seeking to create *the* psychology of the new age. His isolated jottings on ZND should not be wrenched out of this wider context. Particularly, they should be read in the light of an essential feature of his dialectical approach, the qualitative distinctions between different stages of mental development and between different kinds of retardation.

Firstly, the last few years of Vygotskii's life saw him deeply involved in the issue of stages of development. Engels' anthropology and Marx's Historical Materialism gave clear pointers to how dialectical principles could be operationalised in interpreting human phylogenesis and social development: Vygotskii sought to identify an analogous lawful process in human ontogenesis. He was searching for forms of thinking and interaction that would distinguish one such stage from another, because of the enormous practical implications these would have for the optimalisation of upbringing and education. He distinguished, for example, between the 'school-age' stage of development and the stage that immediately preceded it, the 'pre-school-age', for at that earlier stage the child's mental development (as evidenced by the ZND) is most powerfully advanced by symbolic role play (Vygotskii, 1933/1966). The account of ZND quoted at length above is *specifically directed to children of the school-age stage of development* and any attempt to apply it to other stages, higher or lower, would be gravely in error. The practical implications of this distinction are considerable, as Vygotskii himself went on to point out.

> Let us illustrate this in a simple example. As is well known, during the time of the supremacy of the complex system of school teaching in our country this system gave 'educational foundations'. It was affirmed that the complex system was in keeping with the peculiarities

of children's thinking. The basic error was this – the question was wrong in principle. It proceeded from the view that teaching must be oriented towards the yesterday of development, towards charcteristics of the child's thinking that had already matured. By means of the complex system the paedologists proposed to consolidate in the child's development what he ought to have left behind when he came to school. They were oriented towards what the child could do in his thinking on his own and took no account of his ability to transfer from what he knows to what he does not know. They evaluated the state of development like the foolish gardener, only according to the fruit that had already matured. They took no account of the fact that teaching must draw development forward. They took no account of the zone of next development. They were oriented towards the line of least resistance, towards the child's weakness and not towards his strength.

But the situation changes completely when we begin to realise that the complex system is no other than carrying over into school a system of teaching that is suited to the pre-school child, the consolidation of the weak sides of pre-school thinking in the first four years of school teaching, and that this is precisely because the child, who has come to school with functions that have matured in the pre-school years, shows a tendency towards such forms of thinking as correspond to the complex system. This is a system which lags behind child development rather than draws it after itself.

We have seen that teaching and development do not coincide directly, but that they are two processes that are in a very complex inter-relationship. *Teaching is only good when it precedes development.* It then *awakes and calls to life a whole number of functions which are in a state of maturity and which lie within the zone of next development.* In this statement is contained teaching's prime role in relation to development. It is in this that teaching a child differs from training animals. It is in this that teaching a child, the aim of which is his all-round development, differs from teaching specialised technical skills like typing or riding a bicycle which display no essential influence upon development. The formal school discipline of every school subject is the sphere in which this influence of teaching upon development ripens and is accomplished. Teaching would be totally unnecessary if it could use only what had already ripened in development, if it were not itself the source of development, the source of what is new. (Vygotskii, 1934a, 251–2, emphasis in original)

The 'complex' and 'project' systems of education had enjoyed a great vogue amongst progressive Soviet educators of the 1920s, though they had been considerably less popular amongst teachers as a whole (Holmes, 1984). They had involved a breakdown of traditional formal methods and subjects of teaching, a reaching out from the school into the community and considerable reliance upon discovery learning. By the time Vygotskii wrote the above, this educational ideology was officially disapproved and formal school teaching once more firmly supported.

Secondly, Vygotskii continued right up to the end of his life to be deeply interested in the problems of retarded mental development. The defectology that has sprung from Vygotskii's work in this field makes a sharp and fundamental distinction between the educational needs of children who are retarded because of cerebral damage and those whose retardation stems from peripheral causes, physical or social, and are (potentially at least) only 'temporarily retarded' (Sutton, 1980). During the years 1934–5 A. R. Luriya along with F. I. Yudovich conducted a 'natural experiment' at a residential kindergarten attached to a medical genetic institute in Moscow. The experiment involved a pair of retarded twin boys aged 5 years, and the transformation of their development under the influence of rich verbal social interaction with adults was taken as vindication of the Vygotskian position on the transformability of children whose retardation does not stem from a fundamental cerebral flaw (Luriya and Yudovich, 1959). In the post-war years, Luriya returned to this qualitative distinction and took part in the early stages of the long programme of experimental, clinical and pedagogic work that has been necessary to operationalise this straightforward theoretical position (e.g. Luriya, 1961).

Out of a long experience of practice and research within Vygotskii's broad theoretical framework in the USSR there has developed a quite different approach from our own to the definition, assessment and education of unsuccessful school-children (Sutton, 1980). Of particular interest in the present context is the specific technique known as the 'teaching experiment' (*obuchayushchii eksperiment*), a far more convenient way of working than the extensive natural experiment. Standardised Intelligence Testing as we know it, sampling as it does the child's level of *present* rather than *potential* development and presenting its results as though both development and retardation could be unquestionably indexed along a continuum, was not used in the Soviet Union following the 1936 Decree 'Against paedological perversions . . .' – at least until recent years (Sutton, 1983b). On the debit side, Soviet psychology has been starved of the advantages of proper statistical techniques, though in the German Democratic Republic (Witzleck, 1982) considerable progress appears to have been made in bringing together the strengths of the two systems.

ZND IN THE WEST

The remaining discussion deals solely with the Anglo-Saxon West, specifically with Britain and the United States.

Although the concluding chapter of *Myshlenie i rech'* was published in the US in English translation back in the late 1930s (Vygotskii, 1939) it appears to have attracted little interest. Vygotskii remained known to English-speaking psychologists only for his 'blocks' (Vygotskii, 1934c) until the publication of *Thought and Language* (Vygotskii, 1962), an abridged and Bowdlerised edition of *Myshlenie i rech'*, in which the extracts translated above are reduced to four brief paragraphs on pp. 103–4. Not surprisingly perhaps these attracted little or no attention. A year later, however, a much more extensive account appeared, taken from the posthumously published paper 'The problem of teaching and mental development at school age' (Vygotskii, 1934b/1963), as part of a collection published in Britain. Again, this attracted little attention: perhaps the use of the word 'learning' to translate *obuchenie* blunted Vygotskii's sense. Whatever the reason, little explicit attention was directed towards Vygotskii's view of child development, with its profound educational implications, in the English-speaking world – Stones in Britain proving a notable exception (e.g. Stones, 1979/1984, a work so well received in Moscow as to be translated into Russian as a text for teachers in training).

Then in the United States in the late 1970s Cole *et al.* (1979) published an edited collection of Vygotskii's later writings. The editors admitted to taking 'significant liberties', resulting in a mélange 'from which we have omitted material that seemed redundant and to which we have added material which seemed to make his points clearer' (p. x). This collection included versions of two earlier translated papers (Vygotskii, 1934b/1963; 1933/1967) which referred to the zone of next development at the school and pre-school ages, and appears to have been influential in spreading the notion of ZND amongst a sector of American developmental psychology (see Rogoff and Wertsch, 1984). This recent American interest in ZND has been part of a small explosion of interest in Soviet psychology in the United States (e.g. Wertsch, 1985). It has to be admitted, however, that much of this interest has been based on a rather limited range of translations, sometimes rather mutilated ones at that.

Linguistic constraints may indeed prove considerable when seeking access to the writings of Vygotskii and other Soviet psychologists and educators, if one does not read Russian. Further, much of the recent interest in Soviet pschology has been directed towards the academic, 'fun' aspects of Vygotskii's later period, his interest in concepts and the involvement of signs and significance in his developmental theory. The American work on ZND has taken small account of the vital relevance to this of other aspects of Vygotskii's psychology, such as the question of stages of development and the quality of defect, nor of the wider philosophical and political framework of which his psychology is but a part. Thus, the attempt by Brown and French (1979) to incorporate ZND into implicit American models of development, retardation and assessment (within an implicit social philosophy clearly quite distinct from Vygotskii's own) achieves a result that is distinctly odd. The problem of ZND for Anglo-Saxon psychologists and educators, therefore, is not solely one of linguistic translation but also, and perhaps more fundamentally, of the transition of psychological theory and technique from one society and ideology to another.

VYGOTSKII AND US

There are of course obvious parallels between the social contexts of national minorities in the Soviet Union (then and now) and that of cultural minority groups in the English-speaking world. There are also enormous differences between Soviet and Western societies. The developmental psychology that began in the Soviet Union with Vygotskii's Cultural-Historical Theory in the late 1920s is part of a wider view of education, society and humankind that, whatever the particular events of Soviet history, has seen undoubted general improvements in the lot and status of the once under-developed peoples of the former Russian Empire. Could not, therefore, continuingly under-developed and disadvantaged ex-colonial peoples in other parts of the world – including those that live amongst us here in the industrialised West – also share in the apparent benefits of Vygotskiian psychology, living as they do in social and ideological contexts quite different from that in which this psychology has been developed? Could not we all?

How might we in our own societies benefit from ZND and the Cultural-Historical Theory?

Firstly, it is certainly possible to mount specific, practical demonstration in individual instances. Douglas and Sutton (1978), for example, part-replicated the classic twin study of Luriya and Yudovich (1959), transforming the mental development of two young retardates by social, primarily verbal interaction. There is no inherent reason why teachers, schools, parents, communities should not also adopt Vygotskii's understandings and the practical techniques that stem from them. Much of the recent English-language literature on Vygotskii might suggest that his ideas are rarified, abstruse, academic. On the contrary, the fundamental positions of the Cultural-Historical Theory are straightforward and practical and Vygotskii himself went to some trouble to make them widely accessible. They are easily absorbed by like minds and readily and productively adapted to specific practice – *given the wider circumstances that make this possible*. And if circumstances militate against such active demonstration, Vygotskii's theory at least offers fresh understandings of what is going on anyway within our own societies. Thus, though we have nothing analogous to *likbez*, the migration north of American Blacks, from rural to industrialised settings, saw cognitive changes (e.g., Lee, 1951) that Headstart might have been proud of. The sterile 'debate' on Black intelligence has derived from assessments of *present* levels of development and attempts to boost the development of the disadvantaged reduce the basic unit of intervention to below the level of social and cultural change. And within education itself, 'progressive' trends may even have acted to confirm the present levels of development of less advantaged pupils (Sutton, 1981). Right or wrong, Vygotskii and his successors have offered robust and plausible ways of approaching such issues.

Secondly, Vygotskian defectology appears to have made major advances for children who are 'exceptional' or who have 'special educational needs' (e.g. Meshcheryakov, 1979; Suddaby, 1984). Ingenious teaching experiments have been developed, powerful tools to evaluate the effects of education upon the cognitive processes and intellectual potential of a wide range of Soviet pupils (Sutton, 1980). Yet note that these formalised procedures play little part in routine educational and special-educational practice (Stringer, 1984). Rather, the pervasive model of ZND informs individual assessment, pedagogic practice and the direction of the educational system in the same way as the notion of 'intelligence' or 'ability' informs our own. But if we have so far missed out by failing to take account of the experience and achievements of Soviet pedagogic science, we will likely continue to do so if we attempt to benefit solely on the basis of copying technique or method without the underlying understanding of human mental development.

Thirdly, in a culturally diverse world desperate for educational advance, Vygotskii's Cultural-Historical Theory by its very nature offers a basis for a unified understanding of diverse educational achievement and requirements. Specific criticisms of testing method, such as those advanced by Vygotskii in 1929 and by many since, do of course have a place in reviewing our present understanding of human intelligence, but there is a far more fundamental issue. Echoing Lenin, Vygotskii (1929) saw the new era in his country as creating 'entirely new conditions for the development of a single socialist culture in different national forms'. Socialist or not, this distinction between the level and form of culture is essential for considering educational development, both in the Third World and amongst less advantaged people living in the industrialised nations. And this consideration should in no way be seen as applying exclusively to non-European peoples. Vygotskii's approach to psychology was *historical* and, along the historical dimension, the advanced nations, privileged classes, etc., are as accounted as any other (Klix, 1982).

Our own present psychology tends not to be a historical science – which has acted to the detriment of the less culturally advanced peoples to whom it has been applied. Cultural diversity has thrown up challenges to many generally unquestioned givens within our society – not least to our very understanding of human mental development and its determinants. Vygotskian theory offers fresh understandings. Whether or not these can be taken up and operationalised within Western societies may ultimately prove to be not so much a technical matter as a political one.

References

Anderson, B. A., Silver, B. D., Velkoff, V. A. (in press), 'Education of the Handicapped in the USSR: Exploration of the Statistical Picture', *Soviet Studies*.

Brown, A. L., French, L. A. (1979), 'The zone of potential development: implications for intelligence testing in the year 2000', *Intelligence*, **3**, 255–73.

Cole, M., John-Steiner, V., Scribner, S., Souberman, E. (eds) (1979), *Mind in Society: the Development of Higher Psychological Processes*, (Cambridge, Mass.: Harvard University Press).

Dobkin, S. (1982), 'Ages and days': Semyon Dobkin's reminiscences, in *One is Not Born a Personality: Profiles of Soviet Education Psychologists*, (Moscow: Progress, 23–38).
Douglas, J. E., Sutton, A. (1978), 'The development of speech and mental processes in a pair of twins; a case study', *Journal of Child Psychology and Psychiatry*, **19**, 49–56.
Gurova, R. G. (1971), 'A study of the influence of sociohistorical conditions on child development (comparative investigation, 1929 and 1966)'. *Soviet Psychology*, **9**, 189–212.
Holmes, L. (1984), 'Soviet schoolteachers and Moscow: Educational policy and classroom practice, 1921–1931', *Occasional Paper No. 193* of the Kennan Institute for Advanced Russian Studies, (Washington, DC.: The Wilson Center).
Klix, F. (1982), 'On the evolution of cognitive processes and performances', *Animal Mind – Human Mind*, (Berlin: Springer, 226–50).
Lane, D. (1971), *The End of Inequality? Stratification under State Socialism*, (Harmondsworth: Penguin).
Lee, E. S. (1951), 'Negro intelligence and selective migration: a Philadelphia test of the Klineberg hypothesis!, *American Sociology Review*, **16**, 227–33.
Leont'ev, A. N. (1981), *Problems of the Development of the Mind*, (Moscow: Progress).
Luriya, A. R. (1931), 'Psychological expedition to Central Asia', *Science*, **74**, 383–4. Reprinted (1932) in *Journal of Genetic Psychology,* **40**, 241–2.
Luriya, A. R. (1933), 'The second psychological expedition to Central Asia', *Science*, **78**, 191–2.
Luriya, A. R. (1961), 'Study of the abnormal child', *American Journal of Orthopsychiatry*, **31**, 1–16.
Luriya, A. R. (1971), 'Towards the problem of the historical nature of psychological processes', *International Journal of Psychology*, **6**.
Luriya, A. R. (1976), *Cognitive Development; its Cultural and Social Foundations*, (Cambridge, Mass.: Harvard University Press).
Luriya, A. R., Yudovich, F. Y. (1959), *Speech and the Development of Mental Processes in the Child*, (London: Staples).
McLeish, J. (1972), 'The Soviet conquest of illiteracy', *Alberta Journal of* Educational Research, **18**, 307–26.
Meshcheryakov, A. I. (1979), *Awakening to Life: Forming Behaviour and the Mind in Deaf-Blind Children*, (Moscow: Progress).
Petrovskii, A. V. (1973), *Vozrastnaya i pedagogicheskaya psikhologiya*, (Moscow: Prosveshchenie).
Rogoff, B., Wertsch, J. V. (eds) (1984), *Children's Learning in the 'Zone of Proximal Development'*, 'New developments in child development No. 23' (San Franciso: Jossey-Bass).
Shakhlevich, T. M. (1974), 'Bibliografiya trudov L. S. Vygotskogo (k 40 letiyu so dnya smerti)', *Voprosy psikhologii*, **3**, 152–60.
Stones, E. (1979), *Psychopedagogy: Psychological Theory and the Practice of Teaching*, (London: Methuen). Russian translation (1984), *Psikhopedagogika*; *psikologicheskaya teoriya i praktika obucheniya*, (Moscow: Pedagogika).
Stringer, P. (1984), 'Special education in the Soviet Union and the child with learning difficulties', *Journal of the Association of Educational Psychologists*, **6**, no. 4, 2–18.

Suddaby, A. (1984), 'The collective curriculum', *Times Educational Supplement*, 22 June, 20.

Sutherland, J. (1985), 'National language teaching in the Soviet Union: some impressions derived from visits to Union and Autonomous Republics in recent years', *Soviet Education Study Bulletin*, **3**, 33–7.

Sutton, A. (1980), 'Backward children in the USSR' in Brine, J., Perrie, M., and Sutton, A. (eds), *Home, School and Leisure in the Soviet Union*, (London: Allen & Unwin).

Sutton, A. (1981), 'Cultural disadvantage and Vygotskii's stages of development', *Educational Studies*, **6**, 199–209.

Sutton, A. (1983a), 'An introduction to Soviet developmental psychology,' in Meadows, S. (ed.), *Developing Thinking: Approaches to Children's Cognitive Development*, (London and NY: Methuen).

Sutton, A. (1983b), 'Do Communist and Western psychologies show a converging pattern?' paper presented to the Annual Conference of the Centre for Russian and East European Studies, Windsor.

Van der Veer, R. (1984), 'In defence of Vygotskii: an analysis of the arguments that led to the condemnation of the cultural-historical theory' in Bern, S., Rappard, H., van Hoorn, W. (eds). *Studies in the History of Psychology and the Social Sciences*, vol. 2, (Leiden: Psychologich Instituut Van De Rijksuniversiteit).

Vygotskii, L. S. (1929a), 'The problem of the cultural development of the child', *Journal of Genetic Psychology*, **36**, 415–34.

Vygotskii, L. S. (1929b), K voprosu o plane nauchno-issledovatel'skoi raboty po pedologii natsional'nykh men'shinstv', *Pedologiya*, **3**, 367–77.

Vygotskii, L. S. (1933), 'Igra i ee rol' v psikhicheskom rasvitii rebenka; (1967), English translation: 'Play and its role in the mental development of the child', *Soviet Psychology*, **5**, 'Vygotskii Memorial Issue', 6–18.

Vygotskii, L. S. (1934a), *Myshlenie i rech*' Moscow and Leningrad; Sotsekgiz. Reference edition: (1982). Sobranie sochinenii, vol. 2 (Moscow: Pedagogika) 39–361.

Vygotskii, L. S. (1934b), Problema obucheniya i umstvennogo razvitiya v shkol'nom vosraste. English translation: 'Learning and mental development at school age', in Simon, B., Simon, J. (eds) (1963), *Educational Psychology in the USSR* (London: RKP).

Vygotskii, L. S. (1934c), 'Thought in schizophrenia', *Archives of Neurology and Psychiatry*, **31**, 1065–77.

Vygotskii, L. S. (1939), 'Thought and speech', *Psychiatry*, **2**, 29–52.

Vygotskii, L. S. (1962), *Thought and Language*, (Cambridge, Mass.: MIT Press).

Wertsch, J. V. (1981), *The Concept of Activity in Soviet Psychology*, (Armonk, NY: Sharpe).

Wertsch, J. V. (ed.) (1985), *Culture, Communication and Cognition: Vygotskian Perspectives*, (Cambridge: Cambridge University Press).

Witzleck, G. (1982), 'Theory and practice in the construction and application of psycho-diagnostic procedures in the German Democratic Republic', *International Review of Applied Psychology*, **31**, 55–73.

6 Construction of a Test Battery to Measure Learning Potential

Peter Coxhead and Rajinder M. Gupta

DESIGN AND DEVELOPMENT

Design of the test battery

The Learning Efficiency Test Battery (LETB) was developed to meet a real need: this being how to evaluate Asian[2] children's cognitive ability and/or learning efficiency when their experiences and cultural backgrounds are different from children with Western type backgrounds on whom the majority of the commonly used IQ tests have been standardised. Although a large majority of practising psychologists are aware that traditional IQ tests are inappropriate for ethnic minority[5] children (cf. Mackenzie, 1980), they continue to be used as one of the important criteria for the purposes of classification and for placing these children into special schools and units (Tomlinson, 1981; Reschly, 1984). The deficiencies of traditional testing procedures and the advantages of assessing children's learning efficiency have already been outlined in Chapter 1, and there is therefore little need to restate them here. Suffice it to say that our conviction as to the advantages of assessing learning efficiency and our cognizance of the literature highlighting the limitation of IQ tests were the motivating forces behind the development of the Learning Efficiency Test Battery.

It was decided at the outset to develop a test battery rather than a single test. The expectation from a homogeneous test is that it will provide information about a very narrow area of mental processes, whereas a test battery should be able to yield information about a diverse range of mental functioning. Since in assessing children from ethnic minority and disadvantaged populations it is often recommended that one should aim at assessing a wide range of mental processes (see Anastasi, 1961; Davis, 1971; Jensen, 1970), it was this rationale which was the underlying motivation for developing a test Battery, consisting of eight subtests, rather than just a single test.

In the development of the Learning Efficiency Test Battery, there were a number of important design principles which were taken into consideration. The genesis of these principles is from personal experience of assessing both indigenous and ethnic minority children for several years employing a wide variety of psychological tests; first-hand knowledge of child rearing and raising practices in Asian homes; and last, but not least, the insights gained by several experienced workers in the field of assessing children from non-Western cultures (Berry, 1966; Haynes, 1971; Hegarty and Lucas, 1978; Hudson, 1967; Irvine, 1966; Jahoda, 1980; Schwarz, 1961; Winter, 1963; Wober, 1967). Further details of the design principles may be found in Gupta (1983). Briefly, the major objectives were:

1. To discriminate approximately the bottom 5 per cent of a given age group; initially, the target age ranges were 6 year olds to 10 year olds.
2. To provide information, where possible embedded in some mental process theory, to assist in determining the child's future educational needs, in predicting performance in the basic subjects, and in curriculum planning.
3. To include a variety of tests in order to sample a diverse range of learning processes, albeit similar to those required in a classroom-learning situation.
4. To develop a battery whose administration encourages active participation while minimising the use of language either on the part of the administrator or the child.
5. To minimise the impact of the child's previous learning; rather to provide evidence of the ability to learn new tasks based on those learning principles which appear to account for a substantial amount of learning.
6. To use materials and test items which, while reasonably familiar to all children, did not favour one culture over another. (For example, visually complex two-dimensional items and the use of colour were avoided because of evidence suggesting possible cultural differences in pre-exposure.)
7. To produce a practical and usable instrument. (To this end, ease of administration, portability, cost of materials and time were taken into account. For example, although it was believed that items should not be timed, in view particularly of objectives 4 to 6 above, nevertheless the battery should not require an excessive amount of time to administer.)

Although this may seem a formidable and constraining list of objectives, experience gained in a pilot study suggested that it was possible to construct a Learning Efficiency Test Battery with the potential to meet most, if not all, of the objectives.

Model for the administration of the LETB

For the purposes of administering the LETB, a special model was developed. In the development of this model, experiences gained by several other workers who have carried out researches with non-Western populations played an important part (Haynes, 1971; Hegarty and Lucas, 1978; Jahoda, 1956; Lloyd and Pidgeon, 1961; Ortar, 1960; Scott, 1950; Silvey, 1963). The model on which the LETB is based is: Demonstration; Demonstration and Practice; Testing.

Demonstration

The chief function of this phase is to give the child a foretaste of the task. Here the examiner performs the task himself, and the child is not expected to participate but just to observe what the examiner does in front of him. However, the child is not discouraged if he offers to take part in the demonstration. This is an important part of the model as demonstration is considered a vital link in our understanding and learning (Williams, 1958, cited in Lunzer, 1973).

Demonstration and practice

This phase is designed to incorporate teaching and practice of the same task. In addition, this intermediary stage further ensures that the child really understands the task prior to coming to the next phase, Testing. Neither during the first nor the second stage are the child's responses scored, although his way of responding or learning does provide qualitative information about his learning efficiency.

Testing

This is the final phase of the model. Here the testing proper is carried out but not in a fail-pass fashion. Even this phase involves teaching and provides feedback to the child as to whether his response is correct or incorrect. As a result of this teaching and feedback, he has an opportunity to demonstrate that by additional help, he is capable of learning new material. Here the child's responses are scored according to the teaching effort that he required in order to reach the criterion. This enables the LETB to be administered while requiring little use of language either on the part of the examiner or the child. Our experience has shown that it ensures that the child really understands the requirements of the test, and is not being penalised for not fully grasping what he is required to do. In addition, the model also provides a warming-up period prior to the actual assessment and helps to alleviate the child's anxiety (cf. Scott, 1950).

The model is intended to be adhered to even with those children who have satisfactory language familiarity. However, this does not imply that the examiner is not permitted to talk to the child to build rapport or break long silences.

DESCRIPTION OF THE LETB SUBTESTS

The final version of the LETB was designed to have eight subtests. These appear to fall into three categories: tests based on Piaget's work; a short-term memory test; and tests based on associative learning principles.

Piaget-based tests

The Piagetian tasks were selected because a review of some of the representative literature supported the idea that many of his tasks: had the potential to predict the child's future academic success in the basic subjects; were well suited for clinical work; shared important features with criterion referenced testing; could assist in determining future educational needs; and could aid in curriculum planning (Lunzer, 1973; Lunzer and Dolan, 1977; for comprehensive review of the literature see Modgil, 1974; Modgil and Modgil, 1976; Modgil and Modgil, 1980; Schwebel and Raph, 1974). Furthermore, Piagetian tasks: 'are less affected by cultural differences than others . . . Comparisons of children in schools is less likely to be influenced by cultural or class differences using Piagetian measures than by using standardised tests' (Wadsworth, 1978, p. 230).

Yet another advantage of Piagetian tasks is that performance on them is not influenced either by socio-economic status or amount of schooling so long as the tasks are not too dependent upon the quality of verbal responding (Wadsworth, 1978). According to Hathaway and Hathaway-Theunissen (1974), Piagetian tasks assess areas of mental functioning which are of great importance to educators and clinicians – and the children they serve – but more importantly they are areas which are not satisfactorily tested by the prevalent psychometric procedures. There are four tests.

Seriation A

For the purposes of the assessment of this concept the child is required to seriate 10 wooden blocks (in natural wood) presented to him in a random order, either without help ('spontaneously'), or with help ('cues') and feedback. Irrespective of the strategy used, the correct solution is 10 blocks seriated starting from the smallest and progressively increasing to the largest. The length of these blocks range from 3 cm to 8 cm each differing in size by approximately .55 cm.

Seriation B

The same testing materials are used as in Seriation A. The difference is that in order to produce a correct response the 10 wooden blocks need to be arranged in descending order of their magnitude. In order to arrive at the correct response the child is free to use whatever strategy he wishes.

Serial correspondence

While the child is watching, the examiner arranges 10 wooden blocks in front of the child. These are arranged in their serial order, from the smallest to the largest. The child also has in front of him 10 wooden rods placed randomly. The requirement of this task is that the child places each wooden rod underneath the ordinally matching wooden block, either without help or with help and feedback.

The wooden blocks are the same as used for Seriation A and B. The 10 wooden rods are in natural wood, round with flattened edges, 2 cm in diameter; length varying from 2.75 cm to 7.75 cm, each differing in size by approximately .55 cm.

Ordinal correspondence

The materials used for this test are the same as for Serial Correspondence. The major difference between this test and Serial Correspondence is that for this test the 10 test blocks are presented in a randomly prearranged fashion. The child has the 10 wooden rods randomly placed in a sort of pile in front of him – however the child should be able to see each element. The child has to match each wooden rod with its corresponding wooden block so that the ordinal position of the two matches with each other. He can do this either without help or with help and feedback.

Visual sequential short-term memory test

The rationale behind the inclusion of a short-term memory test is that short-term memory seems to be an important school-related ability and the visual sequential aspect of the task has relevance to the written English language. In the written English Language: 'words . . . occur in horizontal orientation, in simultaneous presentation, and in close succession' (Paraskevopoulos and Kirk, 1969). The method of presentation of the stimuli of this test was intended to correspond quite closely to this process.

In certain ways the test used resembles the Visual Sequential Memory Test from the Illinois Test of Psycholinguistic Abilities (Kirk *et al.*, 1976) in the model of presentation. The child is shown a predetermined sequence of abstract designs, each drawn on a 3.5 × 3.5 cm card for a set number of seconds. After the child has seen this sequence the cards are jumbled up and placed in front of him. The child has to reproduce this sequence.

A fixed number of trials are permitted and the items gradually become of increasing difficulty. For instance, the first items consist of 3 cards only and the last items consist of 6 cards.

Tests based on associative learning principles

The Object Picture Association Test, Word Object Picture Association Test and the Symbol Manipulation Test are rooted in the theoretical model of associative learning (Hilgard and Atkinson, 1967; Woodworth and Schlosberg, 1954). Although all learning cannot be explained by the process of assocition, a considerable amount of learning must take place by this process (see Atkinson and Hansen, 1966; Cronbach, 1977; Englemann *et al.*, 1970; Gagne, 1977; Hilgard and Atkinson, 1967), not just in one culture but across various cultures. However it needs to be acknowledged that this claim is, in the main, hypothetical and is not based on a great deal of empirical evidence. Nevertheless, if one looks critically at the processes involved in learning by association, it must be concluded that this type of learning phenomenon is unlikely to be highly culture-specific.

Word object picture association test

The aim of this test is to ascertain the teaching effort that the child would require in order to learn to associate six pictures, each drawn on a card (approximately 4 cm × 4 cm), with their appropriate labels. In selecting the labels, particular attention was paid to ensure that the words should not be familiar – at least not to the large majority of children of the age range selected for the research. This was achieved by ensuring that the words selected for the test were not amongst those lists of words which are commonly used, or read, by children between the ages of 6 to 10 years (Edwards and Gibbon, 1973; Thorndike and Lorge, 1944), and by a trial using a small number of children of the target age range.

Object picture association test

There are some similarities between this test and the Word Object Picture Association Test. This test too requires the child to learn to associate an irregular shaped wooden block with a very familiar object (e.g. tree, cup, face). There are six such associations to be learnt. As the shape of each wooden block is completely irregular it is therefore highly unlikely – almost impossible – for any child to come to the test situation having already learnt one or more associations.

Symbol manipulation

Unlike the rest of the tests, this is a pen and paper test. Although it is mainly a two dimensional test, the manipulation of the stimuli is very simple. The essential requirement is to learn to associate one abstract symbol with another abstract symbol. Throughout the test the stimulus model is always in front of the child. The test starts first with learning to associate one symbol with another, and gradually progresses to four. In other words, the child has to select – in fact draw – four symbols from the stimulus model which correspond with the test items.

PSYCHOMETRIC PROPERTIES OF THE LETB

Introduction

The content of the LETB, discussed above, is derived partly from theoretical considerations and partly from experience with a pilot study. The major research task was to establish whether the battery was acceptable according to the usual psychometric criteria of reliability and validity. A total of 455 children were involved in this part of the study. They included English,[1] Asian[2] and Indian[3] children. Their ages ranged from 6 years to 10 years. Of the 455 children, 385 were drawn from 12 normal junior and infant schools and 40 children were selected from 3 special schools (designated as schools for the Educationally Subnormal – Mild,[4] by the Local Education Authority; see Home Office, 1978 for the new terminology in place of ESN-M in English). The total sample of 455 children also included a small sub-sample of 30 children who were tested in India. For details of the procedure adopted in the selection of schools and children, the interested reader is referred to Gupta (1983).

One difficulty in analysing psychometric data on the LETB was that, by design, item scores were not as 'spread out' as is often found and indeed expected in conventional tests, and were certainly not normally distributed. In this respect, the LETB is very close to mastery learning tests. It is commonly acknowledged that the key point in their design is their: 'appeal to the appropriateness of the content rather than in terms of any experimental or statistical results as would be required for predictive validity or construct validity' (Nunnally, 1978, p. 310).

Procedures to analyse data yielded by mastery learning tests do exist (for example Ferguson and Novick, 1973; Millman, 1974, cited in Anastasi, 1976) but are still at the exploratory stage (Anastasi, 1976), and of uncertain value. It was therefore decided to adhere to more established methods; however, it is important to remember that because these analyses are based on skewed distributions, results should be interpreted with some caution.

Reality of the subtests

In terms of its content, the LETB is easily divided into three groups of eight subtests (see above). However these may not necessarily represent empirically separable skills. The traditional approach to this question is to apply factor analysis to all the items of a battery and then to judge whether the factors obtained do indeed correspond to the pre-defined subtests. To establish the existence of the subtests, initially all race and age groups were combined, giving a sample size of 385. (Later analyses showed that no distortion was produced in this way.) A variety of factor analytic techniques were employed (see Gupta, 1983, for fuller details). The results shown in Tables 6.1 and 6.2 demonstrate most clearly the relationships between the factorial structure and the items of the battery. It would appear that the four Piaget-based 'subtests' are

Table 6.1 Oblique factor pattern matrix of the LETB items (direct oblimin, delta = 0.000)

	Factors (Salients italicised)					
	1	*2*	*3*	*4*	*5*	*6*
PIAGET 1	−04	−03	−03	05	05	*72*
PIAGET 2	09	−02	−07	−05	08	*76*
PIAGET 3	02	−02	12	02	−03	*68*
PIAGET 4	06	15	20	−06	−02	*39*
VSMT 1	−02	*39*	−09	15	04	04
VSMT 2	01	*42*	−12	13	03	12
VSMT 3	02	*61*	−06	01	−04	−00
VSMT 4	03	*58*	−10	04	−02	−06
VSMT 5	07	*55*	10	−07	08	−08
VSMT 6	−03	*64*	09	01	−03	00
VSMT 7	04	*59*	15	−07	06	−07
VSMT 8	−00	*64*	11	−09	10	00
OPAT 1	−02	−02	−00	01	*99*	01
OPAT 2	04	03	−00	02	*85*	03
WOPAT 1	−00	−00	*87*	10	04	06
WOPAT 2	04	04	*85*	05	04	09
SM 1	02	04	10	*90*	05	00
SM 2	16	−01	06	*79*	06	−01
SM 3	*75*	01	09	10	−01	07
SM 4	*79*	01	10	12	01	00
SM 5	*95*	−04	00	02	−00	00
SM 6	*97*	08	−07	−00	−03	02
SM 7	*91*	04	−06	−03	04	−03
SM 8	*89*	−00	−03	−07	03	00

Decimal points omitted.

Key

Piaget 1 to Piaget 4 refers to the four Piaget-based subtests.
VSMT 1 to VSMT 8 refers to the Visual Sequential Short-Term Memory Test items.
OPAT 1 to OPAT 2 refers to the Object Picture Association Test items.
WOPAT 1 to WOPAT 2 refers to the Word Object Picture Association Test items.
SM 1 to SM 8 refers to the Symbol Manipulation Test items.

sufficiently similar as not to warrant separation; in subsequent analyses a *single* Piaget subtest is used in place of the four components described above. The remaining four subtests retain their identity (with some minor adjustment of the Symbol Manipulation test by removing the first two items from the scoring although retaining them in the battery for their practice value). The LETB thus has five distinct subtests.

Table 6.2 Factor correlations of the LETB items

	Factors					
	1	*2*	*3*	*4*	*5*	*6*
Factor 1		34	21	41	48	42
Factor 2			19	23	41	28
Factor 3				–02	23	25
Factor 4					32	35
Factor 5						31
Factor 6						—

Decimal points omitted.

Reliability

Having demonstrated the existence of five subtests within the battery, the issue of their reliability arises. Both an internal consistency method (alpha coefficient) and the test-retest method were used. Table 6.3 summarises both sets of results. (Time constraints meant that the retest sample size was limited to 23.) It will be noted that, with one exception, all subtests show satisfactory reliabilities using both methods.

Validity

Validity is *the* key issue in the design of assessment materials such as the LETB and a great deal of detailed research and analysis was carried out

Table 6.3 Coefficient alphas and test retest reliability coefficients of the LETB subtests

Tests	*Coefficient Alphas* ($n = 385$)	*Test Retest* ($n = 23$)
1 Piaget based	.77 **	.67 **
2 Visual Sequential Short-Term Memory	.80 **	.83 **
3 Object Picture Association	.94 **	.46 *
4 Word Object Picture Association	.93 **	.89 **
5 Symbol Manipulation	.96 **	.98 **

* = significant at the 2 per cent level.
** = significant at the 1 per cent level.

to establish the validity of the LETB and its subtests. Only some of this work can be presented here. The major types of validity considered were construct validity and predictive validity. Hopefully the earlier discussion will have demonstrated the LETB's content validity, as far as the nature of the subtests is concerned. An important content-related issue is that of language dependence.

It was intended that the LETB should be only minimally dependent upon language. After the experience of testing nearly 500 children it can safely be claimed that the LETB, in its administration, requires little use of language either on the part of the examiner or the child. Confirmation of this assertion has also been provided by some professional colleagues who have tried the Battery while still in its developmental stage, as well as by a few teachers who also tried it on small groups of children. Personal experience of administering the Battery has shown that although little language is used in the actual administration of the Battery, children still enjoy taking it. The fact that the LETB can be administered with the minimal use of language cannot be considered a novel feature. There are other tests (e.g. the Learning Ability Test produced by the NFER (Hegarty and Lucas, 1978) which also do not depend upon verbal instructions in their administration. Language-independence is strongly related to the administration model (Demonstration, Demonstration and Practice, Testing). The LETB model owes a good deal to the model used for the administration of the Learning Ability Test.

Construct validity

This refers to the extent to which a test or subtest measures the theoretical traits or constructs which it is intended to measure. One step is to study convergent-discriminant validity: the extent to which the LETB subtests approach and differ from other well-known constructs such as intelligence (as measured by IQ tests) and academic ability (as measured by teacher's ratings) and so on. A range of exploratory and confirmatory factor analysis techniques were used. That the LETB is not simply a measure of intelligence is shown by the results given in Table 6.4. Using the LISREL programme (Joreskog, 1971), it could be demonstrated that a *single* two-factor model fitted data on the LETB and two measures of IQ – Raven's Matrices and the Draw-a-Man test – for *all* age/race groups studied. (The details of this analysis are discussed in more detail later). Table 6.4 shows this common model, after both Varimax and Promax rotations.

Table 6.4 Varimax and promax factor loadings common to four age race groups

	Loadings *Varimax Rotation*		*Loadings* *Promax Rotation*	
	1	*2*	*1*	*2*
Raven	*78*	25	*90*	–12
Draw	*59*	15	*70*	–14
Piaget	*49*	*39*	*45*	22
WOPAT	29	*41*	19	*35*
VSMT	26	*52*	09	*52*
SM	22	*50*	05	*51*
OPAT	12	*76*	–21	*90*
			Factor Correlation	
		Factors 1		69
		2	–	–

Note: Decimals omitted.
Salients italicised.

It is clear that whereas the Piaget subtest does have characteristics in common with conventional IQ tests, the remaining LETB subtests are conceptually and empirically distinct, though correlated.

Another approach to construct validity examines certain group differences (for the underlying rationale of this approach, see Anastasi, 1976; Lewis, 1967; Thorndike and Hagen, 1969). For the purposes of the LETB the contrasted groups were ESN-M children (n = 40) and the rest of the main sample (n = 385). In order to test whether there were significant differences between the performance of these two groups on the LETB, Analysis of Variance was performed. The means and significance test results are shown in Table 6.5 below.

Table 6.5 Means and significance levels of ESN-M children on the LETB subtests

	Main Sample Mean	*ESN-M Mean*	*Sig Level*
(Age)*	52.3	55.9	0.05
Piagetian Test	9.4	1.7	0.001
VSMT	18.6	3.9	0.001
OPAT	32.0	15.7	0.001
WOPAT	18.5	2.9	0.001
SM	22.6	2.9	0.001

*In months over 4 years.

These results clearly indicate that even though the ESN-M group is slightly older than the non ESN-M group, the two categories of children have significantly different means on all subtests of the LETB, thus providing further evidence of its satisfactory construct validity.

Predictive validity

The LETB is clearly designed to provide information to be used to determine a child's *future* schooling; hence it should possess demonstrated predictive validity. Central to the issue of predictive validity is the question of what is to be predicted. Sometimes it is quite difficult to find an appropriate measure of the attributes a test is supposed to index. More often than not with intelligence tests, aptitude tests and learning tests (such as those devised by Haynes, 1971 and Hegarty and Lucas, 1978) their predictive validity coefficient is computed by correlating them with academic tests (e.g. Reading, Maths, Spelling). A discussion pertaining to the difficulties associated with choosing an appropriate criterion for predictive validity can be found in most standard text books on psychometrics; one of the main problems is 'temporal changes' (Anastasi, 1976). This is particularly so if there has been a substantial time lapse between administrations of the predictors and the criterion. Thus we can distinguish concurrent and longitudinal predictive validity.

Concurrent predictive validity

The chosen dependent variables were the Schonell Word Recognition Test (Schonell, 1951) and the Graded Arithmetic-Mathematics Test (Vernon and Miller, 1976). Both were administered at the same time as the subtests of the LETB and the Raven's Coloured Matrices (Raven, 1962) and the Draw-a-Man Test (Harris, 1963), which were treated as independent variables, that is, as able to predict reading and mathematics scores.

The major issue is the effectiveness of the LETB in explaining (predicting) the reading and mathematics scores as compared to the more conventional IQ measures. A prior question which needed to be settled was whether the relationships between the dependent and independent variables differed by age and/or race. The answer to this question was sought by setting up two models using the LISREL-IV programme (Joreskog and Sorbom, 1978). This model allowed *separate* regression coefficients for all the four subgroups by age/race. Then a second model was tried with the constraint that the (unstandardised) regression weights had to be *equal* for all four subgroups. A test of this constraint yielded $\chi^2_{21} = 18.56$, $p > 0.05$ for the Graded Arithmetic-Mathematics Test and $\chi^2_{21} = 20.48$, $p > 0.05$ for the Schonell Graded Word Recognition Test. Thus it appears that the null hypothesis of equal regression weights in all the four subgroups cannot be rejected.

The R^2 values showed (See Table 6.6) that, using a common set of weights for all four subgroups, there was very little difference between the predictive ability of the LETB subtests when compared to two conventional IQ measures – the latter perhaps being marginally better.

Table 6.6 Comparison of predictive validity of LETB and conventional IQ tests

Independent Variables	*Average R^2 values for 4 age/race groups* *DV=Maths*	*DV=Reading*
5 LETB subtests	0.41	0.28
2 IQ measures	0.45	0.30
All 7	0.57	0.38

Longitudinal predictive validity

The concurrent predictive validity of the LETB was examined using the full ability range. A more relevant assessment, perhaps, would be obtained by using only those children whose ability level ought to be discriminated by the LETB, namely the bottom 5 per cent of the population. A small-scale study was set up to test empirically, on a longitudinal basis, the predictive validity of the LETB, and to compare it with conventional assessment procedures (i.e. IQ measures and/or teachers' ratings). One of the key features was a specially selected sample ($n = 27$, of which 78 per cent were Asian) which consisted only of children who, according to conventional assessment procedures were in the bottom 5 per cent of the population, but nevertheless had scores on the LETB subtests comparable to the parent population. (However, it should be added that the criteria for deciding on the bottom 5 per cent included the use of English norms for the Raven's Matrices for Asian children. It is likely that the Asian children were actually of rather higher ability but have been under-estimated due to a bias in the Raven's Matrices (see Gupta, 1983).) The dependent variable was reading score (Schonell Graded Word Recognition Test) which was measured initially (March 1980) and finally (December 1980). Stepwise multiple regression showed clearly that the LETB (particularly the Visual Sequential Short-Term Memory subtest) was a more effective predictor of reading gains over this period than either teachers' ratings or the Draw-a-Man IQ test. (Again, for further details, see Gupta, 1983.) The conclusions that can be drawn from this small study support those who argue that a low IQ *cannot* be viewed as a reflection of low learning ability (Feuerstein, 1979; Guilford, 1967; Haywood *et al*, 1975; Hegarty and Lucas, 1978; Jensen, 1961, 1963, 1967, 1969).

SPECIAL FEATURES AND POTENTIAL APPLICATIONS OF THE LETB

LETB as a culture-fair test

Traditionally, non-verbal IQ tests such as the Raven's Matrices have been thought to be 'fair' when used for assessing children of different cultures. Good norms for the Ravens Matrices for use in the UK do not seem to be available; using one recommended set (Raven, 1962), Gupta (1983) has shown that when Birmingham-based samples of English and Asian children and a sample of Indian children are matched for age (all between the ages of 8–9 years) only 11 per cent of the English children fall in the 'bottom 5 per cent' of the population as assessed by Raven's Matrices and/or Draw-a-Man, whereas by the same criterion, 27 per cent of the Asian children and 27 per cent of the Indian children fall in the 'bottom 5 per cent' of the population. Thus more than twice the number of Asian and Indian children are likely to be classified as being in the bottom 5 per cent of the population or 'mentally defective'. Furthermore, English and Asian children have different intercepts when regression lines are drawn for predicting reading ages from the Raven's Matrices scores. It is well recognised in the literature (e.g. Anastasi, 1976) that children with a higher intercept are discriminated against. Regression analysis results show that the intercept of Asian children is higher than the intercept of English children (see Gupta, 1983). The effect is to underestimate an Asian child's reading age by about 3 months.

As opposed to the Raven's Matrices, which according to the above findings is clearly a culture-based test, all the evidence seems to suggest that, as intended, the LETB is fair to both English and Asian children – although it needs to be added that the construction of it began from the assessment needs of the latter group.

In order to test the culture fairness of the LETB the data was examined in two ways. Firstly, a MANOVA test was performed 'to test the "realness" of the differences among the population centroids' (Cooley and Lohnes, 1971). (In addition to the 5 LETB subtests there were in fact eight other variables as well; but their detail is not pertinent to the present dicussion.) The results showed that the means for the whole set of variables differed among the four groups (Lambda = 0.57; F (39, 1040) = 5.51, significant at the 1 per cent level) so that it was thought legitimate to investigate the differences amongst the means separately. A series of two way analyses of variance (ANOVA) were undertaken as a follow-up for further interpreting the significant MANOVA. The ANOVA results clearly showed that there were non-significant differences (at the 1 per cent level) on 4 out of 5 LETB subtests. The only LETB subtest where significant differences did emerge was the VSMT, where the means favoured Asian children.

The second issue is more complex. A test battery can show differences between groups of children in two quite distinct ways: the subtests can have different means, and/or the relationships amongst the subtests can differ. Differences of the latter kind can also lead to bias: for example one test may be a better predictor of some criterion than another for some race or age groups. One way in which differences in inter-test relationships were examined was through the use of constrained factor analysis using LISREL. The variables used were the five subtests of the LETB, together with the two IQ tests, Raven's Matrices and the Draw-a-Man. The whole sample was divided into four groups defined by race (English or Asian) and age (Top Infants and First Year Junior or Second Year Junior). A two factor model, with the factor loadings and covariances constrained to be equal across the four groups, showed a good fit to the data ($\chi^2 = 89.1, df = 71, p > 0.05$). The LETB thus seems to show similar inter-relationships among its subtests, regardless of race or age.

On the basis of the above analyses, a modest claim is made that the LETB (except the VSMT) can be used with equal confidence for both Asian and English children.

Use of the LETB for determining future educational needs

There is both a theoretical and an empirical justification for using the Piaget-based test of the LETB for identifying children who may have special educational needs. This seems possible to achieve if the child's performance can be interpreted in the light of Piaget and his associates' work. Piaget and his co-workers (Inhelder and Piaget, 1964; Inhelder *et al.*, 1974; Piaget, undated, cited in Gruber and Voneche, 1977) claim that there are three stages in the acquisition of seriation – and this applies to serial and approximately to ordinal correspondence as well. The three stages are:

Stage 1a During this stage the child shows complete lack of understanding of seriation. The child's attempts largely consist of arranging a 'few sticks more or less parallel to each other, horizontally or vertically, in no particular order' (Inhelder *et al.*, 1974, p. 295). This stage is observed when the child is around three to four years of age.

Stage 1b However, during the second subphase of this stage the child attempts to arrange sticks in sub-series or 2, 3 and 4 but he is unable to put them together. Inhelder *et al.*, (1974) describe it as one of the more advanced responses of this phase of the development.

Stage 2 This occurs when the child is around six years of age and the child achieves success in organising the ten elements but only by 'groping'. Although the child is able to make up a seriation, he does not show any understanding of a system of relations which is a marked characteristic of the next stage.

Stage 3 At this stage, which starts at 7–8 years, the child uses a systematic method first by looking for the smallest (or largest) element, then looking for the next one among those remaining and so on. This method of organising the elements is described as 'properly operational' because this method implies an awareness that any given element is both larger than the preceding and smaller than those that succeed it (e.g. $E<D$, C, etc, and $E<F$, G, etc) (Gruber and Voneche, 1977, p. 385).

In the light of the foregoing discussion it seems possible to interpret a child's performance on the Piaget based subtest of the LETB in order to obtain an approximate index of his current level of cognitive functioning and then to employ this information as a guideline for identifying his educational needs. One possible way of interpreting the child's score on the Piaget-based test is to consider a score between 9–12 as being at Stage 3, a score between 6–8 as being at Stage 2, a score between 3–5 as being at Stage 1b and a score between 0–2 as being in Stage 1a.

The availability of information about the performance of the contrasted group, that is ESN-M children, is also useful in comparing with the performance on the LETB of the referred child and then deciding whether such a child should be recommended to stay in the mainstream of education or should be recommended for a transfer to a special school (see Table 6.5 for details of means, etc.).

Results obtained from the child's performance on the LETB, besides being useful in determining the child's future educational needs, can also be used for inferring about the teaching effort he is likely to require in order to master or grasp new concepts or skills. Efficient performance on the various subtests of the LETB is inversely related to the teaching effort; in other words, high scorers on the LETB require less teaching input to reach the mastery level as opposed to the low scorers. In the testing situation, were the child to require an inordinate amount of teaching effort to reach criterion this would suggest that he would be likely to need a substantial amount of teaching help in order to grasp new concepts. For any decision making then the central question would be: can the teacher concerned provide the teaching input the child is likely to require or does the psychologist need to explore some kind of special educational provision where the teaching could be carried out at the child's pace of learning? The interpretation from the LETB is justifiable as its validity is quite satisfactory.

Design of the curriculum and the LETB

In line with current thinking (see Newland, 1973; Toepher, 1981; Woodward, 1970; Ysseldyke and Salvia, 1974, who evaluate some of the current ideas related to assessment), it was also intended that the LETB should be able to assist in designing a curriculum appropriate to the child's level of thinking. This intended characteristic of the LETB is best served by the Piaget-based test. It has been shown above that with the aid of Piaget based test it is possible to estimate a child's level of cognitive processes (approximately between the ages of 3+ and 8+).

Once estimates of the child's current level of mental processes are available, then this information can be usefully employed in designing a curriculum which matches his developmental level. For instance, if on testing one finds that the child is unable to seriate, Piaget's theory would suggest that the child at this stage is pre-numerical or does not yet have stable number concepts. Such a child therefore is not likely to understand certain Mathematics concepts (for details see Wadsworth, 1978). Matching of the curriculum with the child's level of mental processes is absolutely vital to general cognitive development as providing just rich or varied experiences can at best result in rote learning only.

More recently, Toepher (1981) has advanced the view that learning, particularly high level learning, should be matched with the individual's cognitive skills. High IQ and 'satisfactory record' alone are not sufficient to cope with high level learning. Toepher came to this conclusion on the basis of his enquiry based on 1700, 12 to 14 year old children with IQs above 120. Thus the outcome from the Piaget-based test can be employed for designing curriculum for children between the ages of 3+ and 8+ years.

Summary

Bearing in mind the possible difficulties associated with the difference between the LETB and more conventional assessment tests, it is clear that the weight of the psychometric evidence offers a fairly consistent and encouraging picture. Learning efficiency *is* composed of distinct sub-domains, some of which are tested by the LETB. The subtests of the LETB are of more than adequate reliability. Considerations of construct validity show that learning efficiency, as measured by the LETB, is related to but nevertheless not identical to more conventional IQ measurements. When concurrent predictive validity is considered, the LETB is very little if any worse than IQ measures. Longitudinally, the LETB appears to be more effective in predicting achievement gains among the lowest 5 per cent than are IQ measures.

We would certainly not wish to claim that the LETB is the last word in the measurement of learning efficiency or that no further work is required. Rather the LETB offers a useable tool here and now, while pointing the way for future research and development.

Notes

1. *English*: English children are defined as those whose parents were born in the British Isles. These children are referred to as English, although some may well be Welsh, or Scottish either by parentage or birth.
2. *Asian*: An Asian child is defined as one whose parents or grandparents originally came from India, Pakistan or Bangladesh. Although of Asian descent, children of parents who have emigrated from East African countries in recent years were not considered as Asian and were thus not included in the sample. We are inclined to agree with Phillips that this is a 'simple and crude' way of defining ethnic membership, but nevertheless is 'a term which has currency in the field despite its vagueness' (Phillips, 1979, p. 117). Asians as thus defined (irrespective of whether they are

Indian, Pakistani or Bangladeshi) all share common linguistic and social difficulties (Schools Council, 1970).

3. *Indian*: This term refers to those children who were born to Indian parents and who had always lived in India. Neither these children nor their parents had ever left India to live abroad.
4. *ESN-M*: Children who were receiving their education in special schools designated by the Local Education Authority as Schools for the Educationally Subnormal – Mild. (For the criteria employed to recommend children to receive education in special institutions see Chazan *et al.*, 1974; Clarke and Clarke, 1974; Home Office, 1978; Mittler, 1970). With the publication of the Warnock Report (Home Office, 1978) and the new Education Act 1981 (DES 1981, 1983) the terms ESN-M and ESN-S have been replaced by children with moderate and severe learning difficulties. Since the new terminology came into vogue while the present study was more than half way through, it was therefore decided to adhere to the old and well familiar labels.
5. *Ethnic minorities*: This classifactory designation is used for all those children whose parents' original country of origin, values, patterns of thought, language, or customs, are different from the dominant culture in which they live. This term is used in preference to labels like 'culturally handicapped', 'culturally disadvantaged', or 'culturally deprived', as this classifactory terminology implies value judgements. It is unacceptable that people should use prejorative terminology because one culture differs from the dominant culture.

References

Anastasi, A. (1961), 'Psychological tests: uses and abuses', *Teachers College Record*, **62**, 389–93.

Anastasi, A. (1976), *Psychological Testing*, 4th edn (New York: Macmillan Publishing Company Inc.).

Atkinson, R. C., Hansen, D. N. (1966), 'Computer-assisted instruction in initial reading: The Stanford Project', *Reading Research Quarterly*, **2**, 5–26.

Berry, J. W. (1966), 'Temne and Eskimo perceptual skills', *International Journal of Psychology*, **1**, 207–29.

Chazan, M., Moore, T., Williams, P., Wright, J. (1974), *The Practice of Educational Psychology* (London: Longman Group Ltd).

Clarke, A. M., Clarke, A. D. B. (eds) (1974), *The Mental Deficiency: The Changing Outlook*, 3rd edn (London: Methuen).

Cooley, W. W., Lohnes, P. R. (1971), *Multivariate Data Analysis*, (New York: John Wiley).

Cronbach, L. (1977), *Educational Psychology*, 3rd edn (New York: Harcourt Brace Jovanovich).

Davis, W. M. Jr. (1971), 'Are there solutions to the problems of testing black Americans?' in M. M. Meir, 'Some answers to ethnic concerns about psychological testing in the schools', Symposium presented at the American Psychological Association, Washington DC.

Department of Education and Science (1981), *Education Act 1981*, Circular No. 8/81 (London: DES).

Department of Education and Science (1983), *Assessments and Statements of Special Educational Needs*, Circular 1/83 (London: DES).

Edwards, R. P. A., Gibbon, V. (1973), *Words Your Children Use*, (London: Burke Books).

Engelmann, S., Osborn, J., Engelmann, T. (1970), *Distar Language 1 and 2*, (Chicago: Science Research Associates).

Feuerstein, R. (1979), *The Dynamic Assessment of Retarded Performers: The Learning Potential Assessment Device, Theory, Instruments and Techniques*, (Baltimore: University Park Press).

Gagné, R. M. (1977), *The Conditions of Learning*, 3rd edn (New York: Holt, Rinehart & Winston).

Gruber, M. E., Voneche, J. (eds) (1977), *The Essential Piaget*, (New York: Basic Books).

Guilford, J. P. (1967), *The Nature of Human Intelligence*, (New York: McGraw-Hill).

Gupta, R. M. (1983), 'The assessment of the learning efficiency of Asian children', unpublished Ph.D. thesis, University of Aston, Birmingham.

Harris, D. B. (1963), *Goodenough-Harris Drawing Test Manual*, (New York: Harcourt, Brace & World, Inc.).

Hathaway, W. E., Hathaway-Theunissen, A. (1974), 'The unique contributions of Piagetian measurement to diagnosis, prognosis and research of children's mental development', paper presented at the fourth annual conference on Piaget and the Helping Professions, Los Angeles, California.

Haynes, J. M. (1971), *Educational Assessment of Immigrant Pupils*, (Slough: NFER).

Haywood, H. C., Filler, J. W., Shifman, M. A., Chateldnat, G. (1975), 'Behavioural assessment in mental retardation' in P. McReynolds (ed.), *Advances in Psychological Assessment*, vol. 3 (San Francisco: Jossey-Bass Publishers).

Hegarty, S. (1978), *Manual for the NFER Test of Learning Ability*, (individual form) (Slough: NFER).

Hegarty, S., Lucas, D. (1978), *Able to learn? The Pursuit of Culture-Fair Assessment*, (Slough: NFER).

Hilgard, E., Atkinson, B. (1967), *Introduction to Psychology*, 4th edn (New York: Harcourt, Brace and World Inc.).

Home Office (1978), *Special Educational Needs. Report of the Committee of Enquiry into the Education of Handicapped Children and Young People*, (London: HMSO).

Hudson, W. (1967), 'The study of the problem of pictorial perception among unacculturated groups', *International Journal of Psychology*, **2**, 89–107.

Inhelder, B., Piaget, J. (1964), *The Early Growth of Logic in the Child* (London: Routledge & Kegan Paul).

Inhelder, B., Sinclair, H., Bovet, M. (1974), *Learning and the Development of Cognition*, (Cambridge, Mass.: Harvard University Press).

Irvine, S. H. (1966), 'Towards a rationale for testing attainments and abilities in Africa', *British Journal of Educational Psychology*, **36**, 24–32.

Jahoda, G. (1956), 'Assessment of abstract behaviour in a non-Western culture', *Journal of Abnormal Social Psychology*, **53**, 237–43.

Jahoda, G. (1980), 'Sex and ethnic differences on a spatial-perceptual task: some hypotheses tested', *British Journal of Psychology*, **71**, 425–31.

Jensen, A. R. (1961), 'Learning abilities in Mexican-American and Anglo-American children', *California Journal of Educational Psychology*, XII, 4, 147–59.

Jensen, A. R. (1963), 'Learning ability in retarded, average and gifted children', *Merrill-Palmer Quarterly of Behaviour and Development*, **9**, 2, 123–40.

Jensen, A. R. (1967), 'The culturally disadvantaged: psychological and educational aspects', *Educational Research*, 10, 1, 4–20.

Jensen, A. R. (1969), 'Intelligence, learning ability and socioeconomic status' in S. Wiseman (ed.), *Intelligence and Ability*, 2nd edn (Harmondsworth: Penguin Books).

Jensen, A. R. (1970), 'Hierarchical theories of mental ability' in B. Dockrell (ed.), *On Intelligence* (Toronto, Ontario: Institute for Studies in Education).

Joreskog, K. G. (1971), 'Simultaneous factor analysis in several populations', *Psychometrika*, **36**, 409–26.

Joreskog, K. G., Sorbom, D. (1978), *LISREL IV User's Guide*, (Chicago: Illinois: International Educational Services).

Kirk, S. A., McCarthy, J. J., Kirk, W. D. (1976), *Examiner's Manual: Illinois Test of Psycholinguistic Abilities* (Rev. edn, Urbana, Illinois: University of Illinois Press).

Lewis, D. G. (1967), *Statistical Methods in Education*, (London: University of London Press Ltd).

Lloyd, F., Pidgeon, D. A. (1961), 'An investigation into the effects of coaching on non-verbal test material with European, Indian and African children', *British Journal of Educational Psychology*, **31**, 145–51.

Lunzer, E. A. (1973), *Recent Studies in Britain Based on the Work of Jean Piaget*, (New edn, Slough: NFER).

Lunzer, E., Dolan, T. (1977), *Making Sense*, vols 1 and 2. Report to the Social Science Research Council, Nottingham University, School of Education.

Mackenzie, A. (1980), 'Are ability tests up to standard?' *Australian Psychologist*, **15**, 3, 335–48.

Mitler, P. (ed.) (1970), *The Psychological Assessment of Mental and Physical Handicaps* (London: Methuen).

Modgil, S. (1974), *Piagetian Research: A Handbook of Recent Studies* (Windsor: NFER Publishing Company Ltd).

Modgil, S., Modgil, C. (1976), *Piagetian Research: Compilation and Commentary*, vol. IV (Windsor: NFER Publishing Company Ltd).

Modgil, S., Modgil, C. (1980), *Toward a Theory of Psychological Development* (Windsor: NFER Publishing Company Ltd).

Newland, T. E. (1973), 'Assumptions underlying psychological testing', *Journal of School Psychology*, **11**, 4, 316–22.

Nunnally, J. C. (1978), *Psychometric Theory*, 2nd edn (New York: McGraw-Hill).

Ortar, G. R. (1960), 'Improving test validity by coaching', *Educational Research*, **2**, 3, 137–42.

Paraskevopoulos, J. N., Kirk, S. A. (1969), *The Development and Psychometric Characteristics of the Revised Illinois Test of Psycholinguistic Abilities*, (Urbana: University of Illinois Press).

Phillips, C. J. (1979), 'Educational underachievement in different ethnic groups', *Educational Research*, **21**, 116–30.

Raven, J. C. (1962), *Guide to Using the Coloured Progressive Matrices*, (London: H. K. Lewis & Company).

Reschly, D. J. (1984), 'Beyond IQ test bias: the National Academy Panel's analysis of minority EMR over-representation', *Educational Researcher*.

Schonell, F. J. (1951), *Diagnostic and Attainment Testing*, (Edinburgh: Oliver & Boyd).

Schools Council (1970), *Immigrant Children in Infant Schools*, Working Paper 31, (London: Evans/Methuen).

Schwarz, P. A. (1961), *Aptitude Tests for Use in Developing Nations* (Pittsburgh: American Institute for Research).

Schwebel, M., Raph, J. (1974), *Piaget in the Classroom*, (London: Routledge & Kegan Paul).

Scott, G. C. (1950), 'Measuring Sudanese intelligence', *British Journal of Educational Psychology*, **20**, 43–54.

Silvey, J. (1963), 'Aptitude testing and educational selection in Africa', *Rhodes Livingstone Journal*, **34**, 9–22.

Thorndike, R. L., Hagen, E. P. (1969), *Measurement and Evaluation in Psychology and Education*, (New York: John Wiley).

Thorndike, E. L., Lorge, I. (1944), *The Teacher's Word Book of 30,000 Words*, (New York: Teacher's College, Columbia University).

Toepher, C. (1981), in C. Cookson, 'Learning is linked to spurts in development of brain', *TES*, 15 May.

Tomlinson, S. (1981), *Special Education*, (London: Harper & Row).

Vernon, P. E., Miller, K. M. (1976), *Graded Arithmetic-Mathematics Test*, Metric edn (Sevenoaks: Hodder and Stoughton).

Wadsworth, B. J. (1978), *Piaget for the Classroom Teacher* (New York: Longman).

Winter, W. (1963), 'The perception of safety posters by Bantu industrial workers', *Psychology Africana*, **10**, 127–35.

Wober, M. (1967), 'Adapting Witkin's field independence theory to accommodate new information from Africa', *British Journal of Psychology*, **58**, 29–38.

Woodward, W. M. (1970), 'The assessment of cognitive processes: Piaget's approach' in P. Mittler (ed.), *The Psychological Assessment of Mental and Physical Handicaps*, (London: Tavistock Publications).

Woodworth, R. W., Schlosberg, H. (1954), *Experimental Psychology*, (Rev. edn Calcutta: Oxford & IBH Publishing Company).

Ysseldyke, J. E., Salvia, J. (1974), 'Diagnostic prescriptive teaching: two models', *Exceptional Children*, **41**, 181–5.

7 Non-intellective Factors in Dynamic Assessment[1]

David Tzuriel, Marilyn T. Samuels and Reuven Feuerstein

The assessment of non-intellective factors in a test situation is of critical importance for the understanding of a child's test performance as well as for explaining learning difficulties in school and in everyday activities. Elaborated theories have referred to the relationship between intellectual development and various aspects of motivation and personality (Harter, 1978, 1980; Hunt, 1965; McClelland, 1961; White, 1959). Many investigators have related cognitive development and scholastic achievement to intrinsic motivation (Haywood, 1971; Haywood and Burke, 1975), competence motivation (Harter, 1980), locus of control (Stipek and Weisz, 1981; Findley and Cooper, 1983), achievement motivation (Alschuler, 1973; McClelland, 1961) and anxiety (Kirkland, 1971). Surprisingly, however, research on the effects of various non-intellective factors on test performance is scarce especially in the area of dynamic assessment of cognitive performance.

The purpose of this paper is to illuminate the effects of non-intellective factors on test performance and to suggest some ways of modifying their effect during a dynamic assessment procedure. We will refer specifically to the Learning Potential Assessment Device (LPAD), a dynamic approach developed by Feuerstein, Rand and Hoffman (1979).

A brief review of the literature on the effects of non-intellective factors on test performance is presented. This is followed by an introduction to Feuerstein's theoretical and practical approach to assessment of cognitive functioning. A discussion of the examiner–examinee interactions will then be presented followed by a section on the assessment and modification of specific non-intellective factors during dynamic assessment. Finally, some critical Mediated Learning Experience (MLE) criteria that affect non-intellective factors will be discussed.

REVIEW OF LITERATURE

Scarr (1981) argued that any measurement of cognitive functioning also involves measurement of non-intellective factors such as co-operation, attention, persistence and social responsiveness to the testing situation. In fact, Scarr suggests that calling intelligence tests cognitive is misleading because it implies that the non-intellective factors play little role in learning and performance. She suggests that such assessments be referred to as tests of competence as competence is considered to be a more inclusive term for learning and motivation. Zigler and his associates (Zigler and Butterfield, 1968; Zigler, Abelson and Seitz, 1973) have questioned the assumption that the IQ test score is a relatively pure measure of formal aspects of the child's cognitive structure. Zigler and Butterfield (1968) have argued that performance on an intelligence test reflects three distinct factors: cognitive processes, academic achievement unrelated to formal cognitive properties, and motivational factors which involve a wide range of personality variables.

The effects of non-intellective factors on test performance are especially important in assessment of minority groups and retarded performers. Intelligence and other aptitude tests have long been criticised for ignoring the effects of cultural and personality-motivational factors on cognitive performance. Most of the criticism has been related to intelligence test bias against minority groups and culturally deprived and retarded performers (Feuerstein, Rand and Hoffman, 1979; Hilliard, 1979; Mercer, 1973; Reynolds, 1982, 1983; Williams, 1974; Zigler, Balla and Hodapp, 1984). Early works of Zigler and others conclude that children who have suffered negative experiences develop a wariness in interactions with strange adults (Atema, Samle, van Lieshart and Hartup, 1972; Harter and Zigler, 1968; McCoy and Zigler, 1965; Weaver, Balla and Zigler, 1971; Zigler, 1971). As an example Zigler *et al.* (1984) describe a retarded child who has long been shunned and consequently developed feelings of uselessness and high needs for social approval. In testing situations, such a child may be involved in non-task activities such as getting the tester's attention instead of attending to meaningful, task-relevant behaviour. Because of repeated failures, the child might also develop 'learned helplessness' (Seligman, 1975) and not even attempt to solve challenging problems. It should be emphasised that these behaviours observed in test situations may be indicative of behaviour in other situations such as the classroom and hence, further affect learning and performance.

Many children from low socio-economic backgrounds exhibit such wariness in test situations. It has also been shown that this wariness can be overcome if the child learns that the stranger is a non-punishing and/or socially reinforcing person. Other studies have found that culturally deprived children are more motivated toward securing the tester's attention and praise (Stevenson and Fahel, 1961; Zigler, 1963) and less motivated to answer correctly for the sake of correctness alone (Terrell, Durkin and Wiesley, 1959; Zigler and deLabry, (1962). It has also been found that children who lack confidence in their own intellectual abilities tend to rely on concrete situational cues emitted by their examiners rather than on making efforts to form a principle or abstract the required solution (Achenbach and Zigler, 1968; Balla, Styfco and Zigler, 1971; Yando and Zigler, 1971; Zigler and Yando, 1972).

Zigler and Butterfield (1968) presented evidence indicating that the increase found in Stanford-Binet IQ scores following a compensatory education programme was due to the adverse effects of motivational factors on performance during pre-testing rather than to any real change in the children's rate of intellectual development per se. In another study, Zigler, Abelson and Seitz (1973) demonstrated, using the Peabody Picture Vocabulary Test, that disadvantaged children's IQ scores increased 10 points after being retested within a 1–2 week period under typical testing conditions. This finding supports Eisenberg and Connors[2] suggestion that Peabody IQ gains found at the end of a short summer Head Start programme were due to motivational changes rather than real improvement in cognitive functioning. Other findings reported by Zigler *et al.* (1973) suggest that IQ scores of disadvantaged children were underestimates of their cognitive competence as a result of situational wariness. The initial IQ scores became significantly higher when testing was conducted after a pleasant play period.

Deutsch, Fishman, Kogan, North and Whiteman (1964) noted that low socio-economic children as compared to middle-class children, tended to be more fearful of strangers, less self confident, less competitive in the intellectual realm, more 'irritable' and less conforming to middle-class norms. These children may achieve low scores on IQ tests just because they dislike the test's context and because they do not find any relevance to their lives. Feuerstein *et al.* (1979) have strongly emphasised the adverse effects of affective-motivational factors on various phases (input, elaboration, output) of the mental act.

In contrast to other dynamic approaches, Feuerstein *et al.* (1979) presented a comprehensive, systematic and theoretically anchored approach not only for controlling the adverse effects of non-intellective factors on test performance but also for modifying them so that their effects can be separated from cognitive factors.

FEUERSTEIN'S LEARNING POTENTIAL ASSESSMENT DEVICE (LPAD)

Feuerstein's dynamic assessment approach is based on the theory of structural cognitive modifiability (SCM), and the theory of Mediated Learning Experience (Feuerstein, Rand, Hoffman and Miller, 1980). They argue that human organisms have the unique capacity to modify their cognitive functioning in significant ways and to adapt to changing demands in life situations. Feuerstein described three main characteristics that define structural cognitive modifiability: permanence, pervasiveness, and centrality. Permanence refers to the endurance of the cognitive changes across time and space. Pervasiveness is related to a 'diffusion' process in which changes in a part affect the whole. Centrality reflects the self-perpetuating, autonomous, and self-regulating nature of cognitive modifiability. The basic assumptions of the SCM theory are that (a) a human organism is an open system amenable to cognitive changes that affect its functioning, and (b) that cognitive modifiability is best explained by the Mediated Learning Experience (MLE, Feuerstein *et al.*, 1980).

MLE refers to an interactional process in which an adult, usually the parent, intentionally interposes himself between the child and the world and modifies a set of stimuli by affecting its intensity, context, frequency and order, while at the same time arousing in the child a vigilance, awareness and sensitivity to the mediated stimulus. The mediator creates for and with the child temporal, spatial and causal relationships among stimuli. Stimuli that were previously perceived in an episodic, random way become, after successful mediation, more meaningful. The effects of MLE go beyond the immediate situation and are transferred to other situations in terms of time, space and context. Feuerstein has suggested ten criteria of interactional activities that characterise MLE (Feuerstein, Hoffman, Jensen and Rand, 1985). These criteria will be discussed later in relation to the intervention strategies used for modifying non-intellective factors during a dynamic assessment.

Dynamic assessment refers to an approach in which processes of thinking, perception, learning and problem-solving are assessed through an active teaching process aimed at modifying the individual's cognitive functioning. In contrast to the conventional psychometric approach, in which the goal is to measure the manifest level of performance relative to a representative sample of other individuals, the LPAD is geared towards producing changes within the individual during the testing situation and assessing ability to learn and change relative to their own initial level.

The dynamic assessment of learning potential requires that four essential changes be made with respect to current psychometric techniques: (a) a shift from a product to a process orientation; (b) modification of the test structure; (c) change in the test situation; and (d) a shift in focus for interpretation of results. A detailed account of these changes as well as specific goals, procedures, techniques, instruments and mediational processes are discussed elsewhere (Feuerstein *et al.*, 1979; Feuerstein, Rand, Haywood, Hoffman and Jensen[3]). While all four changes relate to the assessment of non-intellective factors during dynamic assessment, for the purpose of this discussion we will emphasise the one most essential change – the test situation. In particular, we will discuss changes in the traditional examiner–examinee relationship that are critical for assessing the effects of non-intellective factors.

The examiner – examinee relationship

In the standard psychometric assessment, the examiner assumes a neutral role with the child. Standardised instructions generally allow only limited feedback, and questions of increasing difficulty are asked until the child has experienced a certain number of consecutive failures. No matter how well the child performs they fail by the end of each subtest. This situation does not generally engage the child nor does it give rise to exploratory or intrinsic motivation. According to Hunt (1965), exploratory behaviour and intrinsic motivation are largely dependent on the experienced incongruity between the child's schemata and the novel information he is exposed to. Without feedback, it is difficult for the child to understand the meaning of the incongruous situation, and such situations may give rise instead to feelings of failure, and avoidance behaviour. For children who lack confidence due to repeated failure, a standard test situation can create anxiety and lead to a lowered level of motivation.

Feuerstein *et al.* (1979) differentiated among three sources of reduced motivation: (a) deficiencies in the prerequisite cognitive conditions needed for arousal of motivation; (b) deficiencies in the need system that would endow cognitive tasks with specific meaning; and (c) an avoidance reaction to tasks that have been associated with repeated experiences of failure. The latter two sources serve to reduce motivation in standard assessment. The importance given by the psychometric approach to the motivational-emotional factors and to the examiner–examinee relationships seems to be rather casual in view of their determining weight. The neutral and even unsympathetic approach which characterises the examiner in standardised test situations does not encourage motivation or feelings of competence. The child's fragmentary grasp of the instructions and the lack of task-intrinsic motivation lead to either vague and imprecise ways of dealing with the presented problems, accompanied by a low level of anxiety and a tuning out of the examiner, or to feelings of threat, low expectations for success and a high level of anxiety.

The apparent lack of interest in the child's success by the examiner might be interpreted by the examinee in one of two ways, both leading to negative reactions: (a) the child might say to himself 'If it doesn't matter to you, why should I care what I do'; or (b) the examiner's neutrality might be interpreted as a manifestation of hostility and an expectation of failure. The result might be a decrease in motivation with lack of expectation for success, and even hostility. Even the examiner's attempts to appear less neutral by smiles and encouragement, might be perceived as insincere, given the lack of feedback as to success and failure, which is what the child really wants to know.

The LPAD test situation differs radically from the conventional psychometric situation in many ways, including the goals, extent and quality of examiner–examinee interaction, their expected roles and the mediational processes used during assessment. The neutral, indifferent role of the examiner is changed into an active, co-operative, teacher–pupil relationship in which the examiner is mainly concerned about the child's success. The examiner, who is totally engaged in the activity, intervenes by making remarks, restraining impulsivity, focusing and preparing the child for difficult problems, requiring the child to give explanations and justification, summing up experiences, and creating reflective, insightful thinking.

The accomplishment of these mediational processes requires that the examiner be alert and sensitive to the examinee's reactions. The examiner conveys to the examinee the feeling that the task is difficult but yet manageable, and that the child is capable of doing the task. The examiner uses various meditional procedures to facilitate feelings of competence, enthusiasm, challenge and interest in the learned material. The result of such an active teaching process is often a change in the child's willingness to attempt tasks. A shift from an extrinsic orientation aimed at pleasing the examiner to a task-intrinsic orientation is often observed during dynamic assessment. The intrinsic motivation is manifested by the child's independent efforts to explore more advanced tasks and the desire to continue to solve problems even during a break. The children begin to show clear signs of pleasure and satisfaction when they grasp the meaning of a problem and begin to obtain some insight into their problem-solving ability.

Feuerstein *et al.* (1979) mentioned that the motivational shift is produced by two factors. The first factor is related to the individual's increased capacity to perceive the nature of the task by integrating a series of criteria at the end of which the tasks he is confronted with become problems to be solved. Second, the child develops a positive approach towards problem solving through increased mastery of tasks. The progressively increasing complexity of tasks in the LPAD immediately raises the child's need to repeat the experience. This repetition has a functional value in consolidating the successful pattern of behaviour and in raising the aspiration level. The shift in motivational pattern is often manifested by the independent activity of the child, which continues after the examiner has finished giving instructions or active teaching. Very often, the examiner manipulates the situation in order to assess the motivational change. The examiner may do this either by withdrawing from participation for a few minutes or by purposely engaging in another activity (e.g., making a telephone call).

It should be noted that the motivational shift is not sufficient to make the examinee's problem-solving behaviour more successful and efficient. Specific feedback regarding performance that transcends the immediate task must also be provided using a variety of communicational modalities. In the static psychometric situation, feedback is not given and the child does not have an opportunity to correct his error. Feedback on items in tests whose structure does not allow inter-item dependency has negative implications for future items. Even if the child is shown how and why he failed, he gains little or nothing that will help him to cope with subsequent items. In the dynamic LPAD situation, on the other hand, feedback is an integral part of the assessment process. The whole spectrum of the child's performance – from the beginning phase of information gathering to strategies of processing information to the final phase of communicating a response efficiently – are commented upon and assisted where necessary. Feedback is not limited to the correction of deficient cognitive functions, the regulation of behaviour (i.e., inhibition of impulsivity), enrichment of mental operations, task-related content, and meta-cognitive strategies, but also to motivational, temperamental, and behavioural characteristics that affect thought processes and performance.

It is our conviction that the examiner–examinee relationship, and the test situation as described above are critical for the assessment of modifiability of both intellective and non-intellective factors in children with learning problems. In the next section, we will discuss frequently observed non-intellective factors that have been found through clinical experience to be crucial in determining the child's performance in a test situation.

SPECIFIC NON-INTELLECTIVE FACTORS

Extensive clinical experience using dynamic assessment procedures has led to the determination of a list of non-intellective factors that need to be identified, controlled and modified in order to adequately assess cognitive performance. Some of these factors have been mentioned previously in the literature in relation to academic and cognitive functioning, whereas others are unique to the dynamic test situation.

Some motivational, affective and personality dimensions can be observed during standard testing (e.g. high need for social approval, anxiety, alienation and apathy, avoidance and fear of failure). These observations, however, are only glimpses of the actual motivational and personality dynamics that are interwoven with the cognitive processes. Indications of motivational and personality patterns are based on rather limited samples of behaviour and there are few opportunities for dynamic, transactional, examiner–examinee relations with all the concomitant, rich information that they provide. The assessment of non-intellective factors in a dynamic testing procedure is of significance not only as an explanation of the child's test performance and school learning, but also for evaluating changes in motivational patterns and effective intervention strategies. One of the most important aims of dynamic testing is to assess the extent to which the various non-intellective factors are modifiable.

Accessibility to mediation

Accessibility to mediation can only be observed in dynamic assessment, but is seen often by teachers in the classroom. Lack of accessibility to mediation is manifested by the child's resistance to accept mediational efforts, either by actively rejecting the examiner's attempts to teach or by passively withdrawing from the situation. Very often, the reason for a lack of accessibility to mediation is related to previous negative experiences with a mediator (i.e., parent or teacher). Some children have been exposed to over-mediation from an adult who has tried desperately to teach the child things that were above his level or to inappropriate mediation by an adult who used ineffective teaching strategies. It is interesting to note that sometimes bright, competitive children have difficulty accepting mediation as they interpret it as a sign of their failure to independently cope with the problems. A lack of accessibility to mediation is observed most often in children who, for various reasons, experienced threat or failure in their interactions with a mediator and generalise this negative situation to the test situation. Lack of accessibility to mediation also may derive from some specific emotional factor that is associated with the learned content. The examiner's role in dynamic testing is to observe this phenomena and to intervene in ways that will allow the child to be more accepting of the examiner's mediation.

Need for mastery

Need for mastery is one of the most important factors determining test results as well as school achievement. Different concepts have been used to refer to need for mastery such as intrinsic motivation (Hunt, 1965; Haywood, 1971; Deci, 1975), competence or effectence motivation (Harter, 1981; White, 1959), curiosity (Maw and Maw, 1970), and exploratory behaviour (Berlyne, 1960; Day, 1971; Nunnally and Lemond, 1973). The need for mastery or intrinsic motivation has been intensively investigated in relation to school achievement (Haywood, 1968, 1971; Haywood and Burke, 1975), effects of extrinsic rewards (Lepper, 1980), and parental child-rearing practices (Baumrind, 1971).

Scarr (1981) suggested that cognitive competence is a result of a 'motivationally determined history of learning', and that motivation and cognition are so intimately related that they form a general competence factor. The need for mastery is defined for our purpose as the individual's striving to cope effectively with cognitive tasks. Operationally, in a testing situation it might be expressed by the examinee's persistence on a task, his attempts to work independently, without the examiner's help, his pleasure when he finds a solution and experiences progress, and his willingness to continue to work on other tasks that are not related to the previous task. The child's need for mastery can be inferred either by an unobtrusive observation of his spontaneous behaviour, by manipulating the test context to examine changes in mastery behaviour or by directly asking the child about his feelings, his wish to continue working on tasks, and his level of aspiration for more difficult problems.

In examining the initial level of need for mastery as well as its modification, one should consider three components that account for actual behaviour: (1) the child's inner resources and characteristics with which he comes to the situation, (2) the examiner's approach, and (3) the nature of the test. Arousal of a need for mastery is usually accomplished by assisting the child to achieve a high level of success, optimising the level of task difficulty while gradually changing its level of complexity, and by using feedback processes aimed at increasing the child's need for challenge, curiosity, exploration and interest. The child's need for mastery cannot be totally separated from the examiner's approach. A sensitive examiner who 'feels' the child's lack of interest can energise the child, focus his attention, confront him with challenges and direct him towards task-intrinsic motivation. Very often, a child's need for mastery is a direct result of the examiner's interest and approach. A passive, apathetic examiner may cause a child to adopt a similar attitude, whereas an enthusiastic examiner can trigger the child's curiosity and achievement needs.

The specific task being used is one of the most important factors in assessment of the child's motivation. For many children, an impaired need for mastery is task-specific and related to previous failures on similar tasks or to difficulties with the operations required by the task. Thus, a different motivational reaction might be shown towards tasks that require analogical thinking, than to tasks that require logical multiplication or hypothetical, probabilistic thinking. Again, it is the examiner's role to modify the child's negative reactions, showing him that even initially 'despised' tasks can be mastered and eventually enjoyed. This modification of the child's attitude is usually managed by transcending the immediate meaning as to the significance of the task (see discussion of MLE categories in the next section).

Frustration tolerance

Frustration tolerance in a dynamic testing context is related to the individual's ability to delay the immediate gratification of finding a quick solution to a problem and being willing to work persistently, even when no clue for a solution is in sight. For some individuals, situations with many unknowns, and problems that require consideration of complex information or conscious mental effort trigger feelings of frustration and anger. The child's frustration tolerance may be expressed by giving up easily after experiencing difficulty, or showing signs of anger when asked to solve another task or to explain and elaborate on an answer. The role of the examiner is to control and 'soften' the child's frustration by ensuring high rates of success, by preparing the child for difficult items and by using various therapeutic procedures. The tester might, for example, tell the child that the way in which he reaches the answer and the attempts he makes are more important than the solution itself. He might also empathise with the child's difficulties, but nevertheless convey to him his belief that he can overcome them. Feelings of success are insured on LPAD tasks as the examiner intervenes to assist the child to use effective problem solving strategies. Incorrect responses are discussed and problems reattempted until a correct solution is reached.

Locus of control

Locus of control (LOC) refers to the individual's perception of himself as responsible for the outcome of his behaviour and for control over life events (Rotter, 1966; Lefcourt, 1976; Phares, 1976). Individuals who feel responsible for things that happen to them (internal LOC) are usually contrasted with those who feel that the outcome of their life is beyond their control (external LOC). The LOC, however, is considered to be a continuous variable with enduring dispositional characteristics, though modifiable, through experience. The literature is replete with evidence showing that perceived control of events is an important determinant of children's academic achievement (see reviews of Findley and Cooper, 1983; Stipek and Weisz, 1981).

Indications of external LOC in a dynamic assessment situation are manifested by the child's sporadic responses, persistent guessing behaviour, passive approach towards problem solution, reliance on task-extrinsic rewards, and expressed surprise about a successful answer.

The examiner attempts to modify this attitudinal orientation by repeatedly showing the child that his correct answers results from his using principles and strategies for solving problems rather than from guessing and chance. It is a common procedure in dynamic assessment to discuss the child's performance, and compare his answers on early tasks to more advanced tasks. After a process of learning, in which the child realises the tasks' difficulty and the successful consequences of those efforts, a change in his LOC is often observed. This is indicated by greater activity, involvement, tendency to rely on task-intrinsic sources of information, and even frustration with self as opposed to blaming others when a mistake is made.

Fear of failure and defensiveness

One of the most debilitating factors in learning and performance is fear of failure and defensiveness. According to Atkinson's conceptualisation (Atkinson, 1964), the need for achievement is separate from avoidance of failure. Both variables, however, interact to determine the level of performance in achievement test situations and risk-taking behaviour. According to Atkinson's theoretical model, both approach and avoidance motivation are influenced by the balance between need for achievement and avoidance of failure, no matter the level of difficulty of the task.

Fear of failure and defensiveness are especially aroused in tasks which remind the child of previous failures, or which seem to be too complicated to deal with. According to the LPAD model, the first tasks presented on each subtest are relatively simple and gradually become more complex. The examiner reinforces the child's performance with specific feedback about what the child did that led to success. This helps him to overcome his fears. It is not unusual to see children who initially approached the tasks very defensively, become less defensive and more willing to take the risk of making hypotheses and entering novel situations.

Confidence in correct responses

Confidence in a correct response refers to the child believing the answer given is correct even when challenged or asked to explain his answer. Uncertainty and lack of confidence might be the result of a lack of crystallisation of the learned material but very often it is related to emotional-attitudinal variables which have little to do with the child's cognition. Some children have great difficulty relying on their inner resources and perceiving themselves as competent generators of information. They may cope successfully with a complex abstract task and reach a correct solution. However, when asked to explain their solution or to give some evidence or justification, they indicate a lack of confidence and change their answer. This particular factor is not easily observed in standardised assessment as the examiner does not question responses. It is an important factor to be aware of however, in both testing and teaching situations, as a lack of confidence in correct performance may be indicative of low self esteem. It may also reflect an outer directedness and dependence on the examiner. The examiner can encourage the child to develop confidence by systematically asking the child to justify answers and by providing specific feedback. For example, when a child gives a correct answer, the examiner might ask 'Are you sure?' The insecure child will doubt his answer initially and even change it to what he thinks the examiner wants or revert to trial and error responding. However, with repeated cognitive analyses of the answers as well as metacognitive explanations, the child will become more confident and consequently more efficient in performance.

Vitality and alertness

Vitality and alertness refer to the level of activity, energy, vividness, attentiveness and interest the child shows in the interaction with the examiner. It is judged subjectively and requires a certain amount of experience with different types of children. While vitality and alertness can be observed during any assessment session, the ease with which this factor can be modified is best ascertained during dynamic assessment. Some children who begin the assessment with an apathetic lifeless approach and a lack of attention and interest, gradually become enthusiastic as they observe their success in solving difficult tasks. This is manifested by an increased willingness to invest effort, an increased responsiveness to humorous remarks, more relaxed body language and greater mental alertness. It should be noted that some children show very little sign of change in their level of vitality and alertness in spite of their success and the examiner's efforts to arouse them, whereas others show much vitality right from the beginning. Vitality and alertness do not necessarily correlate with other non-intellective factors. Children with high vitality and energy might show external locus of control or fear of failure and lack confidence in correct responses.

CRITERIA OF MLE AND NON-INTELLECTIVE FACTORS

Mediated learning experiences begin at the very earliest stage of development in interaction between an adult or older child and the infant. The mediational processes are accomplished during infancy by non-verbal means but, with development, these processes rely increasingly on verbal and symbolic representation. Above and beyond the specific operations undertaken by the adult in a particular situation, there are three essential criteria that define mediated learning interactions: (1) intentionality, (2) transcendence, and (3) meaning. These criteria, operating in conjunction with one another, are always necessary for an interaction to be considered mediated learning as opposed to direct exposure learning. Other criteria of MLE suggested by Feuerstein are: (4) mediation for the regulation of behaviour, (5) mediation for feelings of competence, (6) mediation for sharing behaviour, (7) mediation for individuation and psychological differentiation, (8) mediation for seeking, setting and achieving of goals, (9) mediation for challenge, and (10) mediation for modifiability (Feuerstein *et al.*, 1985). The description of each criterion will be presented next, followed by a discussion of their use in dynamic testing and their effect on various non-intellective factors.

1. *Intentionality*

Interactions characterised by intentionality are those in which the mediator produces a state of vigilance in the learner as evidenced by the increased sharpness and acuity of perception. Intentionality, which can be observed at a very early age in dyadic interactions between the mother and the child, is marked by many signs of mutuality. The mutuality aspect of the interaction is conceptualised as essential for the development of basic feelings of competence and self-determination. Interactions imbued with mutual intentionality assist the child to realise that his actions determine other people's behaviour. The development of the individual's organismic belief that he is the agent of change depends to a large degree on the repetitive interactions of mutual intentionality.

2. *Transcendence*

Transcendence refers to both the character and the goal of MLE interactions. The objective of MLE is to transcend the immediate needs and specific situation and reach out for goals that might have nothing to do with the original activity. For example, a mediator who asks a child to count the number of objects in a game or plan a trip might use this occasion to develop summative behaviour or planning ability. Transcendence depends to a large degree on the intentionality of the mediator. However, when intentionality exists, transcendence becomes a powerful modality for the development and widening of the individual's need system.

3. *Mediation for meaning*

The importance of meaning has long been recognised as a powerful determinant in efficient learning processes (Ausubel, 1968; Postman and Weingartner, 1969). The stimuli that are presented to the child in MLE interactions are not neutral but possess affective, motivational, and value-oriented significance. In later stages of development, the child begins to actively provide meaning to newly-acquired information rather than passively waiting for meaning to come.

4. *Mediation for regulation of behaviour*

In mediation for regulation of behaviour, the mediator controls the rhythm of the child's behaviour by reducing his impulsivity or by speeding up his activity, thus facilitating his efficiency. The introduction of a different rhythm is carried out either by modelling or, more explicitly, by providing metacognitive strategies and by analysing the pattern of responses.

5. *Mediation for competence*

The mediator conveys to the child that he is capable of functioning independently and successfully. Opportunities are organised so that they lead to success, and reasons for success or failure are interpreted to develop feelings of competence and achievement.

6. *Mediation of sharing behaviour*

Sharing behaviour both determines and is determined by the quality of the affective relationship between the child and his/her primary objects of love and attachment. Sharing behaviour represents the energetic principle of MLE which enables the adult to transmit to the child the information he intends to mediate. Mediation of sharing behaviour starts at a very early age with mother–infant eye contact, and develops later in different types of play activities, common experiences, and affective interactions. Sharing behaviour is considered to be the spear head of mediation, due to its emotional quality which ensures the effectiveness of the mediational efforts.

7. *Mediation for individuation and psychological differentiation*

In contrast to mediation of sharing behaviour, the mediation for individuation and psychological differentiation is focused on the child's capacity to differentiate himself from the mediating agents and to create a psychological distance which is so important in the development of individuation and identity formation processes. The mediation for individuation is carried out by encouraging the child to take several perspectives in the perception of an event, by emphasising the child's needs as separate and independent from the adult's needs, and by encouraging the expression of drives, needs and wishes.

8. *Mediation for goal seeking*

In mediation for goal seeking, the mediator encourages the child to set up goals, dissociating between means and goals. Selection of a behavioural path is dictated by the degree to which it is helpful in attaining a specific goal. Goal seeking is characterised very often by awareness, and is contingent upon the individual's needs, values, and attitudes. The mediator usually provides a positive valence to the selected goal and ascribes meaning to it. Mediated seeking of goals and purposeful behaviour goes beyond the individual's cyclic basic needs. It is related to higher order needs for self-actualisation (Maslow, 1968) and ego identity development (Erikson, 1968), and is characterised among other things by commitment and purposefulness (Marcia, 1980; Tzuriel, 1984).

9. *Mediation for challenge*

Mediation for challenge is manifested by seeking novel and complex tasks. Complexity and novelty are among the 'collative variables' suggested by Berlyne (1960) as determinants of psychological arousal and curiosity. Mediation for challenge coupled with mediation for competence are prerequisites for the child's willingness to embark on an adventurous course of action, to take risks, expose himself to the unfamiliar, and overcome feelings of insecurity and anxiety generated by novel tasks, complex instructions, and incongruent conditions.

10. *Mediation for modifiability*

Mediation for modifiability characterises interactions in which the adult inculcates in the child the need to modify his cognitive functioning, not as a means for some definite goal, but rather for its own sake. This is carried out either by modelling or more directly when the significance of learning and developing for self-fulfillment is presented as an ideal. The conception of striving for modifiability is similar to the humanistic conception of becoming (Maslow, 1968; May, 1967; Rogers 1961) in that both perceive the individual as being in a continual process of change and enhancement. The concept of striving for modifiability, however, is more specific and focused on changes in the cognitive system, with possible ramifications to other realms of functioning.

Application of MLE criteria in dynamic assessment

The MLE criteria serve as guidelines for modification of various non-intellective factors during dynamic assessment. The development of the non-intellective factors is determined partially by the nature and extent of the mediational processes in the formative years. Factors such as accessibility to mediation, need for mastery, frustration tolerance, and confidence in correct responses are conceived by us as critically influenced by the type of mediational processes. It is, therefore, the role of the examiner in dynamic assessment to use MLE criteria to assess the modifiability of the various non-intellective factors that affect cognitive performance taking into account, of course, the test situation and the nature of the tasks.

The examiner's efforts to engage the examinee in a mutual process of intentional interaction acts as a 'booster' in arousing the child's attentiveness, alertness, and vividness. The examinee's realisation that his responses are taken seriously for mutual analysis and that his mistakes are not overlooked but rather used for further understanding of his thinking process lead to development of feelings of self-determination and consequently to a need for mastery, internal locus of control, accessibility to mediation, tolerance for frustration and greater confidence in correct responses.

Mediation for transcendence and for meaning is carried out by showing the child how a particular approach is important not only for solving a specific task but also for dealing with future tasks both on the test and in various life situations. For example, systematic and accurate gathering of information and careful planning are important not only for solving an analogy, copying a complex figure, and analysing a three-dimensional stimulus but also for buying a house, planning to build a bridge, and going shopping. Mediation of meaning is characterised by assisting the child to realise that the fragmentary bits of information perceived in a piecemeal way make sense as a whole and that they are related to his previous experience. By encouraging the use of metacognitive strategies, the child becomes aware of how certain patterns of behaviour contribute to his cognitive difficulties.

A strategy used frequently with children is to role play a teacher–student situation in which the child takes the teacher's role. Previous studies have shown that students who learned in order to teach (Benware and Deci, 1984) or actually tutored (Goldschmid, 1970) were more intrinsically motivated than students who learned in order to be tested. The demands on the child in a role play situation are related to mediation of sharing behaviour, mediation for individuation, and mediation for challenge. During dynamic assessment, the examiner mediates for sharing, individuation and challenge by requiring the child to play an active role in explaining how to solve problems and in justifying solutions. The examiner may present an alternative approach and discuss with the child which approach works best and why. Sometimes the child's solution is the preferred one. The child also observes the examiner modelling effective (and sometimes ineffective) problem solving and realises that the examiner must also work systematically and carefully to arrive at the correct solution.

The structure of the tasks in the LPAD is an important element in providing opportunities for mediation. The tasks are structured so that each initial activity brings about success and leads to tasks increasing in their level of complexity and novelty. This allows for mediation for competence, and mediation for challenge, in particular. The combination of the mediational strategies and the test structure, which is unique to the LPAD, is very powerful in modifying the non-intellective factors. The progress in solving the cognitive tasks which gradually become more difficult coupled with the examiner's encouragement and sometimes his enthusiasm and his specific feedback is experienced by the child as real competence rather than mere words or 'reinforcements' aimed at manipulating the child's feelings and motivation. In other words, the simultaneous experience of increasing task difficulty, real progress, and specific feedback, interpreted as growing competence has a strong effect on the whole spectrum of non-intellective factors.

It is important to note that while one can begin to modify non-intellective factors during dynamic assessment through MLE, such changes are temporary. Feelings of incompetence, lack of confidence, fear of failure, etc., are well ingrained attitudes and cannot be changed by a few testing sessions. However, the degree of modifiability observed during the assessment is indicative of the type and amount of intervention that will be needed to make a more permanent change.

SUMMARY

It is apparent that there is a need for research on the transactional relationship between MLE criteria and various non-intellective factors both generally and more specifically in dynamic assessment. A cause and effect relationship in which MLE is the sole determinant of the non-intellective factors cannot be assumed. It is plausible that some non-intellective factors within the child dictate the particular MLE procedures chosen by the mediator. For example, a mediator might choose mediation for regulation of behaviour and mediation for competence more frequently than other MLE criteria when working with a child with low frustration tolerance, as determined previously by temperamental characteristics. An initial fruitful approach for studying the transactional relationship would be the development of an observational technique in which a sequence of children's behaviours and adult's mediational strategies are recorded and analysed. The pattern of interaction might illuminate characteristic sequences at various points in development. The mediational strategies could also be experimentally manipulated with children previously known to exhibit specific non-intellective factors in order to examine the effect of different mediational strategies on these factors.

In summary, it has long been known that non-intellective factors play a role in learning and performance but standardised tests have paid little attention to their effect. The LPAD, a dynamic assessment approach developed by Feuerstein and his colleagues provides opportunities to assess and modify non-intellective factors and to separate the relative effect of these factors from other cognitive factors on performance.

Seven non-intellective factors, observed through clinical experience with the LPAD are discussed. The ten criteria for mediated learning experience are also discussed as they define the type of intervention used in dynamic assessment and have differential effects on the modification of the non-intellective factors.

Notes

1. The authors gratefully acknowledge Social Sciences Humanities Research Council, Canada (grant no. 410–84–0034–R2), for their support of this project and the many people at the Hadassah-WIZO-Canada Research Institute and the Learning Centre who contributed to it.
2. Eisenberg, L., Connors, C. K. (1966), 'The effect of Head Start on developmental processes', presented at the Joseph P. Kennedy, Jr. Foundation Scientific Symposium on Mental Retardation, Baltimore.
3. Feuerstein, R., Rand, Y., Haywood, H. C., Hoffman, M. B., Jensen, M. R. (1986), *LPAD – Learning Potential Assessment Device*: Manual (Hadassah-WIZO-Canada-Research Institute, Jerusalem).

References

Achenbach, T., Zigler, E. (1968), 'Cue-learning and problem-learning strategies in normal and retarded children', *Child Development*, **39**, 827–48.

Alschuler, A. S. (1973), *Developing achievement motivation in adolescents*, (Englewood Cliffs, N.J.: Educational Technology Publications).

Ausubel, D. P. (1968), *Educational psychology: A cognitive view*, (New York: Delta Book).

Atema, J. M., Samle, T. G., van Lieshart, K. F. M., Hartup, W. C. (1972), 'Age of subject, type of social contact, and responsiveness to social reinforcement', *Journal of Genetic Psychology*, **120**, 3–12.

Atkinson, J. W. (1964), *An introduction to motivation*, (Princeton, N. J.: Van Nostrand).

Balla, D., Styfco, S. J., Zigler, E. (1971), 'Use of the opposition concept and outdirectedness in normal, familial retarded and organic retarded children', *American Journal of Mental Deficiency*, **75**, 663–80.

Baumrind, D. (1971), 'Current patterns of parental authority', *Developmental Psychology Monographs*, **4**, 1–101.

Benware, C. A., Deci, E. L. (1984), 'Quality of learning with an active versus passive motivational set', *American Educational Research Journal*, **21**, 755–65.

Berlyne, D. E. (1960), *Conflict, arousal, and curiosity*, (New York: McGraw-Hill).

Day, H. I. (1971), 'The measurement of specific curiosity' in H. I. Day, D. E. Berlyne, D. E. Hunt (eds), *Intrinsic motivation: a new direction in education*, (Toronto: Holt, Rinehart & Winston), pp. 99–112.

Deci, E. L. (1975), *Intrinsic motivation*, (New York: Plenum).

Deutsch, J. A., Fishman, A., Kogan, L., North, R., Whiteman, M. (1964), 'Guidelines for testing minority group children', *Journal of Social Issues*, **20**, 127–45.

Erikson, E. H. (1968), *Identity: Youth and Crisis*, (New York: Norton).

Feuerstein, R., Hoffman, M. B., Jensen, M. R., Rand, Y. (1985), 'Instrumental Enrichment, an intervention program for structural cognitive modifiability: Theory and practice' in J. W. Segal, S. F. Chipman, R. Glaser (eds), *Thinking and Learning Skills*, vol. 1 (Hillsdale, N.J.: Lawrence Erlbaum). pp. 43–82.

Feuerstein, R., Rand, Y., Hoffman, M. B. (1979), *The dynamic assessment of retarded performers*, (Baltimore: University Park Press).

Feuerstein, R., Rand, Y., Hoffman, M. B., Miller, R. (1980), *Instrumental* Enrichment, (Baltimore: University Park Press).

Findley, M. J., Cooper, H. M. (1983), 'Locus of control and academic achievement: A literature review', *Journal of Personality and Social Psychology*, **44**, 419–27.

Goldschmid, M. L. (1970), 'Instructional options: Adapting the large university course to individual differences', *Learning and development*, no. 5 (Montreal: Centre for Learning and Development, McGill University).

Harter, S. (1978), 'Effectance motivation reconsidered: Toward a developmental model', *Human Development,* **21**, 34–64.

Harter, S. (1981), 'A model of intrinsic mastery motivation in children: Individual differences and developmental change', *Minnesota Symposium on Child Psychology*, vol. 14 (Hillsdale, N.J.: Erlbaum).

Harter, S. (1981), 'A new self-report scale of intrinsic versus extrinsic orientation in the classroom: Motivational and informational components', *Developmental Psychology*, **17**, 300–12.

Harter, S., Zigler, E. (1968), 'Effectiveness of adult and peer reinforcement on the performance of institutionalized and non-institutionalized retardates', *Journal of Abnormal Psychology*, **73**, 144–9.

Haywood, H. C. (1968), 'Motivational orientation of overachieving and underachieving elementary school children', *American Journal of Mental Deficiency*, **72**, 662–7.

Haywood, H. C. (1971), 'Individual differences in motivational orientation: A trait approach' in H. I. Day, D. E. Berlyne, D. E. Hunt (eds), *Intrinsic motivation: A new direction in education*, (Toronto: Holt, Rinehart & Winston), pp. 113–27.

Haywood, H. C., Burke, W. P. (1975), 'Development of individual differences in intrinsic motivation' in I. E. Uygins, F. Weizmann (eds), *The structuring of experience*, (New York: Plenum), pp. 235–63.

Hilliard, A. G. (1979), 'Standardization and cultural bias as impediments to the scientific study and validation of "intelligence"', *Journal of Research and Development in Education*, **12**, 47–58.

Hunt, J. McV. (1965), 'Intrinsic motivation and its role in psychological development' in D. Levine (ed.), *Nebraska Symposium on Motivation* vol. 13 (Lincoln: University of Nebraska Press), pp. 189–282.

Kirkland, M. (1971), 'Effects of tests on students and schools', *Review of Educational Research*, 41, 303–50.

Lefcourt, H. M. (1976), *Locus of control: Current trends in theory and research*, (Hillsdale, N. J.: G. Erlbaum).

Lepper, M. (1980), 'Intrinsic and extrinsic motivation in children: Detrimental effects of superfluous social controls', *Minnesota Symposium on Child Psychology*, vol. 14 (Hillesdale, N. J.: Erlbaum), pp. 155–214.

Marcia, J. E. (1980), 'Identity in adolescence' in J. Adelson (ed.), *Handbook of adolescent psychology*, (New York: John Wiley), pp. 159–188.

Maslow, A. H. (1968), *Toward a psychology of being*, (New York: Van Nostrand Reinhold).

Maw, W. H., Maw, E. W. (1970), 'Children's curiosity and parental attitudes', *Child Development*, **41**, 123–9.

May, R. (1967), *Psychology of the human dilemma*, (New York: Van Nostrand Reinhold).

McClelland, D. C. (1961), *The achieving society*, (New York: Free Press).
McCoy, N., Zigler, E. (1965), 'Social reinforcer effectiveness as a function of the relationship between child and adult', *Journal of Personality and Social Psychology*, **1**, 604–12.
Mercer, J. (1973), *Labeling the mentally retarded*, (Berkeley: University of California Press).
Nunnally, J. C., Lemond, L. C. (1973), 'Exploratory behaviour and human development' in L. P. Lipsitt, H. W. Reese (eds), *Advances in Child Development and Behaviour*, (New York: Academic Press).
Phares, E. J. (1976), *Locus of control in personality*, (Morristown, N.J.: General Learning Press).
Postman, N., Weingartner, C. (1969), *Teaching as a subversive activity*, (New York: Delta Books).
Reynolds, C. R. (1982), 'The problem of bias in psychological assessment' in C. R. Reynolds, T. B. Gutkin (eds), *The handbook of school psychology*, (New York: John Wiley).
Reynolds, C. R. (1983), 'Test bias: In God we trust; all others must have data', *The Journal of Special Education*, **17**, 241–60.
Rogers, C. R. (1961), *On becoming a person*, (Boston: Houghton Mifflin).
Rotter, J. B. (1966), 'Generalized expectancies for internal versus external control of reinforcement', *Psychological Monographs*, 80 (1, Whole No. 609).
Scarr, S. (1981), 'Testing for children: Assessment and the many determinants of intellectual competence', *American Psychologist*, **36**, 1159–66.
Seligman, M. E. P. (1975), *Helplessness: On depression, development and death*, (San Francisco: Freeman).
Stevenson, H. W., Fahel, L. S. (1961), 'The effect of social reinforcement on the performance of institutionalized and noninstitutionalized normal and feebleminded children', *Journal of Personality*, **29**, 136–47.
Stipek, D. J., Weisz, J. R. (1981), 'Perceived personal control and academic achievement', *Review of Educational Research*, **51**, 101–37.
Terrell, G. Jr., Durkin, K., Wiesley, M. (1959), 'Social class and the nature of the incentive in discrimination learning', *Journal of Abnormal and Social Psychology*, **59**, 270–2.
Tzuriel, D. (1984), 'Sex role typing and ego identity in Israeli Oriental and Western adolescents', *Journal of Personality and Social Psychology*, **46**, 440–57.
Weaver, J., Balla, D., Zigler, E. (1971), 'Social approach and avoidance tendencies of institutionalized retarded and non-institutionalized retarded and normal children', *Journal of Experimental Research in Personality*, **5**, 98–110.
White, R. W. (1959), 'Motivation reconsidered: The concept of competence', *Psychological Review*, **66**, 297–333.
Williams, R. L. (1974), 'From dehumanization to black intellectual genocide: A rejoinder' in G. J. Williams, S. Gordon (eds), *Clinical child psychology: Current practices and future perspectives*, (New York: Behavioral Publications).
Yando, R., Zigler, E. (1971), 'Outerdirectedness in the problem-solving of institutionalized and noninstitutionalized normal and retarded children', *Developmental Psychology*, **4**, 277–88.

Zigler, E. (1963), 'Rigidity and social reinforcement effects in the performance of institutionalized and noninstitutionalized normal and retarded children', *Journal of Personality*, **31**, 258–69.
Zigler, E. (1971), 'The retarded child as a whole person' in H. E. Adams, W. K. Boardman (eds), *Advances in Experimental Clinical Psychology*, vol. 1 (New York: Pergamon).
Zigler, E., Abelson, W. D., Seitz, V. (1973), 'Motivational factors in the performance of economically disadvantaged children in the Peabody Picture Vocabulary Test', *Child Development*, **44**, 294–303.
Zigler, E., Balla, D., Hodapp, R. (1984), 'On the definition and classification of mental retardation', *American Journal of Mental Deficiency*, **89**, 215–30.
Zigler, E., Butterfield, E. C. (1968), 'Motivational aspects of changes in IQ test performance of culturally deprived nursery school children', *Child Development*, **39**, 1–14.
Zigler, E., de Labry, J. (1962), 'Concept-switching in middle-class, lower-class and retarded children', *Journal of Abnormal and Social Psychology*, **65**, 267–73.
Zigler, E., Yando, R. (1972), 'Outdirectedness and imitative behavior of institutionalized and noninstitutionalized younger and older children', *Child Development*, **43**, 413–25.

8 Arousal, Telic Dominance and Learning Behaviour

Monique Boekaerts

1. INTRODUCTION

Teacher reports as well as empirical evidence lead to the conclusion that there are marked inter-and intra-individual differences in the energy that a pupil is prepared to spend so as to reach specific immediate and long-range goals. In order to come to grips with this variance in individual behaviour a distinction should be made between the individual's normal, or habitual way of performing in a classroom context, and his behaviour in a specific situation.

To illustrate this point reference can be made to the following pupil reports. Pupils *A, B* and *C* are sixth formers of a primary school in Belgium. They all report low levels of anxiety under normal classroom conditions. Pupil *A* reports a tremendous increase in his level of arousal when being confronted with new or difficult problems. He experiences this increase in arousal as unpleasant and labels it as 'anxiety'. Pupil *B* equally reports that he experiences an increase in his level of arousal when being confronted with a new and difficult assignment, but he reports pleasant concommitant feelings such as anticipated excitement of experiencing the feeling of efficacy. Unlike pupils *A* and *B*, pupil *C* does not report an increase in his level of arousal when asked to start on a new or difficult task. However, he reports experiencing mild forms of anxiety under specific conditions such as for example starting to work on tasks which have pass/fail consequences (for example exams). When these threatening consequences are lacking he enjoys problem solving, provided the problem is interesting.

All three pupils were confronted with a new arithmetic task in which they had to do simple calculations so as to figure out how much it would cost to organise a birthday party. Pupil *A* did not immediately start on the task and indicated that he thought the task was too difficult for him to do. However, once he had started the task he continued with great vigour even though he had to ask the teacher for help twice. He even continued with the task when other pupils had already embarked on another, more pleasant activity. Pupil *B* immediately started to work on the set task and seemed to be interested in it. But, as soon as he heard that other pupils had a different problem to solve, which seemed to him more fun to do, he discontinued the problem-solving process and got frustrated when the teacher told him to continue with his own assignment. Finally pupil *C* started the assignment without much enthusiasm. When the teacher informed him that he had selected this problem especially because he knew that he was soon to organise his own birthday party, he seemed to be motivated to put in an effort and he produced an excellent result.

This example may illustrate that the same task may be perceived and appraised differently by various pupils. The amount of arousal which they feel as a result of their appraisal processes as well as the way they label it may be a source of individual differences in motivation and in the quality of the learning process. In the next few pages I will first examine what is meant by arousal, emotional and appraisal processes. In section 2 of this chapter I will describe a method of assessment which aims to gain insight into a pupil's general motivational orientation; in section 3 I will describe some cultural differences in telic dominance and in section 4 the usefulness of the telic dominance concept in explaining and predicting motivated learning behaviour, will be discussed.

1.1 Arousal

In their two-factor theory of emotion Schachter and Singer (1962) state that an *emotion* is the result of the interaction between physiological arousal (the physiological component) and the interpretation of external and internal stimuli leading up to physiological arousal (the cognitive component). Later research (Hamilton, 1979; Levi, 1972) places even more emphasis on the situational context within which increases or decreases in arousal are noted. To date most models depicting emotional processes (Izard, 1977; Lazarus *et al.*, 1970; Leventhal, 1980; Scherer, 1982) focus on four different components: (1) the physiological component which entails changes in bodily processes such an hormonal secretions and increased visceral and/or muscular activity preparing the body for action, (2) the cognitive component which refers to the individual's appraisal of the emotion-arousing situation, (3) the emotional component which reflects the subjective, conscious experience during the emotion and (4) the behavioural component which expresses the behavioural changes due to increased visceral and muscular activity. The relative importance attached to each of these components and their interrelations form the basis for inter-model differences.

Arousal has long been treated as some kind of volume control system. When a person was believed to over-aroused, an overall increase in his energy-level was postulated (and vice versa for low arousal). This change in energy level was believed to be reflected in all responses elicited at that moment. Hockey (1981) proposed an alternative theory of arousal. He holds that the arousal system is a constant source of energy that works selectively on specific aspects of performance. That is, arousal can have both beneficial and detrimental effects on behaviour. Drawing on the work of Näätänen (1975) and Hamilton *et al.* (1977) he further argues that arousal and activation reflect the patterning of a person's physiological state. When the patterning is compatible with task demands, efficient behaviour will occur; when it is incompatible with task demands, performance decrements will result. A person's arousal level may be picked up by behavioural, cortical and autonomic arousal measures. For example, when a person is in a highly aroused state due to perhaps internal or external stress his heart rate, his skin conductance and his pupil dilation may show marked changes, thus indicating a general pattern of sympathetic dominance.

What constitutes physiological activation or arousal, and how it relates to cognitive appraisal processes and performance is beyond our present understanding. The only conclusion that we may draw at present is that changes in internal or external conditions may be perceived by the individual and may produce qualitative changes in his pattern of arousal. The perception and interpretation of both these changes may affect the quality of a person's information processing and as such the quality of his performance (see also Kerber and Coles, 1970; Lang, 1979; Leventhal, 1980; Levine *et al.*, 1978).

1.2 Emotion and appraisal processes

Lazarus and his colleagues at Berkeley developed a cognitive theory of stress and coping which helps us understand the relation between the individual's perception of changes in his level of arousal and his appraisal processes on the one hand; and between his appraisal processes and his behavioural strategies on the other (Lazarus, 1966; Lazarus and Launier, 1978; Lazarus, Kanner and Folkman, 1980; Folkman and Lazarus, 1984a, 1984b, 1985). Lazarus and his colleagues view a *stressful encounter* as a dynamic, unfolding process which reflects a disturbed person-environment relationship. When an individual is confronted with a situation which has significance for his well-being, but which has at that moment the potential for challenge, threat, harm or loss, he will experience stress. Central to the theory is that the way a person perceives a situation and assigns meaning to it gives rise to increases or decreases in his level of arousal and that these changes may be noticed, interpreted and labelled as a *specific emotion* (anxiety, excitement, fear, anger, sadness, and so on). Emotions are the products of how an individual appraises environmental demands (including task demands) in relation to how he appraises his own possible coping resources to meet these demands.

Lazarus *et al.* (1970) made a distinction between three independent types of cognitive appraisal processes, viz. primary appraisal; secondary appraisal and re-appraisal. Primary appraisal processes determine whether an encounter is irrelevant, benign-positive or stressful. If the situation is appraised as stressful, specific emotions are experienced. For example, when the stressful situation is interpreted in a *positive* way, it is experienced as a challenge and positive feelings such as anticipated joy, and excitement will dominate. When the stressful situation is interpreted in a *negative* way it may be experienced as a threat to one's self-esteem; as harmful or as a loss. In this case characteristic emotions such as anxiety, sadness and anger may be experienced. These emotions give rise to secondary appraisal processes addressing the question 'What can I do about it?' In other words, the individual evaluates whether his own coping resources are adequate to deal with the stressful encounter. Hence, coping refers to the individual's efforts to master the stressful situation; either by regulating and controling his emotions (emotion-focused coping); by trying to change the situation (problem-focused coping) or by changing the appraisal processes. As a consequence, the nature, the quality and the intensity of the emotions may change in the course of a stressful encounter. And, these changes reflect the way in which an individual assigns meaning to consecutive events, especially to the changing relation between the task demands and his own attempts to meet these task demands. Finally, reappraisal refers to feedback processes which may change the individual's interpretation of certain person-environments relations. This modified information will form the basis for future primary and secondary appraisal processes.

1.3 **Belief systems and small worlds**

Pupils possess declarative and procedural knowledge, beliefs and opinions that make up their understanding of classroom behaviour. This information which is a subset of their long-term memory structure acts as a frame of reference for perceiving and interpreting learning tasks, and any other form of behaviour that may occur in a classroom setting. In this gradually built-up network of accrued knowledge, which will be refered to as the learner's belief system, information about various aspects of reality is stored in domains, or memory schemata (cf. Anderson and Bower, 1973; Boekaerts, 1979, 1985b; Minsky, 1975). A schemata is not an exact copy of an event. It is a mental composite of the learner's experiences with similar events, persons and objects. On the basis of this stored information a learner can describe and explain causal relations; he can anticipate a learning outcome and the consequences attached to it; and he can plan, execute and evaluate learning strategies.

Hence, the belief system of an individual may be seen as the grand total of his cognitions and his complementary feelings about events, tasks and activities. It is based on past experiences (direct or indirect); on cultural beliefs and on logical deductions. A subset of thes cognitive structures (specific schemata) may be activated in a particular context; for example the classroom, the doctor's office or the hospital. This activated knowledge acts as a *small world*, or frame of reference, for interpreting the learning context, the task demands, one's own competence, and for anticipating probable actions and behavioural outcomes. In other words, the activated subset steers and directs the appraisal processes and *biases* a person's willingness and intention to spend processing resources on a learning task.

1.4 Appraisal processes and task motivation

In current theories of motivation a central role has been assigned to the cognitive and affective intervening processes which are elicited both prior, during and after a learning task has been performed (see for example Heckhausen, 1980). The cognitive and affective intervening processes which are elicited upon confrontation with the task are similar in nature to Lazarus' primary and secondary appraisal processes. I have argued elsewhere (Boekaerts, 1983, 1985a, 1985c) that the first set of cognitive and affective intervening processes reflects the *interaction* between elements of the task-situation complex and the activated small world. They should be seen as a kind of orientation process in which the learner determines whether the learning activity set by the teacher (or freely chosen) is, for instance, challenging, boring, difficult or threatening. After this short orientation process the learner decides what he can/must do in order to cope adequately with the learning demands. Hence, a series of cost-benefit analyses comparing the perceived task demands with one's possibility to meet these demands (that is the learner's perception of his cognitive skills) are postulated. The inferences drawn from these primary and secondary appraisal processes lead to the learner's *situation-specific experiental state* and to his task-specific motivation, or *action tendency*. A substantial relation is postulated between the learner's action tendency and the quality of the learning process. For example, motivational processes affect the degree to which relevant domains of knowledge are explored, and adequate heuristic procedures are selected so as to execute, control, assess and correct the selected learning strategies (cf. Biggs, 1981).

During the performance of a learning activity and when it has been completed the learner evaluates his results and partial results. This second set of cognitive and affective intervening processes (cf. Lazarus' reappraisal processes) consists primarily of causal attribution processes, which relate success or failure to three causal dimensions, viz. locus, stability and control of causality (see Weiner, 1980 and Weiner *et al.*, 1971). Attribution-affect linkages have been well established (Frieze, Hanusa, McHugh and Valle, 1979; Frieze and Snyder, 1980; Frieze and Weiner, 1971; Kukla, 1972). It is important to note, however, that causal attribution processes reflect the *attributional bias* which the learner has acquired on the basis of his past learning history, Heckhausen (1980) demonstrated in this respect that there are two main types of attributional styles used in a classroom context, viz. the success-oriented attributional style and the failure-oriented attributional style. Success-oriented pupils prefer tasks and activities with an intermediate level of difficulty. When they experience success they attribute it mainly to internal factors (effort and ability), which they perceive as stable and controllable. Failure, on the other hand, is considered to be caused by external factors (for example the difficulty level of the tasks; bad luck), which is variable in nature. This attributional bias results in a maximal experience of positive feelings (pleasure, pride) and in a minimal experience of negative feelings (unhappiness, anger, shame and guilt). As such, this attributional bias promotes a realistic success expectancy on future learning occasions.

By contrast, individuals who are failure-oriented, are strongly influenced by prior negative learning experiences. They have a low success expectancy and set themselves unrealistic goals (too high or too low). When they experience failure they attribute it mainly to internal, stable and uncontrollable factors (low ability). However, when they occasionally experience success, they view it as good luck or the result of a too-easy task (variable, uncontrollable, external factors). This attributional bias maximises the negative affects, and minimises the positive effects, which in turn leads to low success expectancies on future occasions, and to an overall low self-concept.

It is important to realise that attribution processes are in fact *post hoc* interpretations which restore the delicate balance between the perception of task demands and one's self-concept. As such they affect a person's *well-being* rather than his learning outcome. Nevertheless, they have a powerful influence on the nature of the learning experience that is going to be integrated into existing long-term memory domains. Indeed a new learning experience may extend, confirm or modify existing memory schemata. Moreover, it may adapt or reinforce the learner's self-efficacy concept and through it his self-esteem. When a learner is presented with the same type of learning opportunity this information will be part of the small world which steers and biases his appraisal processes.

2. AROUSAL IN REVERSAL THEORY

2.1 Telic and paratelic modes

Reversal theory (Apter, 1982; Apter and Smith, 1977; Apter, 1984) places great emphasis on the individual's perception and interpretation of his level of arousal. Arousal is defined as 'the degree of motivational intensity which an individual experiences in consciousness at a given time: the extent to which he *feels* "aroused" in the everyday sense of feeling "worked up" or "stirred up" (Apter, 1982; p. 81). Hence Apter focuses on arousal in a different perspective: he talks about *felt* arousal, or arousal in a phenomenological sense, rather than about arousal in a behavioural or physiological sense. Reversal theory holds that the relationship between *felt* arousal and a person's feelings of well-being is bi-stable rather than homeostatic in nature. This implies that at any moment in time a pupil may be in, or want to be in, any of two optimal (preferred) states of arousal, viz. relaxation (low arousal experienced as pleasant) or excitement (high arousal, experienced as pleasant). As Figure 8.1 shows each state of optimal arousal is situated on top of an inverted U-curve. The right curve symbolises the telic curve; it ranges from *anxiety* (high arousal defined as unpleasant) over *relaxation* (optimal arousal defined as pleasant) to *apathy* (low arousal defined as unpleasant). The left curve, on the other hand, symbolises the paratelic curve. It ranges from *boredom* (low arousal defined as unpleasant) over *excitement* (optimal arousal defined as pleasant) to *over-excitement* (high arousal defined as unpleasant). Each of thes six labels represents a specific meta-motivational state and the two curves depict two distinct and discrete meta-motivational modes, viz. the telic and the paratelic mode, A meta-motivational mode is seen as a characteristic way of perceiving and interpreting the perceptual and phenomenal fields. In other words, not the person's behaviour itself is observed; rather, the person's motives and his way of seeing and appraising situations, and actions is studied.

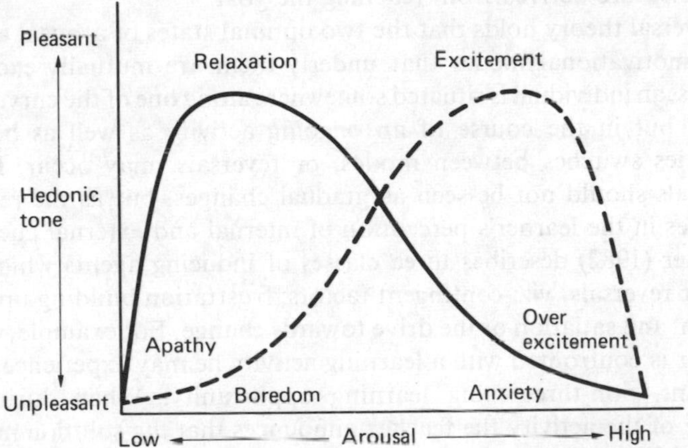

Figure 8.1 The relationship between arousal and hedonic tone for the arousal-avoidance system (continuous line) and for the excitement-seeking system (broken line) over the full range of felt arousal (Apter, 1982)

The distinction between two meta-motivational modes reflects two different ways of experiencing the relationship between means and ends. When a goal is selected, or accepted by the learner, he may undertake activities to reach the goal. Hence, the function of the goal is to steer the individual's behaviour. Another perfectly valid function of a goal could be that it is an excuse for the activity itself. For example, when a pupil writes an essay, the goal of finishing the essay so as to get a mark for his literature course, may not be central to his experience. He may simply enjoy putting his ideas and reflections into words.

When a person is in a *telic* state of mind, serious, goal-directed behaviour and through it the reduction of anxiety is a primary objective. Reaching the goal is essential to him as a person and pleasure is derived from achieving the goal as well as from anticipatory cognitions and feelings during the course of goal attainment. Enjoying the activity itself is secondary to reaching the goal or to gaining mastery. In short, the key components of the telic mode are seriously planning for self-set or teacher-imposed short-term and long-range goals so as to reach the optimal state of relaxation on accomplishing the task.

When the *paratelic* mode is operative, on the other hand, the individual is primarily oriented to search for excitement and to avoid boredom. Activity-oriented behaviour comes first. In other words, here-and-now sensations such as experiencing the feeling of joy, efficacy and interest as well as the anticipation of these sensations are more essential than pleasure derived from reaching the goal.

Reversal theory holds that the two optimal states of arousal and the meta-motivational modes that underly them are mutually exclusive. That is, an individual is situated somewhere along one of the curves at all times, but in the course of an ongoing activity as well as between activities switches between modes, or reversals, may occur. Hence, reversals should not be seen as gradual changes, but as the result of changes in the learner's perception of internal and external cues.

Apter (1982) describes three classes of inducing agents which may trigger reversals, viz. contingent factors; frustration building up in the system; and satiation or the drive towards change. For example, when a learner is confronted with a learning activity he may experience it as a pleasant, non-threatening learning opportunity. When during the course of the activity the teacher announces that the solution must be handed in at the end of the lesson in order to be marked, the pupil may feel that harm may come to his self-esteem. He may experience high arousal, which he labels as 'anxiety' and may switch from the paratelic to the telic mode, or vice versa.

The reversal mechanism receives input from all three classes of inducing agents; each may be powerful enough to instigate a reversal on its own account but more often that not interaction processes will occur and trigger the reversal. Nevertheless, the main cause of a reversal into the telic state will be the imposition on the individual of a goal which he sees as unavoidable or essential. The significance which the learner assigns to these goals and the urgency with which he feels they have to be pursued will ultimately determine the strength of these contingent factors in inducing reversals.

It is noteworthy in this respect, that changes in the meta-motivational systems and in the optimal level of arousal that is experienced as pleasant, may occur from time to time. For example, fatigue, deprivation and feelings of (in)security may temporarily lower or raise the optimum position of the curves. Hence, shifted peaks of the telic or paratelic curves could account for lowered or raised thresholds of 'relaxation' and 'excitement', and give rise to intra-individual differences in what constitutes optimal and sub-optimal states of arousal.

I have already pointed out that a crucial difference between the two meta-motivational modes is the nature of the means–end relationship. Individuals who are in a telic state of mind are primarily oriented towards essential, imposed or unavoidable goals. Their behaviour is guided by and derives significance from these goals and from the position they hold in a complex structure of goals (long-term goals). By contrast, individuals who are in a paratelic state of mind, will engage freely into self-chosen activities; their behaviour is characterised by spontaneity and by lower preferred significance. Apter (1982) considers the arousal system as an integral part of this means–end relation. He argues that when an individual finds himself in a state of sub-optimal arousal he will engage actively either in excitement-seeking or in arousal-avoiding behaviour. In other words, Apter postulates some of kind of arousal regulatory system to restore the perceived imbalance.

2.2 **Telic dominance**

If the inclination to linger predominantly in one of the meta-motivational modes is a relatively stable characteristic of the learner, it could explain why some pupils are prepared to spend long hours mastering skills and executing teacher-set tasks while others are constantly on the look out for here-and-now sensations and do not show any persistance in their work. Dominance of one mode over the other implies consistency in behaviour whereas reversals from one mode to the other puts the emphasis on inconsistency and change. In order to explain this situation I would like to digress for a moment and explain what is meant by the term '*dominance*'.

When one or more learner characteristics (aptitudes) become so dominant that they resemble a pattern of thinking or behaving they acquire the status of an organising and regulating principle. These principles, which have been acquired through individual and social learning experiences, are situated high-up in the information processing system. They reflect the individual's relatively stable strategies (1) to organise and structure aspects of the perceptual and phenomenal fields and (2) to regulate, monitor and evaluate actions. In other words, these organising principles control specific aspects of the information processing system. When no specific information is received regarding the need for change, these control processes will display a *learned bias* to induce the dominant meta-motivational mode and through it the dominant learning or coping strategies. I have already argued that a classroom context and the small world which it activates, may facilitate reversals to the telic mode. The size of this context-effect may be the product of social learning and may be more powerful in some cultures than in others.

The degree of dominance of one meta-motivational mode over the other can be measured by the telic dominance scale (*TDS*). The *TDS* was constructed by Murgatroyd, Rushton, Apter and Ray (1978) for adult, English speaking subjects. It consists of three subscales, viz. serious mindedness (*SM*), planning orientation (*PO*) and arousal avoidance (*AA*). The *SM* subscale measures the degree to which an individual is oriented towards goals seen as essential or important to himself or to others he identifies with, rather than to activities and goals which he considers to be inessential or trivial. The *PO* subscale measures the degree to which an individual plans ahead and organises his activities in pursuit of goals rather than taking things as they come. That is, it is the degree to which a person is oriented towards the future rather than the present; and the extent to which pleasure is gained from the achievement of goals or anticipating goals rather than from immediate behaviour or sensations. The AA subscale measures the degree to which an individual avoids situations which generate high arousal and seeks situations in which arousal levels are not too high.

Boekaerts and Hendriksen (in preparation) adapted the *TDS* to the phenomenal field of 12 year-old pupils. In order to cover the fields of their experiences we introduced a number of school-related situations describing free and imposed learning activities as well as leisure activities in a school and non-school setting. On the basis of several pilot studies, a twenty-seven item questionnaire was constructed (nine items in each subscale). Each item was introduced by a short setting-the-scene statement, and a telic and paratelic alternative was described. The pupils were asked to make a *forced choice* between these alternatives. In addition, they were asked to indicate on a five-point Likert scale how attractive they found each of these alternatives in the situation described by the setting-the-scene statement.

This new version of the *TDS*, which will be referred to as the Nijmegan

TDS (*N–TDS*) was administered to a sample of sixth grade pupils (*N*= 280) so as to determine whether the constructed items did indeed relate to the different features of telic dominance. It was found that the three subscales showed a satisfactory internal consistency (*SM*: 0.81; *PO*: 0.78; *AA*: 0.52 and *TDS*: 0.84). The results of two principal component analyses, performed on the 27 forced choice items and the 54 Likert scales (see Boekaerts and Hendriksen, in preparation), prompted us to slightly alter the definitions for *SM*, *PO* and *AA*. It seems that for twelve year olds *Telic Dominance* is a meta-motivational state in which they recognise an imposed, an unavoidable, an essential or relevant goal; accept responsibility for it and plan ahead to accomplish it. *Serious Mindedness* should be redefined as the learner's inclination to recognise and actively looks for situations in which he can gain in competence (for example, he freely decides to read a book because he wants to acquire more information; or to gain proficiency in a skill he deems important). *Planning Orientation* is redefined as the learner's inclination to accept teacher or adult-imposed goals as his own; or comply with their demands in such a way that he plans ahead in pursuit of these goals. Finally, *Arousal Avoidance* is seen as the learner's inclination to reduce the level of arousal in situations in which there is an unaccomplished goal which he wants to reach.

3. CULTURAL DIFFERENCES IN TELIC DOMINANCE

3.1 Shared beliefs about the significance of a learning opportunity

The teaching-learning process is primarily a social transaction in which goals and objectives depend essentially on explicit or implicit interpersonal definitions. Traditionally the formulation of course objectives, the selection of the content, the teaching method and the evaluation procedures are the province of the teacher. As a chief vehicle for attaining the specified objectives a teacher selects specific learning activities. These teacher-initiated activities can take various forms; they can consist of merely listening or watching the teacher, but more complex skills may also be requested of the pupils; for example, reading comprehension, writing skills, and problem solving.

A learning activity (as different from an experimental task) is part of a stream of ongoing behaviour which the pupils perform during the teaching-learning process. Set learning activities may have *significance* by themselves or they may gain significance by virtue of their learning context (for example, the teacher thinks it is important to reach this learning objective; or my parents deem it important; or it is a final exam requirement). To some extent, teachers and pupils have shared beliefs about what is relevant, although they may (seriously) disagree on the relative importance of specific learning objectives. For example, a pupil may not accept the formulated course objectives and may see a particular learning activity as an irrelevant, unnecessary or threatening step in the teacher-planned learning sequence (see also Boekaerts, 1986a).

The point I want to make, is that the reason why different learners may be inclined to participate in a learning activity may vary. It could for example be the case that the belief system which some pupils have construed about 'learning opportunities' predominantly induces a telic mode in a classroom context. For other pupils, learning activities presented in the restricted environment of the classroom may neither elicit curiosity nor a desire for competence: they perform the set tasks because they perceive them as unavoidable goals. If that is the case one may expect that these pupils happily revert to the paratelic mode whenever the restricted environment of the classroom tolerates it or creates room for it. This raises the question as to whether different socialisation experiences may result not only in a different personal learning history (the contents of various memory domains); but, also in a tendency to switch to and linger in a particular meta-motivational mode when being confronted with a learning opportunity. If true, this assumption could have far reaching consequences for school learning for it could be envisaged that the learner's experimental state at the moment when he appraises a learning opportunity forms his baseline level of motivation to which situation-specific action tendency is added.

In order to gain some insight into the way twelve year old pupils from two different countries may have construed their world the *N–TDS* was administered to 95 Flemish sixth formers and 185 Dutch sixth formers. Using the Chi-square procedures we determined (Boekaerts and Hendriksen, in preparation) for each item whether the percentage of pupils who selected the telic alternative differed significantly in the two samples.

3.2 Differences in the way pupils construe their world

No significant differences ($p<0.01$) were found between the Dutch and the Flemish sample on six *SM* items, six *PO* items and four *AA* items. For a number of these items no clear cut preference pattern for the telic or the paratelic alternative was noted in either sample. For example, 57 per cent of the Dutch pupils and 59 per cent of the Flemish pupils indicated that they would give preference to going to a playing-garden rather than to a museum on a Sunday afternoon. However, on a school trip 57 per cent of the Dutch pupils and 62 per cent of the Flemish pupils prefer to visit an interesting, informative site rather than a fun-fair or a playing-garden. 53 per cent of the Dutch sixth formers and 62 per cent of the Flemish sixth formers would prefer to go swimming so as to get a swimming certificate rather than for fun.

Some other situations elicited a definite telic or paratelic choice in both groups. Sixth formers prefer to do easy arithmetic assignments rather than difficult ones (61–67 per cent). When they have to prepare for an exam 66 per cent of the Dutch and 74 per cent of the Flemish pupils would refrain from watching an interesting film on TV. When given the choice between an interesting, informative TV programme and a funny TV programme 82 per cent of the Dutch and 84 per cent of the Flemish pupils prefer to watch the former programme. In the same vein, these pupils indicate that they would prefer (81–89 per cent) to prepare a talk which required a lot of work, but was informative rather than an easy uninteresting one.

Apart from these non-significant differences, which give us an indication about how twelve year olds construe their world, a number of *significant* differences were found. For example, Dutch sixth formers indicate that when given the choice they would read a book that they think is good fun rather than a book or text from which they can learn a great deal. ($\chi^2 = 7.80$; $p < 0.01$) They also indicate that they prefer to eat what they think is palatable rather than what is good for their health ($\chi^2 = 7.34$; $p < 0.01$).

On three of the *AA* items we notice that Flemish pupils attempt more than their Dutch peers to reduce the level of arousal. Dutch pupils volunteer more to answer difficult questions ($\chi^2 = 20.06$; $p < 0.0000$) than Flemish pupils. They do not mind so much changing teachers during the school year ($\chi^2 = 8.26$; $p < 0.01$), and they enjoy exploring different types of playing-grounds and theatres rather than going to the same place all the time ($\chi^2 = 4.93$; $p < 0.02$). It seems then that Dutch twelve year olds are more independent in the sense that they experience less, or can tolerate more arousal in new, potentially threatening situations. A striking difference was found between these pupils on another *AA* item: Flemish pupils are more inclined to intervene when two or more pupils are having an argument ($\chi^2 = 26.84$; $p < 0.000$). A significant difference between Flemish and Dutch pupils was also noted with respect to their taking responsibility for tidying up their own room. Flemish pupils indicated more frequently that they prefer to tidy up their room regularly rather than do it on command ($\chi^2 = 6.78$; $p < 0.01$).

What can be concluded from these results? Flemish sixth grade pupils seem to be more telically dominant than Dutch sixth grade pupils. Or, to put it differently, Flemish pupils are more inclined to see teacher-imposed or spontaneously encountered learning opportunities as essential and relevant goals. Moreover, they more readily recognise and accept adult-set goals such as taking responsibility for one's possessions. Dutch sixth grade pupils, on the other hand, seem to evaluate imposed goals and freely encountered learning opportunities on the basis of their *personal relevance* (for example obtaining a swimming certificate) their *attractiveness* (having good fun is important) and their *necessity*. Goals which they construe as unnecessary, unimportant, superfluous, trivial, or unwarranted do not trigger the reversal to the telic state. (For example, on a Sunday afternoon it is not necessary to learn; reading a book then should be for the fun of it.)

These reported results should not be taken as evidence for a personality trait, which should be more present in one cultural group than in the other. I am not saying that all Flemish pupils are more telically oriented than Dutch pupils; and even those who are, are not more telically dominant all the time. What I am saying is that the *small world* which is activated when telically dominant pupils are confronted with a situation, in which an essential, unavoidable or imposed goal is presented, forms a *powerful context* for inducing a reversal to the telic mode. Hence, the point I am making, is that telically dominant pupils more easily perceive and interpret a goal as being essential or unavoidable; and that the urgency with which they feel these goals should be reached affects their reported choice of behaviour in free-choice and imposed learning situations.

This leaves us with the question: 'How can we account for the differences between Flemish and Dutch sixth grade pupils?' Although this question cannot be answered on the basis of this research, these differences may have come about by either one or both of the most crucial influences in children's lives, viz. the (extended) family and the school system. Getting good results at school, putting in an effort and enjoying learning in general is valued highly in most cultures. However, there are subtle ways to achieve this end. For example, feeling secure and free of anxiety is a salient goal pursued in Dutch families. From an early age parents encourage their children to control their fearfulness and to be self-determined and self-assured in their decisions to pursue a goal or not. In many Flemish families recognition and acceptance of parents-imposed and teacher-set goals seems to be more important than organising one's life around self-selected goals and self-complacency. Another difference between the Dutch and Flemish school and family environment, which is often quoted in newspaper and magazine articles, is that the former is more tolerant and less restrictive than the latter. It is obvious that such environmental differences – if they do exist – should be reflected in the learner's belief system; and, more specifically, in his perception and appraisal of increases and decreases in his level of arousal. For, as Lazarus argued, whether high or moderate arousal is experienced as *pleasant* or *unpleasant* and how it is consequently labelled, depends on the appraisal of the situation by the individual learner. When a person has learned to tolerate moderate and high levels of arousal, and has acquired the tendency to interpret increased levels of arousal in a positive way, he will interpret a lot of (potentially) stressful situations as 'challenging' situations. The experienced high arousal will then be labelled as 'excitement'. Alternatively, when he has learned to interpret increased levels of arousal in a negative way, he will interpret a lot of stressful situations as 'harmful' to his self-esteem; as 'loss' or 'threat'. This interpretation process will give rise to different emotions; that is, high arousal may be labelled as anxiety, but also as anger, or sadness.

Following this line of argument, it could be the case that cultural differences in parental attitude and in the school environment, created a different learning and socialisation environment for Flemish and Dutch primary school pupils. The Dutch environment could have prompted an early developmental change in the learner's characteristic way of appraising learning opportunities and perceiving goals, imposed on them by the environment. If this line of argument is correct, it could be envisaged that the noted differences in telic dominance may not be as strong between Dutch ten year old and Flemish twelve year olds. In order to investigate this hypothesis the *N-TDS* was administered to a sample of 142 Dutch fourth graders. We found no significant differences between the scores of these pupils and the Flemish pupils on the *TDS* and on the respective subscales. Significant differences were found between the two Dutch samples; (*TDS*: *T*-value 2.27; $p<.02$ / *SM*: *T*-value –2.67; $p<.01$ / *PO*: *T*-value –3.66; $p<.000$ / *AA*: *T*-value –2.44; $p<.02$) (see Boekaerts and Hendriksen, in preparation).

These results are in line with Harter's (1982) finding that there is a developmental change to be noted in the way pupils perceive and appraise learning situations. She found that as pupils grow older their awareness and skill in using internal standards of performance increases and so does their skill in evaluating their own performance. This implies that they are less dependent on external incentives, on feedback and reward; but, more importantly that they get the potential to be more self-sufficient in the learning process. Whether they take the *responsibility* for the organisation and control of the learning process, and are motivated to spend time and effort to master new skills, is quite another matter.

4. AROUSAL, TELIC DOMINANCE AND LEARNING BEHAVIOUR

This brings me to the question: 'how useful is the telic dominance concept in explaining motivated learning behaviour'? It has been argued that essential, unavoidable and imposed goals form a powerful context for inducing the telic mode. At this point I would like to suggest that telic dominance, or the characteristic way a learner perceives the perceptual and phenomenal fields, is based on a *fixed* small world. Activation of this 'fixed' small world automatically gives rise to the learner's baseline level of motivation. This general motivational orientation should be seen as the *stable core* of his motivation to learn. It interacts with situation-specific cues and results in the learner's situation-specific action tendency (his task commitment and his willingness to put energy in the task).

Hence, telic dominance should be seen as an organisation principle, situated high-up in the information processing system; it steers and biases primary appraisal processes. In this light the *N-TDS* is used as a measure of the learner's overall motivational orientation; as a measure of his relatively stable motivational core. This type of motivation should be distinguished from task-specific motivation, or content-oriented interest.

We know from recent research on motivation (see Boekaerts, 1986b; Nenninger, 1986) that in ordinary learning situations (as different from exams) cognitive variables (that is, prerequisite knowledge stored in relevant memory domains and meta-cognitive skills account for approximately 30 per cent of the explained variance in learning outcome. Motivational variables, on the other hand, explain a further 20 per cent. Eigler, Macke and Nenninger (1982) found that when the motivational variance was further subdivided into overall motivation for school tasks and content-specific motivation, the former variable explained 3–7 per cent of the variance and the latter 8–20 per cent.

In my own research (Boekaerts, 1985c) I found that measures of overall motivation contribute only a small portion of unique variance to action tendency (1.5–4.7 per cent); whereas task-related appraisal processes accounted for 57 per cent of the variance in action tendency on a reading task, 42 per cent on a drawing task and 34 per cent on an arithmetic task. I also investigated by means of a MANOVA repeated measures design (Boekaerts, 1986b) whether action tendency for three different types of learning activities was affected by the pupil's telic dominance score. The results demonstrated that whether or not a sixth form Flemish pupil ($N = 241$) was telically dominant or not, did not have a significant effect on his action tendency for any of the tasks (reading comprehension task, arithmetic task; drawing task). However, telic dominance had a significant effect on the learner's task-specific success expectancy judgement ($F = 17.92$; $p < .0001$); his task-specific attractiveness judgement ($F = 9.06$; $p < .01$) and his task-specific self-efficacy judgement ($F = 6.91$; $p < .01$).

Because no task × telic dominance interaction effects were found, it was assumed that the telic dominance effect is caused by the learner's *overall* self-efficacy judgement, his *overall* success expectancy judgement and his *overall* attractiveness judgement about schooltasks.

More research is necessary to gain insight into the way a learner assigns meaning to learning tasks and how he perceives the changing relations between task demands and his own resources to meet these demands. To adequately address these issues, it will be necessary to study primary and secondary appraisal processes at a greater level of specificity than is possible with the *N-TDS*. Clearly, the *N-TDS* has potential value for gaining insight in the way various pupils construe their world. However, the reported research (see also Boekaerts, 1986b) suggests that the *N-TDS* may be of greatest value when used as an adjunct to on-line instruments measuring task-specific appraisal processes. In developing a comprehensive model of motivation to learn, such a dual approach is necessary.

References

Anderson, J. R., Bower, G. H. (1973), *Human Associative Memory*, (Washington: Winston).

Apter, M. J. (1982), *The Experience of Motivation: The Theory of Psychological Reversals*, (New York/London: Academic Press).

Apter, M. J., Smith, K. C. P. (1977), 'Humour and the theory of psychological reversals' in Chapman, A. J., Foot, H. C. (eds), *It's a Funny Thing, Humour*, (Oxford: Pergamon).

Apter, M. J. (1984), 'Reversal theory and personality: a review', *Journal of Research in Personality*, **18**, 265–88.

Biggs, J. B. (1981), *The Process of Learning*, (Sydney: Prentice-Hall).

Boekaerts, M. (1979), *Towards a Theory of Learning Based on Individual Differences*, (Ghent: Communication and Cognition).

Boekaerts, M. (1983), 'Motivatie en onderwijs: Theorieën en modellen op een rijtje gezet' in Dijkstra, S., Dudink, A., Takens, J. R. (eds). *Psychologie en onderwijs* (Lisse: Swets & Zeitlinger).

Boekaerts, M. (1985a), 'Some developments in the study of motivational processes in a classroom context' in D'Ydewalle, G. (ed.), *Cognition, Information Processing, and Motivation*, XXIII International Congress of Psychology, vol. 3 (Amsterdam: North Holland).

Boekaerts, M. (1985b), 'Problem solving behaviour: New perspectives for ecologically valid research', *Journal of Structural Learning*, **8**, 195–224.

Boekaerts, M. (1985c), 'Situation-specific judgements of elements of the task-situation complex versus overall measures of motivational orientation' in De Corte, E., Lodewijks, J. G. L. C., Parmentier, R., Span, P. (eds), *Learning and Instruction*, (Oxford: Pergamon Press).

Boekaerts, M. (1986a), 'Motivation in theories of learning', *International Journal of Educational Research*, **2**.

Boekaerts, M. (1986b), 'The measurement of state and trait motivational orientation: Refining our measures' in van den Bercken, J. H. L., De Bruyn, E. E. J., Bergen, Th. C. M. (eds), *Achievement and Task Motivation*, p. 22 (Lisse: Swets North-America and by Swets & Zeitlinger).

Boekaerts, M., Hendriksen, J. (in preparation). *A Telic Dominance Scale for Primary School Pupils.*

Eigler, G., Macke, G., Nenninger, P. (1982), 'Mehr dimensionale Zielerreichung in Lehr-Lern-Prozessen', *Zeitschrift für Pädagogik*, **28**, 397–423.

Folkman, S., Lazarus, R. S. (1984a), 'Coping and adaptation' in Gentry, W. D. (ed.), *The Handbook of Behavioural Medicine*, (New York: Guildford).

Folkman, S., Lazarus, R. S. (1984b), *Stress, Appraisal and Coping*, (New York: Springer Publishing).

Folkman, S., Lazarus, R. S. (1985), 'If it changes it must be a process: study of emotion and coping during three stages of a college examination', *Journal of Personality and Social Psychology*, **48**, 1, 150–70.

Frieze, I., Hanusa, B., McHugh, M., Valle, V. (1979), 'Attributions of the causes of success and failure as internal and external women barriers to achievement in women' in Sherman, J., Denmark, F. (eds), *Psychology of Women*, (New York: Psychological Dimensions).

Frieze, I., Snyder, H. (1980), 'Children's beliefs about the causes of success and failure in school settings', *Journal of Educational Psychology*, **72**, 186–96.

Frieze, I., Weiner, B. (1971), 'Cue utilization and attributional judgements', *Journal of Personality*, **39**, 591–606.

Hamilton, P., Hockey, R., Rejman, M. (1977), 'The place of the concept of activation in human information processing theory' in Dornic, S. (ed.), *Attention and Performance*, vol. 6 (New York: Academic Press).

Hamilton, V. (1979), 'Personality and stress' in Hamilton, V., Warburton, D. M. (eds), *Human Stress and Cognition*, (Chicester: John Wiley).

Harter, S. (1982), 'A developmental perspective on some parameters of self regulation in children' in Karoly, P., Kaufer, F. H. (eds), *Self-Management and Behaviour Change From Theory to Practice*, (New York: Pergamon Press).

Heckhausen, H. (1980), *Motivation und Handeln*, (Berlin: Springer Verlag).

Hockey, R. (1981), 'Stress and the cognitive components of skilled performance' in Hamilton, V., Warburton, D. (eds), *Human Stress and Cognition: An Information Processing Approach*, (New York: John Wiley).

Izard, C. E. (1977), *Human Emotions*, (New York: Plenum Press).

Kerber, K. W., Coles, M. G. (1970), 'The role of perceived physiological activity in affective judgements', *Journal of Experimental Social Psychology*, **14**, 419–33.

Kukla, A. (1972), 'Attributional determinants of achievement-related behaviour', *Journal of Personality and Social Psychology*, **21**, 166–74.

Lang, P. J. (1979), 'A bio-informational theory of emotional imagery', *Psychophysiology*, **16**, 495–512.

Lazarus, R. S., Averill, J. R., Opton Jr., E. M. (1970), 'Toward a cognitive theory of emotions' in Arnold, M. (ed.), *Feelings and Emotions*, (New York: Academic Press).

Lazarus, R. S. (1966), *Psychological Stress and the Coping Process*, (New York: McGraw Hill).

Lazarus, R. S., Launier, R. (1978), 'Stress-related transactions between person and environment' in Pervin, L. A., Lewis, M. (eds), *Perspectives in Interactional Psychology*, (New York: Plenum).

Lazarus, R. S., Kanner, A. D., Folkman, S. (1980), 'Emotions: a cognitive-phenomenological analysis' in Plutchik, R., Kellerman, H. (eds), *Theories of Emotion*, (New York: Academic Press).

Leventhal, H. (1980), 'Toward a comprehensive theory of emotion' in Berkowitz, L. (ed.), *Advances in Experimental Social Psychology*, vol. 13 (New York: Academic Press).

Levi, L. (1972), 'Stress and distress in response to psychosocial stimuli', *Acta Medica Scandinavia*.

Levine, S., Weinberg, J., Ursin, H. (1978), 'Definitions of the coping process and statement of the problem' in Ursin, H., Boade, E., Levine, S. (eds), *Psychobiology of Stress: A Study of Coping Stress*, (New York: Academic Press).

Minsky, M. (1975), 'A framework for representing knowledge' in Winston, P. H. (ed.), *The Psychology of Computer Vision*, (New York: McGraw Hill).

Murgatroyd, S., Rushton, C., Apter, M., Ray, C. (1978), 'The development of the telic dominance scale', *Journal of Personality Assessment*, **42**, 5, 519–28.

Naatanen, R. (1975), 'The inverted-U relationship between activation and performance a critical review' in Rabbit, P. M. A., Dornic, S. (eds), *Attention and Performance*, vol. 5 (New York: Academic Press).

Nenninger, P. (1985), 'How stable is motivation by contents?' in De Corte, E., Lodewijks, H., Parmentier, R., Span, P. (eds), *Learning and Instruction* (in press, 1985).

Schachter, S., Singer, J. E. (1962), 'Cognitive, social and physiological determinants of emotional state', *Psychological Review*, **69**, 379–99.

Scherer, K. R. (1982), 'Emotion as a process: function, origin and regulation', *Social Science Information*, **21**, 555–70.

Weiner, B. (1980), 'The role of affect in rational (attributional) approaches in human motivation', *Educational Researcher*, **9** (7), 4–11.

Weiner, B., Frieze, I. H., Kukla, A., Reed, L., Rest, S., Rosenbaum, R. M. (1971), *Perceiving the Causes of Success and Failure*, (New York: General Learning Press).

Name Index

Subject Index